# Frommer's

# Best Beach Vacations

## *Florida*

BY CHELLE KOSTER WALTON

A Beachscape Publishing, Inc. production for
MACMILLAN TRAVEL U.S.A.

# Frommer's Best Beach Vacations: *Florida*

**Publishers/Editors** Gary Stoller and Bruce Bolger
**Managing Editor** Martin Everett
**Design Director** Audrey Razgaitis
**Beach Consultant** Dr. Stephen Leatherman
**Senior Editor** Nicola S. Coddington
**Copy Editor** Ann LaForge
**Research Editors** Betty Villaume and Teresa Stoller
**Map Designer** John Grimwade
**Cartographer** Joyce Pendola
**Graphic Design** Sun Design/Lauri Marks

*Frommer's Best Beach Vacations: Florida* is produced for Frommer's by Beachscape Publishing, Inc. Please address any comments or corrections to Beachscape at 145 Palisade St., Dobbs Ferry, N.Y. 10522; tel. 914-674-9283.

## Special Sales

Bulk purchases (10+ copies) of Frommer's Travel Guides are available to corporations at special discounts. The Special Sales Department can produce custom editions to be used as premiums and/or for sales promotions to suit individual needs. Existing editions can be produced with custom cover imprints such as corporate logos. For more information, write Special Sales, Macmillan Travel, 1633 Broadway, New York, NY 10019-6785.

**Also Available:**
*Best Beach Vacations: California*
*Best Beach Vacations: Hawaii*

**Coming in 1996:**
*Best Beach Vacations: New England*
*Best Beach Vacations: New York to Washington, D.C.*
*Best Beach Vacations: Carolinas & Georgia*

**Macmillan Travel**
A Simon & Schuster Macmillan Company
1633 Broadway, New York, NY 10019-6785

Library of Congress No. 95-79416
ISBN 0-02-860496-2

Manufactured in the
United States of America

10 9 8 7 6 5 4 3 2 1

First Edition

# About the author

Chelle Koster Walton has lived on Sanibel Island, Florida, for nearly fifteen years. She has written two previous Florida travel guidebooks and is a contributing editor of *Caribbean Travel & Life* magazine. In 1994 she won the Bahamas Discovery Award, and in 1993 she won the Society of American Travel Writers' Lowell Thomas bronze award for best guidebook. Her articles appear in the *Miami Herald*, *Florida Travel*, and other publications.

# A word from the author

Not exactly a day at the beach—as some have suggested. Researching this book required the help, patience, support, and understanding of many people. First and foremost in the support and understanding department comes my husband, Rob, who single-parented our five-year-old son Aaron during my long jaunts to the beach. Aaron, who helped research several beaches, rated St. Joseph Peninsula highest in the "ghost crab" category. Ron and Mindy Koster helped me judge the softness and snoozability of a few beaches.

Besides family, I am indebted to Stephen Leatherman, who contributed his expertise on local beaches and taught me all sorts of fun things about sand, dunes, erosion, and the importance of volleyball nets. Then there are the people behind the scene who hekped package my research in the most friendly format possible: Martin Everett, the patient editor; Gary Stoller, the juggler; Joyce Pendola, the talented mapmaker, and Nikki Coddington, the eleventh-hour pinch-hitter. Special thanks to Jane Wooldridge at the *Miami Herald*.

Other dedicated people to whom I am indebted for assistance include: Rose Drye at Accommodations St. George; Lee Daniel at the St. Petersburg/Clearwater Area Convention & the Visitors Bureau; Tamara Laine at Gulf County Chamber of Commerce; Leslie Benz at the Pensacola Convention & Visitor Information Center; Marcia Bush at Panama City Tourism; Rosetta Land Stone and Jan Tully at the Florida Tourism Bureau; Lynn Peterson, Traci Greenberg, Mia Casey, Amy Rankin, Beth Preddy, Patti Hendrix, Kathleen Martin, Julie Perrin, Susan Phillips, Deborah Roker-Weintraub, Ellie Brady, Captain Carl Johnson, and the countless people who answered my many questions.

# Table of

# Contents

## Southern Florida

## North Atlantic Coast

## Beach Locator Maps

# The Best Beach Vacations Rating System

**G**oing to the beach is a great American pastime. Whether for a vacation or just a day, Americans flock to the nation's shores in search of the inexplicable pleasure that comes with a stay by the water. That's about all we have in common regarding our love of beaches, for each person has his or her own special tastes. Some come for serenity, others for action, and there are a hundred variations in between. *Best Beach Vacations* is designed to help you find the beach experience that's right for you, be it for a day, a weekend, or an entire vacation.

*Best Beach Vacations* uses a unique rating system that systematically evaluates each beach area according to the categories that matter most to beach lovers: **Beauty, Swimming, Sand, Hotels/Inns/B&Bs, House Rentals, Restaurants, Nightlife, Attractions, Shopping, Sports,** and **Nature**. A quick review of the ratings will help you quickly narrow your selection. The overview and service information in each chapter provide everything you'll need to start planning your beach experience.

To select the beaches featured in this book, we began with information gathered by professor Stephen Leatherman, sometimes called Dr. Beach, a coastal geologist and director of the University of Maryland's Laboratory for Coastal Research. For years, Leatherman has collected information on water quality, scenic beauty, sand conditions, surf, temperature, and tourist amenities at beaches around the United States, data he uses to determine an overall rating for each beach. Using that data, along with their own knowledge and input from regional and local sources, the authors visited each beach and combed nearby areas to personally evaluate all of the

| | |
|---|---|
| Beauty | A |
| Swimming | B |
| Sand | C |
| Hotels/Inns/B&Bs | B |
| House rentals | A |
| Restaurants | B |
| Nightlife | B |
| Attractions | B |
| Shopping | C |
| Sports | A |
| Nature | A |

other important elements that go into a beach experience.

The ratings at the beginning of a chapter summarize the entire area. Within each chapter, individual beaches are listed. Each has its own description with more specific ratings. It's easy to use the rating system, because it's based on the A through F scale that's used for grade-school report cards; if you see NA (not applicable) in a ratings category, it means that that particular feature does not apply to this beach.

Here are the criteria used to formulate a grade for particular aspects of each beach or beach area.

*Beauty:* overall setting, sand, and views offshore.

*Swimming:* water quality, temperature, and wave conditions.

*Sand:* texture, color, and cleanliness.

*Amenities:* rest rooms, food concessions, lifeguards, and sports equipment.

The grades for all other categories are based on the quality and quantity of offerings in or around the beach area. The rating for *Attractions*, for example, assesses the quality and quantity of all types of things to do in the area surrounding the beach.

*Best Beach Vacations* makes every attempt to warn readers of specific safety concerns in each area. However, readers should visit all beaches mindful of the potential dangers posed by water, wave, and sun, and take appropriate precautions.

We hope you have a wonderful beach vacation.

—*Gary Stoller and Bruce Bolger*

# Best Beach Vacations:

**F**lorida is a land of seductive beaches flavored with a taste of the tropics. Sand covers 1,200 of the state's 8,000 miles of shoreline, and with three diverse coastlines, it boasts a variety of beach character and culture unmatched by other coastal states. Most of Florida's beaches lie on barrier islands, which, separated from the mainland, often enhance the beach experience by offering a sense of isolation from reality. You immediately slow down to island time, in which tides and nature rule. So don't try to rush it—relax and savor the experience.

In the northwest corner, where Florida meets the Deep South, the Panhandle boasts the world's whitest sands, along with towering dunes, history, great fishing, and locals with an outgoing friendliness delivered with a Southern twang. Here, temperatures are cooler than in most other areas of the state.

On the long Gulf Coast, beaches begin below the so-called Big Bend (also known as the Armpit by those who rue its lack of beaches). Shells are the Gulf Coast's great gift from the sea. This is the calmest of the coasts in terms of wave action, and the mood is laid-back.

The Atlantic Coast, divided into South Florida and North Florida in this book, is the most crowded and developed (with some exceptions). From the quirky Florida Keys and action-packed Miami up to Victorian Amelia Island, an entire range of personality changes await.

No matter what your beach prejudice—soft sand, roaring surf, isolation, great hotels, top restaurants, exciting nightlife, excellent shopping, or water sports—you'll find something in almost every part of the state.

# Overview

## WHEN TO GO

**WINTER:** This is peak season in the Keys and in the south of Florida, with many warm, sunny, and dry days, and lots of people. However, an occasional cold front can bring downright chilly weather, even as far south as Miami. There is little snow in the north of Florida, but the days rarely get hot enough for swimming.

**SPRING:** The entire state warms up, and the first waves of intense humidity and tropical showers begin affecting the south.

**SUMMER:** Hot and humid throughout the state.

**FALL:** This is probably the best time to visit Florida. The heat eases, and the summer vacationers are

## BEACH RANKINGS

*Here are Florida's 25 best beach areas, ranked in the order of the author's personal preference:*

1. Santa Rosa Island
2. Hutchinson Island
3. Pass-A-Grille
4. Grayton Beach
5. St. George Island
6. Caladesi/Honeymoon
7. St. Joseph Peninsula
8. Sanibel/Captiva
9. Playalinda
10. Amelia Island
11. North Naples
12. Bonita
13. Fort DeSoto
14. Bahia Honda Key
15. Perdido Key
16. Fort Pierce
17. Clearwater
18. Key Biscayne
19. Manasota Key
20. North Palm Beach
21. Sebastian Inlet
22. Siesta Key
23. Destin
24. Miami South Beach
25. St. Andrews

gone. However, hurricane season is August through November, so be attentive to any watches or warnings.

Water temperatures in the south range from the 60s to the 70s in winter and are in the 80s in summer. Water temperatures in the north range from the 50s to the 60s in winter and reach the 80s in summer.

# HOW TO GET THERE

Most major U.S. airlines fly to Florida. Gateways include Miami, Orlando, Tampa, Fort Lauderdale, Fort Myers, Sarasota, Jacksonville, and Tallahassee. Amtrak offers service from the East Coast of the United States and from some points in the West.

Florida is linked to its neighboring states by three major interstate highways: I-95, which enters from Georgia and serves Florida's east coast; I-75, which also enters through Georgia and serves the west coast; and I-10, which enters from Alabama and traverses the northern part of the state. The most scenic beach routes are Highway 98 along the Panhandle, Highway 41 (Tamiami Trail) along the southern Gulf Coast, and the storied Route A1A along the Atlantic Coast. Route 1 through the Florida Keys also passes through scenic areas.

# SERVICE INFORMATION

Here are a few notes about the service information provided in this book, as well as the author's choice of the chapter(s) that offer the best in each category.

# HOTELS/INNS/B&Bs

Because Florida is a family-oriented destination, accommodations often provide kitchen facilities in a condominium, suite, villa, or apartment setting. If you don't mind cooking some of your own vacation meals, consider the amount of money you can save in restaurant tabs.

Lodging falls into four price categories, based on double-occupancy peak-season nightly rates (before taxes):

| | |
|---|---|
| Very expensive | More than $180 |
| Expensive | $111 to $180 |
| Moderate | $76 to $110 |
| Inexpensive | $75 or less |

Best lodging: Chapter 25, Amelia Island.

# HOUSE RENTALS

Best house rentals: Chapter 4, Grayton Beach.

# RESTAURANTS

If you're determined to eat like the natives, try:

**Dolphin**—Not the mammal made famous by Flipper, but a slightly stronger-flavored fish also called mahimahi or dolphin fish.

**Stone crab claws**—In season from October 15 to May 15, it's considered a delicacy in Florida and is served either steaming hot with drawn butter or chilled with mustard sauce.

**Key lime pie**—Made from tiny yellow limes, egg yolks, and sweetened condensed milk, and topped with meringue or whipped cream.

**Floribbean cuisine**—A fusion of Latin, Caribbean, and North American influences.

Restaurants fall into four price categories, based on the approximate cost of an appetizer, main course, and dessert for one person at dinner (not including drinks, tax, and tip):

| | |
|---|---|
| Very expensive | More than $50 |
| Expensive | $31 to $50 |
| Moderate | $16 to $30 |
| Inexpensive | $15 or less |

Best restaurants: Chapter 25, Amelia Island, and Chapter 19, Miami South Beach.

# NIGHTLIFE

Best nightlife: Chapter 19, Miami South Beach.

# ATTRACTIONS

Best attractions: Chapter 5, St. Andrews.

# SHOPPING

Best shopping: Chapter 16, North Naples.

# SPORTS

## FISHING

Best fishing: Chapter 3, Destin.

## BOATING

Best boating: Chapter 9, Clearwater.

## SURFING

Best surfing: Chapter 23, Sebastian Inlet.
Another excellent area: Chapter 2, Santa Rosa Island.

## DIVING

Best diving: Chapter 17, Bahia Honda.
Another excellent area: Chapter 6, St. Joseph Peninsula.

## GOLF

Best courses: Chapter 20, North Palm Beach.

# HISTORY

Best history: Chapter 2, Santa Rosa Island.

# NATURE

Best natural attractions: Chapter 5, Grayton Beach; Chapter 6, St. Joseph Peninsula; Chapter 8, Caladesi/Honeymoon.

# SAFETY TIPS

Any dangers associated with Florida beaches are minimized by awareness and care. Too often, travelers let their guard down at beaches, but a few simple precautions can reduce the chances of a problem.

Sea creatures can pose a threat, although shark attacks are rare. More common are encounters with sting rays, sea lice, fire coral, jelly fish, Portuguese men-of-war, and other stinging creatures. Upon entering the water (especially during the summer), shuffle your feet to scare off any sting rays nesting along the shore. If you see jelly fish or other gelatinous floating organisms in the water, it's best to get out. Sea lice—actually jelly fish larvae—are a problem on the east coast. They can cause itching.

Rip currents can easily drown a weak swimmer. Unless you're a good swimmer, stick to beaches with lifeguards. Pay attention to posted warnings, and never swim alone.

Crime is a reality in metropolitan areas and areas frequented by tourists. Keep hotel and car doors locked at all times, keep your car windows rolled up to prevent car-jacking, and don't take valuables to the beach.

While protecting yourself, also be aware of how to protect the beaches. Use boardwalk paths over the dunes, don't step on any underwater coral, and don't litter. Please be considerate of the wildlife as well. Leave sea turtle nests alone, and don't feed alligators, birds, or any wildlife.

# Chapters 1–7

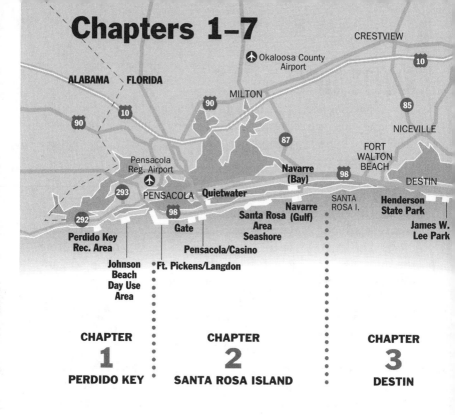

CRESTVIEW

Okaloosa County Airport

ALABAMA  FLORIDA

MILTON

NICEVILLE

Pensacola Reg. Airport

FORT WALTON BEACH

PENSACOLA  Quietwater

Navarre (Bay)

DESTIN

SANTA ROSA I.

Navarre (Gulf)

Henderson State Park

Perdido Key Rec. Area

Gate

Santa Rosa Area Seashore

James W. Lee Park

Pensacola/Casino

Johnson Beach Day Use Area

Ft. Pickens/Langdon

CHAPTER
1
PERDIDO KEY

CHAPTER
2
SANTA ROSA ISLAND

CHAPTER
3
DESTIN

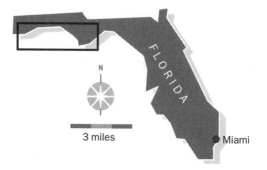

FLORIDA

N

3 miles

Miami

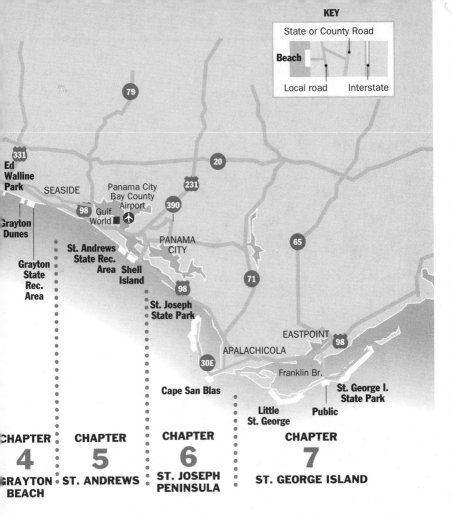

**KEY**

State or County Road

Beach

Local road    Interstate

79

331

**Ed Walline Park**

SEASIDE

**Grayton Dunes**

98 Gulf World

Panama City Bay County Airport

20

231

390

**Grayton State Rec. Area**

**St. Andrews State Rec. Area** Shell Island

PANAMA CITY

65

71

98

**St. Joseph State Park**

EASTPOINT

98

APALACHICOLA

30E

Franklin Br.

**Cape San Blas**

**St. George I. State Park**

**Little St. George**

Public

CHAPTER

**4**

**GRAYTON BEACH**

CHAPTER

**5**

**ST. ANDREWS**

CHAPTER

**6**

**ST. JOSEPH PENINSULA**

CHAPTER

**7**

**ST. GEORGE ISLAND**

N

3 miles

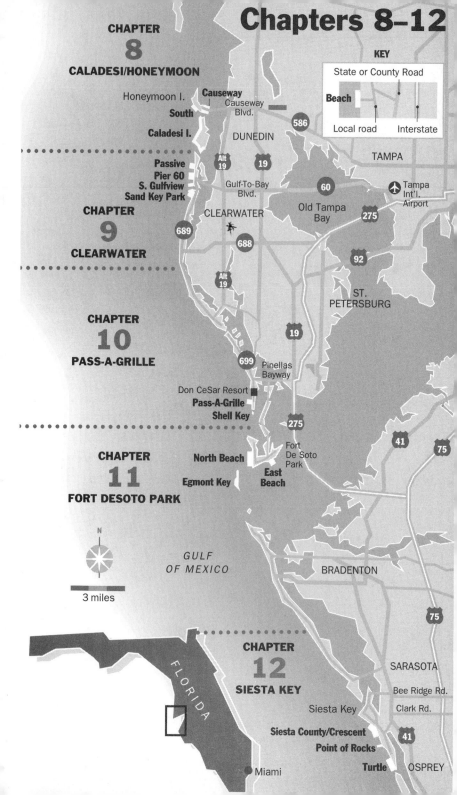

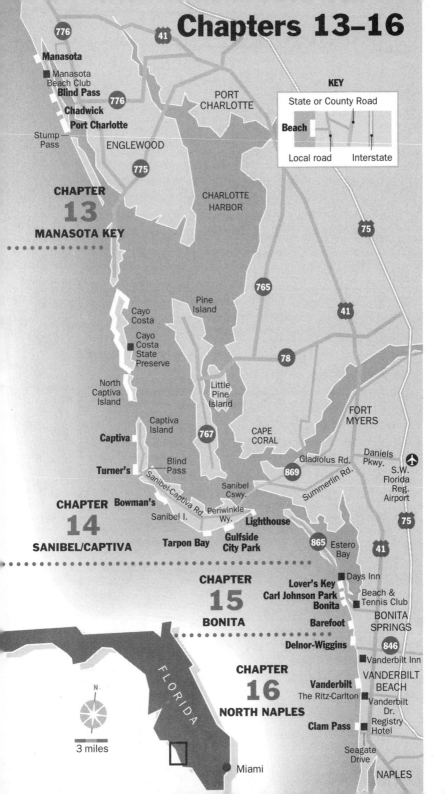

# Chapters 13–16

**Manasota**
- Manasota Beach Club
**Blind Pass**
**Chadwick**
**Port Charlotte**

Stump Pass
ENGLEWOOD

PORT CHARLOTTE

### KEY
State or County Road
**Beach**

Local road        Interstate

## CHAPTER 13
### MANASOTA KEY

CHARLOTTE HARBOR

Cayo Costa
Cayo Costa State Preserve

North Captiva Island

Pine Island

Little Pine Island

Captiva Island

**Captiva**

**Turner's**

Blind Pass

**Bowman's**

Sanibel-Captiva Rd.

Sanibel Cswy.
Sanibel I.        Periwinkle Wy.

**Lighthouse**

## CHAPTER 14
### SANIBEL/CAPTIVA

**Tarpon Bay**        **Gulfside City Park**

FORT MYERS

CAPE CORAL

Gladiolus Rd.

Summerlin Rd.

Daniels Pkwy.

S.W. Florida Reg. Airport

Estero Bay

## CHAPTER 15
### BONITA

**Lover's Key**
**Carl Johnson Park        Bonita**
**Barefoot**
**Delnor-Wiggins**

Days Inn
Beach & Tennis Club
BONITA SPRINGS

## CHAPTER 16
### NORTH NAPLES

**Vanderbilt**
The Ritz-Carlton
**Clam Pass**

Vanderbilt Inn
VANDERBILT BEACH
Vanderbilt Dr.
Registry Hotel

Seagate Drive

NAPLES

FLORIDA

N

3 miles

Miami

# Chapter 17

Everglades
National Park

*GULF OF MEXICO*

Great White
Heron Nat'l. Wildlife Refuge

Marathon
Airport

Vaca Key

Little
Torch
Key

Bahia
Honda
Key

Seven-Mile
Bridge

MARATHON

Ramrod
Key

Summerland
Key

Little
Palm I.

Big Pine
Key

Caloosa
Sandspur

**CHAPTER**
**17**
**BAHIA HONDA KEY**

Key West

**KEY**

State or County Road

**Beach**

Local road     Interstate

N

FLORIDA

9 miles

Miami

Key
West

**XVIII**

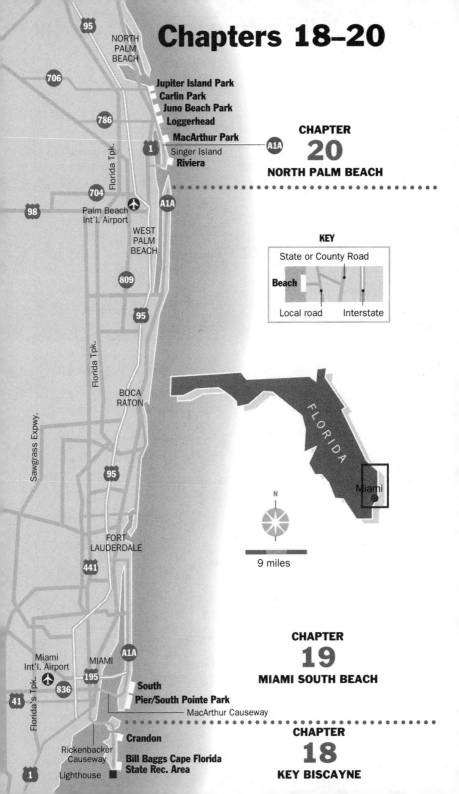

# Chapters 18–20

NORTH PALM BEACH

**Jupiter Island Park**
**Carlin Park**
**Juno Beach Park**
**Loggerhead**
**MacArthur Park**
Singer Island
**Riviera**

A1A

## CHAPTER
## 20
### NORTH PALM BEACH

Palm Beach Int'l. Airport

WEST PALM BEACH

A1A

BOCA RATON

FLORIDA

Miami

N

9 miles

**KEY**

State or County Road

Beach

Local road          Interstate

FORT LAUDERDALE

## CHAPTER
## 19
### MIAMI SOUTH BEACH

Miami Int'l. Airport

MIAMI

A1A

**South**
**Pier/South Pointe Park**
MacArthur Causeway

**Crandon**
Rickenbacker Causeway
**Bill Baggs Cape Florida**
**State Rec. Area**
Lighthouse

## CHAPTER
## 18
### KEY BISCAYNE

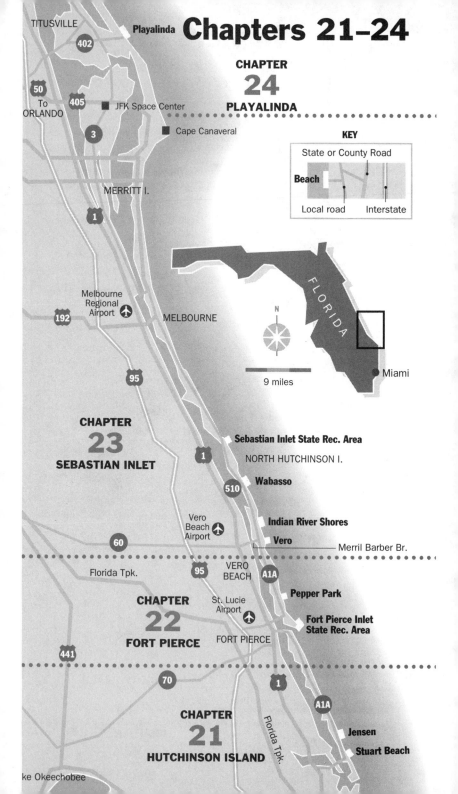

# Chapters 21–24

TITUSVILLE

402

Playalinda

50
To
ORLANDO

405

■ JFK Space Center

3

## CHAPTER
# 24
## PLAYALINDA

■ Cape Canaveral

MERRITT I.

1

### KEY
State or County Road

**Beach**

Local road    Interstate

Melbourne
Regional
Airport ✈

192

MELBOURNE

FLORIDA

N

9 miles

● Miami

95

## CHAPTER
# 23
## SEBASTIAN INLET

1

**Sebastian Inlet State Rec. Area**

NORTH HUTCHINSON I.

510

**Wabasso**

Vero
Beach
Airport ✈

**Indian River Shores**

**Vero**

60

Merril Barber Br.

Florida Tpk.

95

VERO
BEACH

A1A

## CHAPTER
# 22
## FORT PIERCE

St. Lucie
Airport ✈

FORT PIERCE

**Pepper Park**

**Fort Pierce Inlet
State Rec. Area**

441

70

1

A1A

## CHAPTER
# 21
## HUTCHINSON ISLAND

Florida Tpk.

**Jensen**

**Stuart Beach**

ke Okeechobee

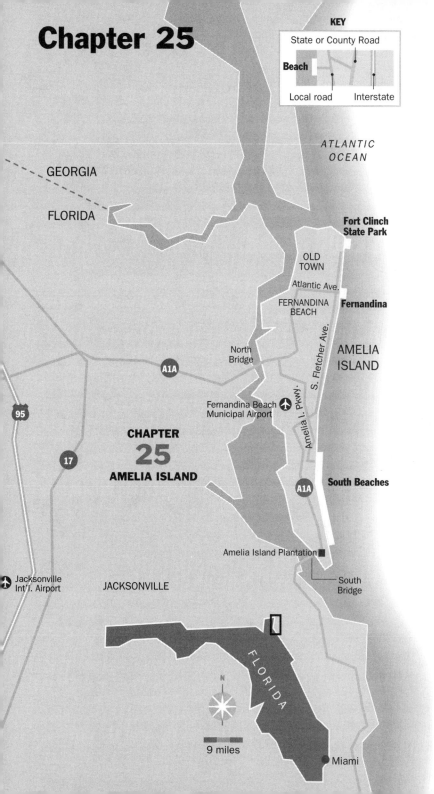

# Chapter 25

ATLANTIC
OCEAN

GEORGIA

FLORIDA

**Fort Clinch
State Park**

OLD
TOWN

Atlantic Ave.

FERNANDINA
BEACH

**Fernandina**

North
Bridge

AMELIA
ISLAND

S. Fletcher Ave.

A1A

Fernandina Beach
Municipal Airport

Amelia I. Pkwy.

**CHAPTER
25
AMELIA ISLAND**

95

17

A1A          **South Beaches**

Amelia Island Plantation

South
Bridge

Jacksonville
Int'l. Airport

JACKSONVILLE

FLORIDA

N

9 miles

Miami

## CHAPTER 1

# Perdido Key

**S**panish explorers aptly named it Perdido ("Lost Land"), and that still is true today. At the western tip of Florida, it feels like the edge of the world, with its whiter-than-white sand that drifts into a dreamy landscape of dunes. Like most of the Panhandle, it exudes a Deep South culture that contrasts with the rest of Florida. Folks are friendly, unhurried, and speak with a twang. They're on Central Time, not Eastern. Food usually comes fried, and temperatures rarely reach the 90s in summer.

| | |
|---|---|
| Beauty | B+ |
| Swimming | A |
| Sand | A+ |
| Hotels/Inns/B&Bs | C- |
| House rentals | B |
| Restaurants | B- |
| Nightlife | C- |
| Attractions | B |
| Shopping | C |
| Sports | A- |
| Nature | A |

Florida shares the island with Alabama, whose resort town of Orange Beach is rampant with development. Fortunately, large tracts of the Florida portion are part of the Gulf Islands National Seashore, which was created to preserve coastland from Florida to Mississippi. There is commercial development, too, but it has been well-planned. Tall condo buildings are spaced apart and interspersed with lower structures.

Beach enthusiasts coming to Perdido Key have their choice of two delightful spots: one primitive, and another that offers the usual park amenities. If you prefer the former, turn left after you come onto the island and drive two miles to the end of the road. This brings you into the·National Seashore, which extends for six miles on the island's east end. Explore it on foot. It's worth the effort: Beaches don't get any prettier than this.

Camping is permitted at primitive sites (*see* Nature).

If you're not bent on exploring, turn right after arriving on the island and drive two miles to Perdido Key State Recreation Area. About midway down the 16-mile-long island, this preserve is devoted equally to beach play and nature.

Between the state park and the National Seashore there are stores, restaurants, and a few resorts clustered at the island's entrance. What you won't find here are amusement parks and other tourist attractions characteristic of many resort communities in the Panhandle.

If you tire of sun-splashed days and quiet nights, you can head off-island for adventure. The Pensacola Naval Base offers some nearby. Just across the bridge from Perdido is Big Lagoon State Recreation Area, which has extensive nature trails and camping facilities. Downtown Pensacola lies only a half-hour away, with its historic sites, shops, and entertainment (*see* Chapter 2, Santa Rosa Island).

# GULF BEACHES
## GULF ISLANDS NATIONAL SEASHORE

Nearby development detracts from some of the scenic beauty, but don't let that deter you from exploring the pristine sands that lie beyond the entrance. At the end of the road, you'll find parking and facilities at the Johnson

| | |
|---|---|
| Beauty | A- |
| Swimming | A |
| Sand | A+ |
| Amenities | B |

**HOW TO GET THERE**

◆ From Pensacola Regional Airport (about one hour from Perdido Key), take Airport Blvd. and turn left on Ninth Ave. (Rte. 289). Turn right on Brent Lane (Rte. 290/296), which changes names to Beverly Pkwy. and Michigan Ave. Continue for 2 3/4 miles and turn left on Millview Rd. (Rte. 297), which changes to Blue Angel Pwy. (Rte. 173). After 3 mi., turn right on Rte. 292 and continue 4 mi. to the Perdido Key Bridge.

Beach Day Use Area. It's frequently crowded here, but you can get away from it all by walking. A quarter-mile nature trail begins across the road. Beyond that, approximately six miles of deserted beach provide an opportunity for people who like to do more strenuous hiking. You will see the ruins of Fort McRee along the way. *Open 8-sunset. At the east end of Johnson Beach Rd.*

*Swimming:* Water is shallow, but there's considerable wave action and, sometimes, undercurrents. Avoid the east end where currents are strong.

*Sand:* The wide beach is carpeted with the Panhandle's patent brilliant white sand.

*Amenities:* Rest rooms, bathhouses, picnic shelters, board-walks. During the summer, there are food concessions, and lifeguards are on duty.

*Sports:* No concessions in park.

*Parking:* Park in lot or along the road. Entry to the park costs $4 per car; $1 for bikers or hikers.

## PERDIDO KEY STATE RECREATION AREA

This park spans the island from the Gulf to Old River, giving visitors a chance to explore a variety of natural habitats. For most of the year, there's just one access to the one mile of Gulf beach here, but another one is opened during the summer

| Beauty | B |
| --- | --- |
| Swimming | A |
| Sand | A+ |
| Amenities | B+ |

months. Both are nicely maintained. Boardwalks cross shrub-studded dunes. Fewer people come here than to the National Seashore beach. Shops, bars, and water-sports concessions are nearby. *Open 8-sunset. On Perdido Key Dr.*

*Swimming:* The water is generally calm, with strong wave action at times.

*Sand:* A wide, fluffy carpet of quartz-crystal sand that builds into a striking landscape of dunes.

*Amenities:* Rest rooms, showers, picnic facilities, boardwalks to the beach. No lifeguard.

*Sports:* A parasailing concession and waverunner rentals are near the beach.

*Parking:* Costs $2.

# HOTELS/INNS/B&Bs

♦ **Perdido Bay State Recreation Area** (moderate). Golf is the focus here, but this small resort on the mainland also has a pool, tennis courts, restaurants, and a lounge. Nine four-bedroom cottages can be divided into single guest rooms or two-bedroom villas. Cottages and villas run in the expensive to very expensive range; each has a kitchen, wet bar, screened porch, and living area. Cottage No. 6 has the nicest view of the golf course, and has recently been redecorated. *1 Doug Ford Dr., Pensacola, FL 32507; tel. 904-492-1213, 800-874-5355. Off Rte. 292, about 2 mi. before the bridge to Perdido Key.*

♦ **Big Lagoon State Recreation Area** (inexpensive). The park has more than 75 campsites with modern facilities. Excellent nature-study programs. *12301 Gulf Beach Hwy., Pensacola, FL 32507; tel. 904-492-1595. On the mainland, 2 mi. east of Perdido Key.*

♦ **Best Western** (inexpensive). Close to the beach, it has 100 rooms, a hot tub, an outdoor pool, and free continental breakfast. *13585 Perdido Key Dr., Pensacola, FL 32507; tel. 904-492-2755, 800-554-8879.*

# HOUSE RENTALS

Rental houses are scarce on Perdido Key because property values were too high to build single homes when the area was developed in the 1980s. The few houses available must be reserved far in advance. In summer, they rent for around $1,000 a week, and a three-night to one-week minimum is required. Condominium and townhouse rentals are plentiful. Summer rates range from $500 to $1,200 a week.

♦ **Century 21 Leib & Associates.** Rents condos, townhouse units, and a few vacation homes. *14620 Perdido Key Dr., Pensacola, FL 32507; tel. 904-492-0744, 800-553-1223. Open Mon.-Sat.*

♦ **Perdido Management Services.** Rents condo and townhouse units for vacations and houses for stays of six months or more. *14110 Perdido Key Dr., Pensacola, FL 32507; tel. 904-492-2315, 800-232-6010. Open Mon.-Sat.*

4

# RESTAURANTS

◆ **Oyster Bar Restaurant** (expensive). Overlooking the Oyster Bar Marina, it has lots of windows on the water and is nicely decorated with wood and plush carpet. Seafood dominates the menu. The gumbo and oyster stew are tops. *13700 River Rd., Pensacola, FL 32507; tel. 904-492-0192. Open Tue.-Sun. for lunch and dinner. Alongside the bridge to Perdido Key. Take your first left after you come onto the island.*

◆ **Characters Caribbean Cafe** (moderate). Dine inside in the pleasant, air-conditioned dining room, sit at the lunch counter, or eat outside on the porch and enjoy the Caribbean art. The menu is mainly Caribbean but has everything from ham on rye to char-grilled salmon. Specialties include snapper pie (a fish quiche) and Havana salad with grilled chicken breast. *14110 Perdido Key Dr., Pensacola, FL 32507; tel. 904-492-2936. Open daily for lunch and dinner. At Colours on the Key shopping area.*

◆ **Keenan's Barbecue** (inexpensive). Genuine pit-barbecue favorites (pork, chicken, ribs, turkey, and beef) are served on picnic tables in a simple dining room. *13818 Perdido Key Dr., Pensacola, FL 32507; tel. 904-492-6848. Open Mon.-Sat. for lunch and dinner.*

# NIGHTLIFE

Don't expect any wild nights on Perdido Key. Everything is tastefully low-key. Cross the Florida state line into Alabama if you want to find some more action.

◆ **Flora-Bama Lounge.** Country tunes twang regularly from the stage of this local good-time bar. It also presents blues and jazz concerts. *17401 Perdido Key Dr., Pensacola, FL 35207; tel. 904-492-0611. Open nightly. Admission. At the Florida-Alabama state line on Perdido Key.*

# ATTRACTIONS

◆ **National Museum of Naval Aviation.** One of the world's largest air and space museums, it displays more than 100 historic aircraft and traces the history of aviation and space exploration. *Pensacola Naval Air Station, Pensacola, FL 32507; tel. 904-453-6289, 800-327-5002. Open daily 9-5. From Perdido Key, take Rte. 292A to Blue Angel Pkwy. (Rte. 173) and turn right.*

◆ **Pensacola Greyhound Track.** Matinee and night races, plus simulcasts of thoroughbred racing. *Hwy. 98 W., Pensacola, FL 32507; tel. 904-455-8595. Call for racing schedule. Admission. Take Rte. 292 off the island for 2 3/4 mi. and turn left on Dog Track Rd.*

# SHOPPING

Souvenir and clothing shops are interspersed throughout the island. A charming mid-island complex called Colours on the Key carries the  most unusual merchandise.

◆ **Frazier's Gifts.** Beach-motif souvenirs include jewelry, home accessories, toys, T-shirts, and insulated glasses. *14110 Perdido Key Dr., Pensacola, FL 32507; tel. 904-492-1671. Open daily. At Colours on the Key shopping area.*

◆ **Tony's Locker.** Wildlife gifts, clothing, and nautically themed items. *13700 River Rd., Pensacola, FL 32507; tel. 904-492-0192. Open Tue.-Sun. At the Oyster Bar Marina.*

◆ **White Wolf Emporium.** Native American art, crafts, jewelry, dolls, and books are the specialty here. *14620 Perdido Key Dr., Pensacola, FL 32507; tel. 904-492-2008. Open daily.*

# BEST FOOD SHOPS

**SANDWICHES:** ◆ **Subway.** *13390 Perdido Key Dr., Pensacola, FL 32507; tel. 904-492-7171. Open daily.*

**SEAFOOD:** ◆ **Nix Bros. Seafood.** *13470 Perdido Key Dr., Pensacola, FL 32507; tel. 904-492-1234. Open daily. On the mainland, alongside the bridge to Perdido Key.*

**FRESH PRODUCE:** ◆ **Delchamps.** *13390 Perdido Beach Blvd., Pensacola, FL 32507; tel. 904-492-1198. Open daily.*

**BAKERY:** ◆ **Delchamps.** *13390 Perdido Beach Blvd., Pensacola,*

*FL 32507; tel. 904-492-1198. Open daily.*
**BEVERAGES:** ◆ **Tom Thumb Food Store.** *14254 Perdido Key Dr., Pensacola, FL 32507; tel. 904-492-2376. Open daily.*
**WINE:** ◆ **Flora-Bama Lounge and Package.** *17401 Perdido Key Dr., Pensacola, FL 32507; tel. 904-492-0611. Open daily.*

# SPORTS
## FISHING
Charter-boat companies will take you to local and deep waters in search of redfish, bluefish, flounder, and sea trout.
◆ **Gray's Bait & Tackle.** Buy your fishing license, bait, tackle, and other fishing items here. *13013 Sorrento Rd., Pensacola, FL 32507; tel. 904-492-2666. Open daily. Off island, on Rte. 292.*
◆ **Holiday Harbor Marina.** Sells tackle, bait, and other supplies. *14050 Canal-A-Way, Pensacola, FL 32507; tel. 904-492-0555. Open daily. Off River Rd., by the west side of the bridge.*
◆ **Oyster Bar Marina.** Full- or half-day bottom-fishing trips; full-day offshore trips to deeper Gulf waters. *13700 River Rd., Pensacola, FL 32507; tel. 904-492-0192. Open daily. Alongside the bridge to Perdido Key. Take your first left as you come onto the island.*

## BOATING
Big Lagoon State Recreation Area on the mainland has a public ramp, but you must pay to get into the park. On Perdido Key, you can launch small vessels at the National Seashore. There's an admission there also, and it's difficult to launch at low tide.
◆ **Edgewater Rentals.** Rents pontoon boats year-round; center-console boats in summer. *Oyster Bar Marina, 13700 River Rd., Pensacola, FL 32507; tel. 904-492-7272. Open daily. Alongside the bridge to Perdido Key. Take your first left as you come onto to the island.*
◆ **Oyster Bar Marina.** Sightseeing trips for up to 50 passengers. *13700 River Rd., Pensacola, FL 32507; tel. 904-492-0192. Open daily. Under the bridge to Perdido Key. Take your first left as you come onto the island.*

## BICYCLING

Bike-riding along Perdido Key's lightly traveled roads is a real pleasure. The National Seashore's two-mile road is the best spot. There is no place to rent a bicycle on the island, however.

## GOLF

◆ **Perdido Bay Golf Resort.** Tee off at an attractive, semi-private 18-hole championship course. *1 Doug Ford Dr., Pensacola, FL 32507; tel. 904-492-1223, 800-874-5355. Open daily. Admission. Take Rte. 292 off the island and turn left on Doug Ford Rd.*

## TENNIS

There are no public tennis courts on the island. The closest courts are 25 minutes away in Pensacola.

# HISTORY

◆ **Fort Barrancas.** Built between 1839 and 1844 to protect Pensacola Harbor, it commands a strategic position overlooking the bay. Hence the fort's name, which means "bluffs" in Spanish. The National Park Service maintains it as part of the Gulf Islands National Seashore. There's a picnic area and a half-mile woodland nature trail. You can choose between guided and self-guided tours of the historic fort. *Gulf Islands National Seashore, 1801 Gulf Breeze Pkwy., Gulf Breeze, FL 32561; tel. 904-934-2600. Open daily. Admission. At Pensacola Naval Air Station. From Perdido Key, take Rte. 292A to Blue Angel Pkwy. (Rte. 173) and turn right.*

◆ **Fort McRee Battery ruins.** Hikers can explore the site where one of Pensacola's early-19th-century forts once stood. It has since slipped into the water. Still upright, however, are the ruins of the batteries. *From the Gulf Islands National Seashore parking lot, walk east along the beach.*

# NATURE

◆ **Big Lagoon State Recreation Area.** Salt spray has gnarled and dwarfed much of the vegetation in this 698-acre coastal community. The sand beaches on Big Lagoon and the salt marshes on Grand Lagoon host a variety of flora and fauna. You can see it all from an observation tower, or get up close via nature trails. Among the residents: gray foxes, raccoons, opossums, cardinals, towhees, and nut hatches. There are interpretive exhibits, and you can enjoy a guided walk. *12301 Gulf Beach Hwy., Pensacola, FL 32507; tel. 904-492-1595. Open daily. Admission. 2 mi. from Perdido Key on Hwy. 292A.*

◆ **Gulf Islands National Seashore.** Perdido Key's segment of this 150-mile system of preserved coastland offers beach exploration, primitive camping, and a quarter-mile nature trail. *1801 Gulf Breeze Pkwy., Gulf Breeze, FL 32561; tel. 904-934-2600. Open 8-sunset. Admission. At the east end of Johnson Beach Rd.*

◆ **Perdido Key State Recreation Area.** Opened in 1980 to pro-tect 247 acres of fragile barrier island ecology, it provides vis-itors the opportunity to bird-watch, enjoy the beach, fish, and study nature. Bounded on one side by the Gulf and on the other by Old River, it's a popular resting spot for birds migrating across the Gulf. Low-to-the-ground dunes vegeta-tion dominates the landscape. *c/o Big Lagoon SRA, 12301 Gulf Beach Hwy., Pensacola, FL 32507; tel. 904-492-1595. Open daily. On Perdido Key Dr.*

# SAFETY TIPS

Hikers exploring the National Seashore's secluded area should be careful about overexertion. The island's soft sand tires legs more quickly than conventional hard-sur-face hiking. Take plenty of water wherever you go and use a lot of sunscreen.

# TOURIST INFORMATION

◆ **Pensacola Area Convention & Visitor Bureau.** *1401 E. Gregory St., Pensacola, FL 32501; tel. 904-434-1234, 800-343-4321; fax 904-432-8211. Open daily 8-5.*

◆ **Perdido Key Area Chamber of Commerce.** *15500 Perdido Key Dr., Box 34052, Pensacola, FL 32507; tel. 904-492-4660. Mon.-Fri. 9-4.*

# Santa Rosa Island

**S**anta Rosa Island stretches 43 miles long and back more than 400 years into history. Of the three communities and two national parks on this intriguing island, the town of Pensacola Beach is best known. It has a reputation among families and the spring-break crowd not only for value and a great beach, but also for its proximity to downtown Pensacola's nightlife and historic districts.

| | |
|---|---|
| Beauty | A- |
| Swimming | B+ |
| Sand | A+ |
| Hotels/Inns/B&Bs | B+ |
| House rentals | B |
| Restaurants | A |
| Nightlife | A |
| Attractions | A+ |
| Shopping | A |
| Sports | A+ |
| Nature | A |

History is encapsulated on the island, mainly at Fort Pickens National Park, where the once-proud fort, completed in 1834, overlooks lush beaches, bicycle paths, and a fishing pier. Local history goes back much farther, to 1559, when the Spanish explorer Don Tristan DeLuna established the first settlement in North America on Pensacola Bay, six years before the founding of St. Augustine, America's oldest city, on the east coast of Florida.

The colony of 1,000 lasted only two years, but the Spaniards returned in 1698 and held the territory until the British routed them in 1763. Pensacola became a U.S. territory in 1821.

The various cultural influences brought a diversity of style to the colonial architecture, which has been beautifully preserved in and around Pensacola. This is something of a contrast to the development of Pensacola Beach, which, with its plentiful restaurants, clubs, shops, hotels, and a newly upgraded beach, is the island's prime resort area.

Fortunately, much of the region's natural beauty has been preserved. Most of the 150 miles of protected land and waters in the Gulf Islands National Seashore is in the Pensacola area, and some 14 miles are on Santa Rosa Island. Ground-quartz sand, as fine and white as sugar, sifts into mountainous dunes that give way to wide, wonderful beaches. Dazzling in bright sunlight, the famous Panhandle sand is awe-inspiring on Santa Rosa.

Santa Rosa Island gives beachgoers several options. Driving east a short way from Pensacola Beach, you'll come to a section of National Seashore that offers solitude and unparalleled bird-watching. Farther along is Navarre Beach, a less-glitzy version of Pensacola Beach. Beyond that, and closed to the public, is a section of Eglin Air Force Base. On the other side of the base, the town of Fort Walton Beach, reachable only from the mainland, occupies the eastern end of the island.

Late spring and summer are the island's true tourist seasons. Temperatures peak around 82 degrees in July, with water temperatures registering around 84. In winter, when the mercury may go as low as 53, venturing into the water takes bravery, and on rough days, it's inadvisable. A sign at the Bob Sikes Bridge reports on swimming conditions year-round. Gulf temperatures, normally warmer than land readings, dip into the mid-60s.

## HOW TO GET THERE

◆ From Pensacola Regional Airport (25 min. from Pensacola Beach), follow Airport Blvd. and turn left on Rte. 289 (9th Ave.). Follow it for 2 1/4 mi. until you see the sign for Hwy. 98. Turn left on Hwy. 98 and cross the Pensacola Bay Bridge (also called Three-Mile Bridge) to the town of Gulf Breeze. In about 1 mi., Hwy. 98 swings east, but you go straight to the Bob Sikes Bridge ($1 toll), which takes you to Pensacola Beach on Santa Rosa Island.

Pensacola, like most of the Panhandle, is on Central Time. The rest of Florida is on Eastern time.

# GULF BEACHES
## PENSACOLA BEACHES

The town of Pensacola Beach has just completed a $6-million improvement project, in which roads were widened, power lines submerged, and beach amenities upgraded. At the town center, there's more parking and an open-air

| | |
|---|---|
| Beauty | B+ |
| Swimming | B+ |
| Sand | A+ |
| Amenities | A+ |

pavilion for concerts. To the west of the main beach are a series of accesses with parking and a boardwalk, but no other facilities. Just before you come to the entrance to Fort Pickens, there's the Gate Beach, a beach park in the old style.

*Swimming:* Waves get big enough to attract surfers some days. Other times, the gradual shelf and calm, clear waters make this a haven for swimmers.

*Sand:* Very wide beach with beautiful, bright white sand.

*Amenities:* Casino Beach has rest rooms and food concessions. At the Gate Beach, there are small picnic shelters and grungy rest rooms. There are lifeguards on duty at the Casino Beach, but none at the Gate Beach.

*Sports:* A good surfing beach when conditions are right. Snorkeling is good, particularly at Casino Beach, where the artificial Jacobi Reef attracts marine life. There's a fishing pier at the beach's east end.

*Parking:* Free parking. Casino Beach's lot is being expanded to accommodate more than 500 cars.

### Casino Beach

Named for the dance pavilion that welcomed visitors until the late 1960s, it's also referred to as just Pensacola Beach. It benefited most from the recent improvements. *On Via De Luna near the Bob Sikes Bridge.*

### Gate Beach

This does not have a proper name, but locals call it the Gate

Beach. With cement shelters and groomed sand, it's not as natural as the beaches inside the national park, but it's free. The
dunes come close to the shoreline, making the beach impassable
in spots at high tide. *Off Fort Pickens Rd., just before you get to Fort
Pickens National Park.*

## FORT PICKENS NATIONAL PARK

This is the island's loveliest showcase of
what's natural and historic about the area.

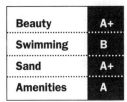

| Beauty | A+ |
| Swimming | B |
| Sand | A+ |
| Amenities | A |

There's parking at several points along the
seven-mile stretch of untainted sand.
Some accesses provide a boardwalk; others only a footpath. Fort ruins loom at
several spots along the Gulf beach and on the opposite side of
the island by the bay. Grasses and wild flowers decorate rolling
dunes. Some areas have oaks and pines. *From the Bob Sikes
Bridge, take a right at the stoplight on Fort Pickens Rd. and continue
3 1/4 mi. to the park entrance. Open 8-sunset.*

*Swimming:* The waves get wild, and the undercurrent is strong
in Pensacola Pass, at the park's western end.

*Sand:* Dunes range from low to fairly high. The wide beach
is a carpet of talcum-soft white sand, with the faintest tinge
of beige.

*Amenities:* Langdon Beach has rest rooms, outdoor showers,
and a picnic pavilion. Lifeguards on duty in summer. No facilities at other accesses.

*Sports:* Anglers fish from shore on both the Gulf and the bay. A
fishing pier near the fort juts into the sound, and jetties thrust
into the pass. Hiking and bike trails wind through the park.
Some diving sites off the west end can be reached from the
beach. Divers should beware of strong currents and remember
to display a diver's flag on the surface.

*Parking:* Entry to the park is $4 per car; $1 per walker or biker.

### Langdon Beach

Safely removed from the island's resort activities, this makes a
wonderful getaway. It's just across the road from a picnic area
with a bike trail.

## Other Accesses

Plant life is supplemented here with oaks and slash pines. All you can see from the beach is sand, dune grasses, agaves, a range-finder tower, and a few people. Unfortunately, many visitors walk on the dunes, trampling the fragile environment. instead of using the boardwalks to get to the beach. Cyclists must leave their vehicles in the bike rack.

## SANTA ROSA AREA SEASHORE

Desolate and surreal, seven miles of wind-sculpted dunes and sparse vegetation are preserved by the Gulf Islands National Seashore. Several Gulfside accesses are the only signs that this land has been discovered by humans. Even there, the low,

| Beauty | A |
| --- | --- |
| Swimming | B+ |
| Sand | A+ |
| Amenities | B |

wooden structures blend well with the landscape. These beaches, where the dunes and desolation can make you feel as though you're walking on the moon, are great for solitude-seekers. *From the Bob Sikes Bridge, turn left on Via De Luna and continue 7 mi. east of park entrance. Open 8-sunset.*

*Swimming:* This beach has its share of large waves, so use caution, especially when the lifeguard is off-duty.

*Sand:* High dunes with fine, white sand. Beach narrows in spots.

*Amenities:* Rest rooms, indoor and outdoor showers, picnic shelters, and barbecue grills. Food concessions, exhibit areas, and a souvenir shop are open May-September and on busy weekends in the off-season. Lifeguards on duty only at peak periods.

*Sports:* There are no beach concessions.

*Parking:* Plenty of parking. When entrance station is manned, you must pay $4 per car; $1 per cyclist or walk-in.

## NAVARRE BEACH (GULF)

Facilities show their age here, but the beach is a good one for walking. It's usually crowded. *From Pensacola Beach, head east 15 mi. on Via De Luna (Rte. 399).*

*Swimming:* Generally quiet, shallow waters, but whipped-up waves and strong

| Beauty | B |
| --- | --- |
| Swimming | B+ |
| Sand | A |
| Amenities | B |

currents make swimming hazardous at times.

*Sand:* Soft, white sands, but dunes are less impressive than those to the west.

*Amenities:* Rest rooms, outdoor showers, a pavilion with two cement tables, and plenty of nearby dining and recreational facilities.

*Sports:* There's a fishing pier next door and boating facilities nearby.

*Parking:* Free and plentiful.

# BAY BEACHES
## QUIETWATER BEACH

The name says it all. Waves are calm at this beach on Santa Rosa Sound, which is tucked into the crook where the Bob Sikes Bridge meets the town of Pensacola Beach. Near to shops, marinas, and restaurants, convenience is Quietwater Beach's long

| | |
|---|---|
| Beauty | B+ |
| Swimming | A- |
| Sand | A |
| Amenities | A+ |

suit. It begins just east of the bridge, where there's a park with picnic and parking facilities. Around the bend, it borders the Quietwater Beach Boardwalk shopping complex, a hive of community life, complete with boardwalks, a pier, and a scallop-shell bandstand.

*Swimming:* Protected by the island, waters are bathtub calm and clear. Gentle slope as you enter the water. Buoys protect swimmers from boat traffic.

*Sand:* The beach is widest around the shopping complex. Sand is fine and cushy.

*Amenities:* Outdoor showers, picnic shelters along the bridge approach, and an abundance of restaurants, bars, and shops. Lifeguard on duty.

*Sports:* Near the shopping complex, you will find volleyball nets set up on the beach. Water-sports rentals are on the bridge approach.

*Parking:* A long parking lot borders the beach by the bridge. You can also park in the shopping-complex lot, but that fills up faster.

## NAVARRE BEACH (BAY)

Right by the Navarre Beach Bridge, this beach stretches a long way along Santa Rosa Sound. A good place for families, it provides ready access to food and recreational facilities. *Take the Navarre Beach Bridge to Hwy. 98 and turn left following the signs.*

| | |
|---|---|
| Beauty | B |
| Swimming | B+ |
| Sand | B |
| Amenities | B+ |

*Swimming:* The water is calm, but gets deep quickly.

*Sand:* A long, narrow beach with clean, white sand.

*Amenities:* Cement picnic shelters dot the beach. Across the road are shops, restaurants, and recreation concessions.

*Sports:* Across the road, there's a boat launch, a sailing-lessons concession, and waverunner rentals.

*Parking:* A small, unpaved lot runs along part of the beach.

# HOTELS/INNS/B&Bs

Pensacola Beach has a lot of places to stay, but nothing outstanding. Some of the motels have character, however. On the mainland, there are a variety of hotels in Pensacola.

◆ **Clarion Suites Resort** (expensive). Remarkable individuality in its 86 suites. Dressed in varying shades of pastel clapboard, they embody different design elements, creating a feeling of community. Right on the beach, the resort has a boardwalk to the sands, a pool, and a well-laid-out commons area. Continental breakfast. The best suites are Nos. 143-158, because they're closest to the Gulf. *20 Via De Luna, Pensacola Beach, FL 32561; tel. 904-932-4300, 800-874-5303.*

◆ **The Dunes** (moderate). Part old, part new. The new is an Art Deco tower with modern rooms; the old a motel-like structure with dated but comfortable accommodations. Each entity has its own pool, and they share a stretch of beach. There are 140 units in all. Children's program shared with the nearby Holiday Inn. Golfers should ask about the play-around package. *333 Fort Pickens Rd., Pensacola Beach, FL 35261; tel. 904-932-3536, 800-833-8637.*

◆ **Fort Pickens Campground** (inexpensive). Five separate camp areas hold 200 sites for RVs and tents. Most are shaded by tall slash pines and live oaks. Loop A is closest to the beach. Campsites are issued on a first-come basis; no reservations. These fill up beginning in March. Maximum stays are enforced according to season. Electricity and dumping facilities are provided. *Fort Pickens National Park, 1400 Fort Pickens Rd., Pensacola Beach, FL 32561; tel. 904-934-2621. Open daily. Check-in 8-sunset. In Fort Pickens National Park, at the west end of Santa Rosa Island.*

◆ **New World Inn** (inexpensive). Part of Pensacola's historic waterfront warehouses, its 16 modern rooms and suites are decorated in themes recalling such local historical personages as Geronimo and Andrew Jackson. Restaurant and pub. Continental breakfast. *600 S. Palafox St., Pensacola, FL 32501; tel. 904-432-4111. From the Pensacola Bay Bridge, veer left on Bayfront Pkwy. Turn right on Palafox St.*

# HOUSE RENTALS

In July and August, a one-week minimum rental is often required, normally from Saturday to Saturday, for homes in Pensacola Beach. Rates range from $495 to $1,150 a week. In Navarre Beach, condo and home rentals are your best option. Homes along the Gulf rent from $1,000 to $3,000 for a week. Away from the beach, you can pay as little as $600 a week.

◆ **Gulf Properties.** *8460 Gulf Blvd., Navarre Beach, FL 32566; tel. 904-939-2311, 800-821-8790. Open Mon.-Sat.*

◆ **Pensacola Beach Realty.** *649 Pensacola Beach Blvd., Pensacola Beach, FL 32561; tel. 904-932-5337, 800-874-9243. Open Mon.-Sat.*

# RESTAURANTS

◆ **Flounder's Chowder and Ale House** (expensive). This place is pure fun—and the food is great. Exterior is slapped together like an old fish house. Inside, one room spoofs library ambience. Excellent seafood and steaks. The house specialty, the Florida Seafood Platter, samples the best of the region: char-grilled fish, shrimp scampi, fried oysters, fried scallops, and stuffed blue crab. Known also for Sunday brunch. *800 Quietwater Beach Rd.,*

*Pensacola Beach, FL 32561; tel. 904-932-2003. Open daily for lunch and dinner.*

◆ **Jubilee** (expensive). A restaurant complex on the bayside beach, it caters to various budgets with its Beach Island Bar, casual Beachside Cafe (inexpensive), and formal TopSide (expensive). Sandwiches, salads, and burgers are served downstairs in a festive atmosphere. Upstairs, soft music, gold-and-white linen, and windows on the bay set a fine-dining mood for new-Florida style seafood and steaks with a Cajun influence. Popular entrees include blackened grouper and shrimp scampi. *400 Quietwater Beach Rd., Pensacola Beach, FL 32561; tel. 904-934-3108, 800-582-3028. Open Mon.-Sat for breakfast, lunch, and dinner; Sun. for brunch and dinner. At the Quietwater Beach Boardwalk.*

◆ **McGuire's Irish Pub and Brewery** (moderate). A legend for its tasty burgers, steaks, and home-brewed beers, served among moose heads, antiques, and nearly 100,000 autographed dollar bills. *600 E. Gregory St., Pensacola, FL 32501; tel. 904-433-6789. Open daily for lunch and dinner. Take the Pensacola Bay Bridge (Hwy. 98), which becomes Gregory St.*

◆ **Peg Leg Pete's Oyster Bar** (moderate). A seaworthy place, it appeals to casual boaters, families, and youths on spring break. Long tables and booths, country music set the tone. Specialties: snow crab served in buckets, oysters done nine ways, and Cajun dishes. The red beans and rice studded with sausage makes a hearty, inexpensive meal. *1010 Fort Pickens Rd., Pensacola Beach, FL 32561; tel. 904-932-4139. Open daily for lunch and dinner. At Lafitte Cove Marina.*

# NIGHTLIFE

Pensacola Beach holds it own in the nightlife department, with several clubs catering to the under-30 crowd. Older night crawlers should head to Pensacola for concerts and clubs.

◆ **Flounder's Chowder and Ale House.** Reggae is the trademark sound from Flounder's outdoor band stand. Dance barefoot in the sand. *800 Quietwater Beach Rd., Pensacola Beach, FL 32561; tel. 904-932-2003. Open daily. Live music Wed.-Sun.*

◆ **McGuire's Irish Pub and Brewery.** Known for Irish entertainment and fine, home-brewed ales, porters, and stouts. *600 E. Gregory St., Pensacola, FL 32051; tel. 904-433-6789. Open daily. Take the Pensacola Bay Bridge (Hwy. 98), which becomes Gregory St. (Hwy. 98).*

◆ **Pensacola Civic Center.** Part of the Pensacola Civic Center complex, it stages entertainment from boxing to rock concerts. *201 E. Gregory St., Pensacola, FL 32501; tel. 904-432-0800, 800-488-5252 for Ticketmaster. Admission. Take the Pensacola Bay Bridge (Hwy. 98), which turns into Gregory St.*

◆ **Saenger Theatre.** Housed in a 1920s vaudeville theater, it hosts local performing groups, such as Kaleidoscope Dance Theatre, Pensacola Symphony Orchestra, and Pensacola Opera, as well as internationally known performers. *118 S. Palafox St., Pensacola, FL 32501; tel. 904-444-7686, 800-488-5252 for Ticketmaster. Box office open Mon.-Fri. Admission. From the Pensacola Bay Bridge, veer left onto Bayfront Pkwy. Turn right on Palafox.*

◆ **Seville Quarter.** A complex of bars and restaurants housed in historic digs. Rosie O'Grady's features Dixieland. Phineas Phogg's does dance tunes.*130 E. Government St., Pensacola, FL 32501; tel. 904-434-6211. Open nightly. Admission. From the Pensacola Bay Bridge, veer left onto Bayfront Pkwy., which becomes Main St. Take a right on Tarragona St., then a left on Government St.*

◆ **Under Where? Bar.** A lighted sand volleyball court and live country music attract the young crowd. *1010 Fort Pickens Rd., Pensacola Beach, FL 32561; tel. 904-932-4139. Open daily. Below Peg Leg Pete's Oyster Bar.*

# ATTRACTIONS

◆ **Pensacola Museum of Art.** Exhibitions are confined in Pensacola's Old City Jailhouse, built around 1906. *407 S. Jefferson, Pensacola, FL 32501; tel. 904-432-6247. Open Tue.-Fri. 10-5; Sat. 10-4; Sun. 1-4. From the Pensacola Bay Bridge, go left on Bayfront Pkwy., then turn right on Jefferson St.*

◆ **The Zoo.** More than 700 animals, including two white tigers, dwell on 50 acres of natural landscapes and botanical gardens. Japanese garden, daily elephant and bird shows, petting zoo, newborn nursery. *5701 Gulf Breeze Pkwy., Gulf Breeze, FL 32561; tel. 904-932-2229. Open daily 9-5 in summer; 9-4 in winter. Admission. Take the Navarre Beach Bridge to Hwy. 98 in Gulf Breeze. Turn left on Hwy. 98 and continue for about 7 mi.*

# SHOPPING

The best shopping on the island is at the Quietwater Beach Boardwalk, on the bay and to the left of the Bob Sikes Bridge as you enter Pensacola Beach. Another strip of shops is on Via De Luna. Off-island, downtown Pensacola holds many surprises in its historic districts, particularly Seville Square and Quayside Market.

◆ **Flea Market.** A thrift-seeker's outdoor mall of antiques, produce, furniture, crafts, and used merchandise. *5760 Gulf Breeze Pkwy., Gulf Breeze, FL 32561; tel. 904-934-1971. Open Sat.-Sun. From the middle of the island, take Navarre Beach Bridge to Hwy. 98. Turn left on Hwy. 98 and continue for 7 mi. Located across the street from the Zoo.*

◆ **Fort Pickens Bookstore.** Great selection of books and videos about Pensacola, Civil War days, the military, national parks, and the South. *Fort Pickens National Park, 1400 Fort Pickens Rd., Pensacola Beach, FL 32561; tel. 904-934-2600. Open daily.*

◆ **Go Fish T-Shirt & Sole Co.** It has two store fronts at Quietwater Beach Boardwalk. One sells colorful T-shirts, jewelry, toys, and gifts. The other is a factory outlet selling lovely women's batik and cotton fashions at great prices. *400 Quietwater Beach Rd., Quietwater Beach Boardwalk, Pensacola Beach, FL 32561; tel. 904-934-5251, 904-934-0274. Open daily.*

◆ **Quayside Art Gallery.** The South's largest co-op gallery, featuring the work of more than 200 local artists. Housed in an 1873 fire house. *Plaza Ferdinand, 17 E. Zaragoza St., Pensacola, FL 32501; tel. 904-438-2363. Open daily. From the Pensacola Bay Bridge, go left on Bayfront Pkwy. Turn right on Jefferson St., then left on Zaragoza.*

# BEST FOOD SHOPS

SANDWICHES: ◆ **Sandshaker Sandwich Shop.** *731 Pensacola Beach*

*Blvd., Pensacola Beach, FL 32561; tel. 904-932-0023. Open daily.*
**SEAFOOD:** ◆ **Fish Peddler Seafood.** *333 Gulf Breeze Pkwy., Gulf Breeze, FL 32561; tel. 904-932-9613. Open daily.*
**BAKERY:** ◆ **Chan's Market Cafe.** *16 Via De Luna, Pensacola Beach, FL 32561; tel. 904-932-8454. Open daily.*
**ICE CREAM:** ◆ **Lum's Deli.** *400 Quietwater Beach Rd., Quietwater Beach Boardwalk, Pensacola Beach, FL 32561; tel. 904-934-0520. Open daily.*
**BEVERAGES:** ◆ **Tom Thumb Food Store.** *22B Via De Luna, Pensacola Beach, FL 32561; tel. 904-932-2201. Open daily.*
**WINE:** ◆ **Chan's Liquor & Wines.** *16 Via De Luna, Pensacola Beach, FL 32561; tel. 904-932-8454. Open daily.*

# SPORTS

## FISHING

The Bob Sikes Fishing Pier, which extends along the bridge between Santa Rosa Island and Gulf Breeze, is a favorite place to dangle a worm. Other piers are located along the bridge between the mainland and Gulf Breeze and at Pensacola Beach, Fort Pickens, and Navarre Beach. Fishermen also cast along the beach and from the jetty at Fort Pickens' west end.
◆ **Gray's Tackle & Guide Service.** Fishing charters. *207 Gulf Breeze Pkwy., Gulf Breeze, FL 32561; tel. 904-934-3151. Open daily.*
◆ **Gulf Breeze Bait & Tackle.** Sells fishing licenses and other fishing necessities. *825 Gulf Breeze Pkwy., Gulf Breeze, FL 32561; tel. 904-932-6789. Open daily.*
◆ **Lo-Baby.** Charter fishing excursions. *38 Highpoint Dr., Gulf Breeze, FL 32561; tel. 904-934-5285. Open daily.*
◆ **Navarre Fishing Pier.** Tackle and bait shop with restaurant on-site. *8577 Gulf Blvd., Navarre Beach, FL; tel. 904-939-5658. Open daily.*
◆ **Pensacola Beach Fishing Pier.** *Casino Beach Boardwalk, Pensacola Beach, FL 32561; tel. 904-932-0444. Open daily.*

## BOATING

Boat launches are located just east of Fort Pickens Park on Santa Rosa Sound, at Quietwater Beach, and at the Navarre Beach Bridge.
◆ **Key Sailing.** Rents pontoon boats and catamarans. *400 Quietwater Beach Rd., Pensacola Beach, FL 32561; tel. 904-932-*

*5520. Open daily.*

◆ **Lo-Baby.** Excursion, dolphin, and dive cruises aboard a 41-ft., 22-passenger boat. *38 Highpoint Dr., Gulf Breeze, FL 32561; tel. 904-934-5285. Open daily.*

◆ **Radical Rides.** Rents personal watercraft, sailboats, and sailboards. *444 Pensacola Beach Blvd., Pensacola Beach, FL 32561; tel. 904-934-9743. Open daily.*

## DIVING

◆ **Lo-Baby.** Dive cruises aboard a 41-ft., 22-passenger boat. *38 Highpoint Dr., Gulf Breeze, FL 32561; tel. 904-934-5285. Open daily.*

## BICYCLING

Seven miles of bike paths run parallel to lengths of Via de Luna and Fort Pickens Road. Miles of unpaved bike trails wind through the ruins and natural flora at Fort Pickens National Seashore.

◆ **Island Video & Ice Cream.** Rents bikes for a two-hour minimum. *12 Via De Luna, Pensacola Beach, FL 32561; tel. 904-934-5007. Open daily.*

◆ **Paradise Scooter & Bicycle Rental.** Rentals for two-hour minimum; also weekly. *715 Pensacola Beach Blvd., Pensacola Beach, FL 32561; tel. 904-934-0014. Open daily.*

## GOLF

◆ **The Club at Hidden Creek.** 18-hole championship course. *3070 PGA Blvd., Navarre, FL 32566; tel. 904-939-4604, 800-239-2582. Open daily. Admission. Cross the Navarre Beach Bridge to Hwy. 98 in Navarre. Turn right and go to Water St. Turn right. Follow the signs.*

◆ **Tiger Point Golf Course.** A 36-hole tournament course. *1255 Country Club Rd., Gulf Breeze, FL 32561; tel. 904-932-1333, 800-477-4833. Open daily. Admission.*

## TENNIS

◆ **Gulf Breeze Recreation Center.** You can volley on one of six hard-surface courts. *800 Shore Line Dr., Gulf Breeze, FL*

*32561; tel. 904-934-5140. Open daily. Take the Bob Sikes Bridge to Gulf Breeze and turn left on Shore Line Dr.*

# HISTORY

**D**owntown Pensacola has a wealth of preserved structures in the Seville and Palafox Historic districts, and in the North Hill Preservation District.

◆ **Fort Pickens.** Ruins of the circa-1830 fort are spread throughout the island, but the major portion is at the western end. A Union outpost during the Civil War. In 1886, Geronimo and other Apaches were held here. Candlelight tours and Civil War demonstrations on weekends. *Fort Pickens National Park, 1400 Fort Pickens Rd., Pensacola Beach, FL 32561; tel. 904-934-2600. Open daily 8-sunset. Guided tours Mon.-Fri. at 2; Sat.-Sun. 11 and 2. Admission. At the west end of Fort Pickens Rd.*

◆ **Historic Pensacola Village.** Part of the Seville Historic District in downtown Pensacola, it encompasses museums, historic homes, and the Colonial Archaeological Trail. The T.T. Wentworth, Jr., Florida State Museum, has a variety of exhibits, including Discovery!, a hands-on children's museum. Julee Cottage, once the home of a free African-American, houses a museum of black history. *205 E. Zaragoza St., Pensacola, FL 32501; tel. 904-444-8905. Open daily 10-4; closed Sun. Labor Day-Easter. Admission. Take the Pensacola Bay Bridge and turn left on Bayfront Pkwy. Drive about 1 mi. to S. Tarragona St. Turn right and go 1 block to Zaragoza St. Follow signs to the ticket office in Tivoli House.*

◆ **Pensacola Historical Museum.** Housed in an 1832 church, it concentrates on local history. *405 S. Adams St., Pensacola, FL 32501; tel. 904-433-1559. Open Mon.-Sat. 9-4:30; Sun. 1-5. Admission. From Pensacola Bay Bridge, veer left onto Bayfront Pkwy. Turn right on Adams St.*

# NATURE

◆ **Fort Pickens National Park.** The park contains a small museum that explains local flora and fauna. A 1,600-foot boardwalk takes visitors through grasses and wild flowers with interpretive signposts. *1400*

*Fort Pickens Rd., Pensacola Beach, FL 32561; tel. 904-934-2600. Open daily. Admission. At the west end of the island.*

◆ **Naval Live Oaks.** Part of the Gulf Islands National Seashore, its 1,378 acres include lovely stands of live oak and are home to birds, reptiles, and an occasional bobcat or red fox. More than five miles of nature trails. *1801 Gulf Breeze Pkwy., Gulf Breeze, FL 32561; tel. 904-934-2600. Open daily.*

◆ **Santa Rosa Area Gulf Islands National Seashore.** A prototype of maritime forest ecology, this seven miles of unspoiled coastland is a bird-watcher's paradise. *Navarre Beach Rd., Navarre Beach, FL 32566; tel. 904-934-2600. Open daily. Admission. From Pensacola Beach, head east on Rte. 399, which changes into Navarre Beach Rd.*

# SAFETY TIPS

Gulf waters can get rough here with tricky currents and undertow. Heed warnings posted at the toll booth on the Bob Sikes Bridge. Never swim alone or when tired. Also, beware of jellyfish, sea nettles, Portuguese men-of-war, and other stinging nuisances. Vandalism does occur at Fort Pickens National Park, usually after hours, so lock your car.

# TOURIST INFORMATION

◆ **Gulf Islands National Seashore.** *1801 Gulf Breeze Pkwy., Gulf Breeze, FL 32561; tel. 904-934-2600. Open daily 8:30-4:30. At Naval Live Oaks Visitor's Center. From Pensacola Beach, take the Bob Sikes Bridge to Gulf Breeze Pkwy. (Hwy. 98) and turn right.*

◆ **Pensacola Beach Visitor Information Center.** *735 Pensacola Beach Blvd., Pensacola Beach, FL 32561; tel. 904-932-1500, 800-635-4803. Open Mon.-Sat. 9-5; Sun. 9-3.*

◆ **Pensacola Convention & Visitors Information Center.** *1401 E. Gregory St., Pensacola, FL 32501; tel. 904-434-1234, 800-874-1234. Open daily 8-5. On the mainland, at the foot of the Pensacola Bay Bridge.*

◆ **South Santa Rosa County Information Center.** *Box 5337, Navarre, FL 32566; tel. 904-939-2691, 800-480-7263. Open Mon.-Fri. 9-5; Sat.-Sun. 10-4. From the island, take Navarre Beach Bridge to Hwy. 98 and turn left. The office is on the left.*

## CHAPTER 3

# Destin

Although some people refer loosely to the entire Panhandle as the Emerald Coast, the beach towns of Destin and Fort Walton Beach claim the designation as their own, and it's easy to see why. The sun playing on the Gulf waters here makes the surface sparkle like a gem, thanks to a concentration of blue-green algae. The color goes perfectly with the blinding white sands that roll and stretch lazily to meet the sea.

| | |
|---|---|
| Beauty | A- |
| Swimming | A |
| Sand | A+ |
| Hotels/Inns/B&Bs | A- |
| House rentals | B+ |
| Restaurants | A |
| Nightlife | A |
| Attractions | A+ |
| Shopping | A- |
| Sports | A+ |
| Nature | B+ |

A relative newcomer to the tourist trade, Destin is separated from the bright lights of Fort Walton Beach by the waters of East Pass and by a radically different attitude toward development. The area has grown steadily in the past decade, but hotels, inns, restaurants, and even fun parks are done in good taste.

Location alone is enough to explain Destin's strong ties to sea and sand. The town clings to the western tip of a long peninsula separated from the mainland by wide Choctawatchee Bay. Much of its activity clusters around the west-end harbor, where charter boats and seafood restaurants abound. Indeed, because of the excellent deep-sea fishing off its shores, Destin proclaims itself the World's Luckiest Fishing Village. Restaurants not only have grouper and other deep-sea species on the menu, but should you happen to hook one yourself, they'll gladly cook it for you.

Boating is popular here, too, along with the complete array

of water sports. Scuba divers find much to explore, including several offshore wrecks and a submerged petrified forest known as Timber Hole.

East of town, Destin's beaches provide a relaxing environment for wading, swimming, or sunbathing. They have fine sand that's the whitest on the Panhandle. Farther along, the residential community of Sandestin offers its guests a full agenda of water and land sports.

# GULF BEACHES
## CRYSTAL BEACH

This sparkling span of beach begins well beyond Destin's area of commercial development. Henderson Beach State Recreation Area sets the tone with an undeveloped beachfront and an aura of natural solitude. James W. Lee Park tends to attract larger numbers of people but is lovely nonetheless.

| | |
|---|---|
| Beauty | A- |
| Swimming | A |
| Sand | A |
| Amenities | A |

*Swimming:* Great wading for kids in the shallow, clear water. Waters maintain a refreshing coolness in the summer. The brave even swim them in winter.

*Sand:* This could be the whitest sand you've ever seen, so bring your sunglasses! Outside the state park, the sand is groomed.

*Amenities:* Rest rooms, outdoor showers, picnic decks and shelters, shops, and restaurants. Several boardwalks cross the dunes to the

## HOW TO GET THERE

◆ From Fort Walton Beach/Okaloosa County Airport (25 minutes from Destin), follow Rte. 85 south 9 mi. through Fort Walton Beach. When you reach Hwy. 98, veer left to cross Santa Rosa Sound onto Okaloosa Island. Continue east on Hwy. 98 for 6 1/2 mi. until you reach the East Pass Bridge. Cross the bridge into Destin. To reach the beaches, continue east for about 5 mi.

beach. Lifeguards on duty at James W. Lee Park, but not at Henderson Beach State Recreation Area.

*Sports:* Jet Ski and parasailing concessions are less than three miles away.

*Parking:* Henderson Beach State Recreation Area, which has two large lots with plenty of parking spaces, charges a $2 entrance fee on the honor system. Parking, however, is free at James W. Lee Park, and the lot often fills quickly.

## Henderson Beach State Recreation Area

Dunes edge the contours of this mile-long beach, which is not as wide as that at James W. Lee Park. A condo development spoils the view to the west, but development is more subdued to the east. Picnic shelters and other park structures are relatively attractive. *Open 8-sunset. Entrance on Hwy. 98E.*

## James W. Lee Park

A wide, dazzling beach that, because it is free, is likely to be crowded on good beach days during the summer. It offers such on-site amenities as a gift shop, a restaurant, and an ice cream parlor, all housed in New England-style buildings with tin roofs and cupolas. *From the entrance to Henderson Beach State Recreation Area, drive 3/4 mi. east on Hwy. 98E. Turn south on Mathew Blvd. Turn left and drive 2 1/2 mi. on Old Hwy. 98.*

# HOTELS/INNS/B&Bs

◆ **Henderson Park Inn** (very expensive). Built in 1993 to resemble a New England inn and furnished with antique reproductions, it's one of the few Florida B&Bs right on the beach. The 20 suites have microwaves, refrigerators, and Gulf porches. The inn also has family-style villas (expensive range) made over from a motel. Complimentary breakfast. *35000 Emerald Coast Pkwy., Destin, FL 32541; tel. 904-837-4853, 800-336-4853. East of Destin on Old Hwy. 98.*

◆ **Sandestin** (expensive). A 2,400-acre residential resort community with all the ingredients for an ideal beach vacation. Accommodations range from hotel rooms in the 175-unit Inn to four-bedroom villas.

Most popular is Beachside Towers, whose suites and other units are priced in the very expensive category. There are 63 holes of golf, 14 tennis courts, workout facilities, bike rentals, recreational programs, and a 98-slip marina that offers fishing charters and water-sports rentals. Security gate at the entrance. *9300 Hwy. 98 E., Destin, FL 32541; tel. 904-267-8000, 800-277-0800; fax 904-267-8222.*

# HOUSE RENTALS

Though condominiums and townhouses are more plentiful, the Destin area also has a nice selection of homes to rent. Rates run from $1,200 to $4,500 for a week in summer. Some properties require a weekly Saturday-to-Saturday rental.

◆ **Abbott Realty.** Free catalog. *Box 30, 35000 Emerald Coast Pkwy., Destin, FL 32541; tel. 904-837-4853, 800-336-4853. Open daily.*

# RESTAURANTS

Variety of seafood is wider than in most of Florida because restaurants serve local triggerfish and amberjack. Although the fish are commonly deep fried, steamed, or broiled, chefs are turning increasingly to char-grilling and blackening.

◆ **Harbor Docks** (expensive). Local seafood specialties get an Oriental tweak here, where the sushi bar is famous and dishes smack of Thai fire. The interior is decorated with antique rod and reels. *538 Hwy. 98 E., Destin, FL 32541; tel. 904-837-2506. Open daily for lunch and dinner.*

◆ **A.J.'s Seafood & Oyster Bar** (moderate). Harbor views and fresh seafood add to the flavor of this longtime favorite, which serves everything in its name and much more. The smoked yellowfin tuna dip appetizer is wonderful. House specialties include fried Florida lobster, gumbo, and soft-shelled crab. There is seating indoors and out. *116 Hwy. 98E., Destin, FL 32541; tel. 904-837-1913. Open daily for lunch and dinner. Just east of the Destin Bridge.*

◆ **Fudpucker's** (moderate). The motif is shipwreck; the cuisine deep-water. Try the squashed crab soup and char-grilled tuna. Salads and burgers sate the non-seafood seeker. Music and fun charge the atmosphere. *20001-A Emerald Coast Pkwy., Destin,*

*FL 32541; tel. 904-654-4200. Open daily for lunch and dinner.*

◆ **Harry T's Boathouse** (moderate). One of the town's most popular restaurants, it offers everything from blackened grouper (a large, meaty fish) to New York Strip and fajitas. The decor is classy, the harbor overlook spectacular; the dress casual. *320 Hwy. 98 E., Destin, FL 32541; tel. 904-654-4800; fax 904-654-4329. Open Mon.-Sat. for lunch and dinner; Sun. for brunch and dinner. At the Destin Yacht Club.*

◆ **Lucky Snapper Grill & Bar** (moderate). Overlooking Destin Harbor, it will tempt you with such local catches as triggerfish, mackerel, amberjack, and grouper prepared char-grilled, pan-fried, deep-fried, and with creative sauces. Try whatever's in season. *76 Hwy. 98 E., Destin, FL 32541; tel. 904-654-0900. Open daily for lunch and dinner. At the foot of the Destin Bridge at Harbor Walk. Turn right after Hooter's.*

# NIGHTLIFE

◆ **Destin Lanes.** This massive center of nightlife has 24 bowling lanes, restaurant, bar, lounge, dance floor, 80 video games, bingo, billiards, and gym. *34876 Hwy. 98 E., Destin, FL 32451; tel. 904-654-5251. Open daily.*

◆ **Fudpucker's.** Local and imported bands play rock and roll. *20001-A Emerald Coast Pkwy., Destin, FL 32541; tel. 904-654-4200. Open nightly.*

◆ **Harry T's Boathouse.** Live reggae, jazz, and local rock bands. *320 Hwy. 98 E., Destin, FL 32541; tel. 904-654-4800. Open nightly. At the Destin Yacht Club.*

◆ **Lucky Snapper.** Go for happy hour and watch the sun set over the bridge. After dark, the open-air bar hosts live country and rock bands. *76 Hwy. 98 E., Destin, FL 32541; tel. 904-654-0900. Open daily. Live music Wed.-Sun. Admission. At the foot of the Destin Bridge at Harbor Walk. Turn right after Hooter's.*

# ATTRACTIONS

The Emerald Coast provides plenty of family entertainment. Destin has a few of the area's trademark amusement parks. In nearby Fort Walton Beach, they're wall-to-wall.

◆ **Air Boingo.** Top adventure: bungee jumping. *1127 Hwy. 98 E., Destin, FL 32541; tel. 904-654-9306. Open daily in summer. Hours vary. Closed in winter. Admission.*

◆ **Big Kahuna's.** Entertainment for all ages. The sand dune buggy track is a fun novelty, plus there are carnival games, a sky coaster, 54 holes of miniature golf, and a mega-waterpark. *1007 Hwy. 98 E., Destin, FL 32541; tel. 904-837-4061. Open daily. Admission.*

◆ **The Track.** A family fun park with bumper boats, bumper cars, go-carts, and two 18-hole miniature golf courses. *1125 Hwy. 98 E., Destin, FL 32541; tel. 904-654-4668. Open daily. Hours vary. Admission.*

# SHOPPING

◆ **Artz.** A studio that sells watercolors and pastels of artist Donna Burgess. *120-B Hwy. 98 E., Destin, FL 32541; tel. 904-837-1887. Open daily.*

◆ **Silver Sands Factory Stores.** Factory-outlet discounts at more than 60 shops, including Dansk, Laura Ashley, Reebok, Lenox, and Calvin Klein. *Hwy. 98 E., Destin, FL 32541; tel. 904-864-9780, 800-510-6255. Open daily.*

◆ **The Market at Sandestin.** More than 25 shops sell upscale products, from kitchen wares to swimwear. *Sandestin Resort, Destin, FL 32541. Open daily. At the Sandestin Resort entrance on Hwy. 98 E.*

◆ **The Zoo Gallery.** Wildlife books, prints, pottery, clothing, and jewelry. *868 Hwy. 98 E., Destin, FL 32541; tel. 904-837-7554. Open daily.*

# BEST FOOD SHOPS

**SANDWICHES:** ◆ **Donut Hole II.** *6745 Hwy. 98 W., Santa Rosa Beach, FL 32459; tel. 904-267-3239. Open daily. 2 1/2 mi. east of Sandestin.*

**SEAFOOD:** ◆ **Destin Ice House Seafood Market.** *210 Hwy. 98 E., Destin, FL 32541; tel. 904-837-8333. Open daily. 1/2 mi. east of the Destin Bridge.*

**FRESH PRODUCE:** ◆ **Delchamps.** *Hwy. 98 E. and Main St., Destin, FL 32541; tel. 904-837-8527. Open daily. At Shores Shopping Center.*

**BAKERY:** ◆ **Donut Hole II.** *6745 Hwy. 98 W., Santa Rosa Beach, FL*

*32459; tel. 904-267-3239. Open daily. 2 1/2 mi. east of Sandestin.*

**ICE CREAM:** ◆ **Parrots Sweet Shop.** *3500 Old Hwy. 98 E., Destin, FL 32541; tel. 904-654-5344. Open daily. On the beach at James W. Lee Park.*

**BEVERAGES:** ◆ **Ritz Food Store.** *34884 Hwy. 98 E., Destin, FL 32541; tel. 904-654-5861. Open daily.*

**WINE:** ◆ **Sands Liquors & Wine.** *1105 Hwy. 98 E., Destin, FL 32541; tel. 904-837-9550. Open daily.*

# SPORTS
## FISHING

Calling itself "The World's Luckiest Fishing Village," Destin makes the most of its proximity to the 100-fathom fishing ground offshore. In summer, sailfish, marlin, dolphinfish, and wahoo are the prized catches. Fishing charters charge around $30 per person for a half-day, including license and, sometimes, cleaning services. Fishing licenses may also be obtained at Wal-Mart and K-mart.

◆ **Backcountry Outfitters.** Fishing charters in local waters, half-day and full-day. *East Pass Marina, Destin, FL 32541; tel. 904-585-3321. Open daily.*

◆ **Half-Hitch Tackle.** Sells fishing tackle and licenses. *621 Hwy. 98 E., Destin, FL 32541; tel. 904-837-3121. Open daily.*

◆ **Moody's.** Five-hour fishing cruises to deep water. Staff cleans your fish, and you get a special price at A.J.'s restaurant to have it prepared. *Box 68, 194 Hwy. 98 E., Destin, FL 32541; tel. 904-837-1293. Open daily. Behind A.J.'s restaurant.*

## BOATING

Destin boasts the largest charter boat fleet in Florida. More than 140 vessels set sail for party, fishing, and sightseeing excursions.

◆ **Blackbeard Sailing Charters.** Sightseeing and sunset cruises with a pirate theme aboard a 54-foot schooner. *Hwy. 98 E., Destin, FL 32541; tel. 904-837-2793. Open daily. East of the Destin Bridge, behind A.J.'s Restaurant.*

◆ **Glass Bottom Boats.** Sightsee above and below the water, while you learn about local bird and marine species. *304 Hwy. 98 E., Destin, FL 32541; tel. 904-654-7787. Open daily. At Capt. Dave's Marina.*

◆ **Premier Powerboat Rentals.** Rents powerboats by the day or half-day. *302 Hwy. 98 E., Destin, FL 32541; tel. 904-837-7755. Open daily. 1/2 mi. east of Destin Bridge on Destin Harbor.*

## DIVING

Diving in Destin waters is excellent. Dive shops run trips that specialize in such things as spear-fishing, shell collecting, and lobstering.

◆ **ScubaTech.** Diving and snorkeling charters and scuba certification courses. *312 Hwy. 98 E., Destin, FL 32541; tel. 904-837-2822. Open daily. At Capt. Dave's marina.*

## BICYCLING

There are no bike rentals in the Destin area, but the Sandestin Resort has bike trails and rentals for guests.

## GOLF

◆ **Emerald Bay Golf Club.** A top-rated 18-hole course. *40001 Hwy. 98 E., Destin, FL 32541; tel. 904-837-5197. Open daily. Admission. On Hwy. 98, 4 mi. east of Destin.*

◆ **Indian Bayou Golf and Country Club.** Choose from three nine-hole courses. *Country Club Dr., Destin, FL 32541; tel. 904-837-6191. Open daily. Admission. From Hwy. 98 E., turn north on Rte. 30F (Indian Bayou Trail, which becomes Country Club Dr.).*

◆ **Seascape Resort.** 18-hole course. *100 Seascape Dr., Destin, FL 32541; tel. 904-837-9181, 800-874-9106. Open daily. Admission. On Old Hwy. 98.*

## TENNIS

◆ **Buck Destin Park.** *724 Legion Dr., Destin, FL 32541; tel. 904-654-6060. Open daily.From Hwy. 98 E., turn north on Main St., then left on Legion Dr.*

# HISTORY

◆ **Museum of the Sea and Indian.** Contains the nation's largest collection of Southeastern Native American ceramic artifacts. Also, live animals and exhibits about marine life. *686 Old Hwy. 98 E.,*

*Destin, FL 32541; tel. 904-837-6625. Open daily. Summer 8-7; winter 9-4. In Dec., schedule is limited. 8 mi. east of Destin on Beach Hwy. (Old Hwy. 98).*

◆ **Old Destin Post Office Museum.** Simple and to-the-point, it recalls the town's pioneer days. *Stahlman Ave., Destin, FL 32541; tel. 904-837-8572. Open Wed.Turn north on Stahlman Ave. 1/4 mi. east of Destin Bridge.*

# NATURE

◆ **Henderson Beach State Recreation Area.** Plenty of scrub vegetation such as Southern magnolia and dunes rosemary. This is the last stop for flocks of birds as they head south in the fall. *17000 Emerald Coast Pkwy., Destin, FL 32541; tel. 904-837-7550. Open daily 8-sunset. Admission.*

# SAFETY TIPS

The whiter-than-white sand of the Emerald Coast reflects the sun's rays like a mirror. Wear sunscreen, hat, and sunglasses at all times. Tourist attractions in Destin and Fort Walton Beach are magnets for those who prey on visitors. Take special care of your belongings in these places.

# TOURIST INFORMATION

◆ **Destin Chamber of Commerce.** *Box 8, Destin, FL 32541; tel. 904-837-6241. Open Mon.-Fri. 9-5. Across from the Holiday Inn on Hwy. 98.*

◆ **Emerald Coast Convention & Visitors Bureau.** *Box 609, Fort Walton Beach, FL 32549; tel. 904-651-7131, 800-322-3319. Open Mon.-Fri. 8-5. At 1540 Hwy. 98 E.*

## CHAPTER 4

# Grayton Beach

One of Florida's oldest beach towns, Grayton Beach is the focal point of a coast as diverse as it is beautiful. Some 26 miles of shoreline stretch along the Gulf in Walton County: snow-white dunes giving way to wide strands lapped gently by spring-clear waters. Not far off the beach, however, pine forests and fresh-water lakes suddenly put you in a woodland setting. The contrast is more than enough to convince you that you've "gotten away from it all," a feeling enhanced by the expanse of Choctawhatchee Bay separating the long peninsula from the mainland.

| | |
|---|---|
| Beauty | A |
| Swimming | A |
| Sand | A |
| Hotels/Inns/B&Bs | B- |
| House rentals | A+ |
| Restaurants | B+ |
| Nightlife | C- |
| Attractions | B |
| Shopping | B+ |
| Sports | B- |
| Nature | A |

Skirting the Gulf shore, Route 30A traces its scenic, back-road way from one quiet beach settlement to the next. Grayton Beach, off the highway on a side road, is the most appealing, with a generous number of old beach houses along its twisty, sand lanes. Developed in the 1920s, it has long attracted surfers, artisans, and free spirits. Although the arrival of young professionals and businesspeople may have tamed some of the town's raw energy in recent years, much of the old spirit remains. A sign at a local cafe reads, "Hours may vary depending on the quality of the surf."

This flavor has been influenced, nonetheless, by the overnight success of Seaside, a planned resort community that sprang up less than five miles away in the early 1980s. Conceived as the embodiment of beach-town memories—a place where people rock on front porches and children play in the surf—Seaside got rave reviews as a model community and established a chic presence among the area's historic cottages and humble beach abodes. Pastel houses line the private, brick-paved streets in this rendition of Florida-vernacular Victorian. Every home, by mandate, has a picket fence of original design.

If change has brought gentrification to the Grayton Beach area, it has also brought many benefits for visitors. Restaurants and lodging are first-class, and many people come here to shop in the small, beguiling stores, studios, and galleries. Prime season runs from Memorial Day through Labor Day. That's when temperatures hover in the low 90s and crowds surge.

Surfers-in-the-know still show up at Grayton Beach, but water sports are generally limited to swimming, fishing, and sailing. (For suggestions on scuba diving, *see* Chapter 3, Destin, and Chapter 5, St. Andrews.) Golf, tennis, and even croquet opportunities are ample. For children's entertainment or non-stop nightlife, one need only travel the 45 minutes to Panama City Beach.

## HOW TO GET THERE

◆ Grayton Beach is just under an hour by car from either the Fort Walton Beach or Panama City airport. From Fort Walton Beach/Okaloosa County Airport, follow Rte. 85 south 9 mi. through Fort Walton Beach. When you reach Hwy. 98, veer left to cross Santa Rosa Sound onto Okaloosa Island. Continue east on Hwy. 98 for about 19 mi. Turn right on Rte. 30A and follow signs for Grayton beaches.

◆ From Panama City Airport, take Airport Rd. to Hwy. 98 and turn right. Continue west on Hwy. 98 for about 25 mi. Turn left on Rte. 30A and drive 9 mi., following signs for Grayton beaches.

# GULF BEACHES
## GRAYTON BEACH

**B**uffed and bleached by centuries of river travel from the Appalachian Mountains to Florida's Gulf shore, Grayton Beach's quartz sand is as white as snow. It crunches when you walk on it, because the granules are round and polished.

| | |
|---|---|
| Beauty | A+ |
| Swimming | A |
| Sand | A+ |
| Amenities | B |

For day visitors, the best way to get on the beach is to base at Grayton Beach State Recreation Area. Its dunes and forests are glorious, and the facilities are top-notch. In the village of Grayton Beach, public accesses are meant for residents and overnight visitors, so parking is tight. Down the road in Seaside, attractively designed beach walkovers take residents and guests to the wonderful white sands. Technically, the beach, like all Florida beaches, is public, but there is no designated public access.

*Swimming:* Water is clear, shallow, and inviting. Waves build in storm season.

*Sand:* A deep, sparkling white carpet of fine sand that builds into high dunes.

*Amenities:* Grayton Beach State Recreation Area has rest rooms, showers, and picnic facilities. In town, you'll find restaurants and shops. No lifeguard.

*Sports:* Surfers like these beaches when the waves cooperate. The nearest water-sports concessions are in Seaside (*see* Boating). There's lake and Gulf fishing. A boat ramp provides access to the brackish lake at Grayton Beach State Recreation Area.

*Parking:* With luck, you may get one of the few spots at Grayton Dunes, but the town isn't prone to accommodating day visitors. Local businesses emphasize that their lots are for customers, not beachers. Grayton Beach State Recreation Area has lots of parking. Entry fee: $3.25 a car; $1 for hikers and bikers.

### Grayton Dunes

There's a large tidal lake and a Gulf front where you can swim. Both boast wide, wonderful, luxurious sand. *Downtown Grayton Beach, near the Corner Cafe.*

## Grayton Beach State Recreation Area

Sheltered from development, this is as pristine as they come. Wide, fluffy beaches graduate into 20-foot dunes with a cool, forested backdrop. A nature trail winds through its 400 acres. In the fall, thousands of monarch butterflies flutter through on their way to Mexico. *Open daily 8-sunset. On Rte. 30A, east of Rte. 283.*

## SANTA ROSA BEACHES

Don't be confused by Pensacola's Santa Rosa Island to the west—these beaches are just around the corner from Grayton Beach on Route 30A. Some have rest rooms and other facilities, and some don't. Such communities as Santa Rosa Beach,

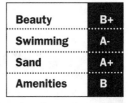

| Beauty | B+ |
|---|---|
| Swimming | A- |
| Sand | A+ |
| Amenities | B |

Blue Mountain Beach, and Dune Allen Beach, though poised for growth, are still small towns. Their parks are small, too, and the residents take pride in keeping them trim and clean.

*Swimming:* Generally safe waters that range from bathtub calm to waves fit for surfing. Summer storms can bring wave action.
*Sand:* Plenty of fine, quartz-white Panhandle sand.
*Amenities:* Rest rooms and picnic shelters at Ed Walline Park. No lifeguard.
*Sports:* No sports concessions.
*Parking:* Limited parking.

## Ed Walline Park

A small-town beach park that takes you back in time and provides a pleasant stopover for families. Quaint picnic shelters are done in Victorian style, with a white picket-fence border. *East of Dune Allen Beach at the intersection of Rtes. 30A and 393.*

# HOTELS/INNS/B&Bs

Grayton Beach has just a few low-rise condominiums, cottages, and tiny B&Bs. But to the west are high-rise condos and, to the east, more bed-and-breakfasts and Seaside's vacation rentals (*see* House Rentals and Tourist Information).

◆ **Josephine's Bed & Breakfast** (expensive). White-columned and Old-South elegant, its seven rooms have basic kitchen amenities (fridge, wet bar, microwave). Most have fireplaces. An intimate dining room serves complimentary breakfast, plus other meals. *101 Seaside Ave., Seaside, FL 32459; tel. 904-231-1940, 800-848-1840.*

◆ **Grayton Beach State Recreation Area** (inexpensive). Campground has 37 wooded sites, some lakeside. Grills, picnic tables, water, electricity. Reservations recommended March through September. *357 Main Park Rd., Santa Rosa Beach, FL 32459; tel. 904-231-4210.*

# HOUSE RENTALS

Many rentals require a two-day to one-week minimum stay. Rates in season range from $450 to $2,500 a week around Grayton Beach and Blue Mountain Beach to the west, and from $775 to $3,000 in the resort community of Seaside.

◆ **Abbott Realty.** Major lister of condominiums and houses along the coast. *35000 Emerald Coast Pkwy., P.O. Box 30, Destin, FL 32541; tel. 904-837-4853, 800-336-4853. Open daily.*

◆ **Monarch Realty.** Most of its local listings are in Seaside. *P.O. Box 4788, Seaside, FL 32459; tel. 904-231-1938, 800-475-1843; fax 904-231-4196. Open daily.*

◆ **Rivard of South Walton.** Lists homes and cottages in Grayton Beach and Blue Mountain Beach, plus villas, condos, and duplexes. *15 Pine St., Santa Rosa Beach, FL 32459; tel. 904-231-4446, 800-423-3215. Open daily.*

◆ **Seaside Cottage Rental Agency.** Oversees Seaside's inventory of 150 homes, plus its motor court suites and honeymoon cottages. Renters may use all resort facilities: tennis courts, three swimming pools, beaches, croquet lawn, shuffleboard, playground. *Box 4730, Seaside, FL 32459; tel. 904-231-1320, 800-277-8696. Open daily.*

# RESTAURANTS

◆ **Bud & Alley's** (expensive). Go for sunset drinks in the second-story bar, then ask for a gazebo table. Menu changes seasonally.

If it's offered, try the pan-fried Louisiana redfish with smoked tomato roast corn sauce and fried sweet onions. Reservations recommended. *Box 4760, Seaside, FL 32459; tel. 904-231-5900. Open daily for lunch and dinner in summer; closed Tue. in off-season. On Rte. 30A, about 3 mi. east of Rte. 283.*

◆ **Criolla's** (expensive). A soothing atmosphere pervades even as you enter through a lovely garden. The eclectic cuisine has an emphasis on New Orleans and Caribbean dishes. Ask for the snapper butter pecan or barbecue shrimp even if they're not on the menu. Reservations are recommended. *170 E. Hwy. 38, Grayton Beach, FL 32459; tel. 904-267-1267; fax 904-231-4568. Open for dinner Mon.-Sat. Closed in winter.*

◆ **Goatfeathers** (moderate). A popular seafood house that's perfect for families. Try the steam buckets. Extensive menu also lists chicken, steaks, sandwiches, soup, salad, and children's selections. *Rte. 30A, Santa Rosa Beach, FL 32459; tel. 904-267-3342. Open daily except Wed. for lunch and dinner. On Rte. 30A, west of Grayton Beach.*

◆ **Grayton Corner Cafe** (inexpensive). For sandwiches, grilled seafood, and oysters, find your way to this local eatery. *1 Hotz Ave., Grayton Beach, FL 32459; tel. 904-231-1211. Open Wed.-Sat. for lunch and dinner. Off Rte. 283, near the beach.*

# NIGHTLIFE

◆ **A.J.'s Seafood & Oyster Bar.** Live entertainment is mainly beach rock and reggae. *Grayton Beach, FL 32459; tel. 904-231-4102. Open daily. At the corner of Rtes. 30A and 283.*

◆ **Bud & Alley's.** Watch sunsets from its upstairs bar. On weekends, there is live jazz and rhythm-and-blues acts to liven things up around the herb garden. *Box 4760, Seaside, FL 32459; tel. 904-231-5900. Open daily in summer; closed Tue. in off-season. On Rte. 30A, about 3 mi. east of Rte. 283.*

# SHOPPING

Shopping is a major draw for visitors to the area. An artistic atmosphere pervades the studios, galleries, and boutiques in Grayton Beach and Seaside.

◆ **Magnolia House.** A charming, tin-roofed home stuffed with gifts and home furnishings. *2 Magnolia St., Grayton Beach, FL 32459; tel. 904-231-5859. Open Mon.-Sat.*

◆ **Patrone's.** A collection of small studios filled with creative endeavors, from handmade cypress furniture to jewelry. Kids like the Barnyard Zoo's live goats, pigs, and other animals. *307 DeFuniak St., Grayton Beach, FL 32459; tel. 904-231-1606. Open daily.*

◆ **Per-spi-cas-ity.** A gaily painted marketplace of tiny shops and stalls by the road in Seaside. Handcrafted gifts, baskets, jewelry, and clothing. *Seaside, FL 32459. Open daily, weather permitting. Along the south side of Rte. 30A.*

◆ **Ruskin Place.** This street in Seaside is designed with the row houses of London's Soho in mind. Local artists and artisans exhibit their wares here and offer workshops for children and adults. *Seaside, FL 32459. Open daily Memorial Day-Labor Day; Thu.-Sat. off-season. North of Central Sq.*

◆ **Sundog Books.** This tiny shop is wall-to-wall with books that beg you to browse. *Box 4692, Santa Rosa Beach, FL 32459; tel. 904-231-5481. Open daily. On the south side of Rte. 30A, in downtown Seaside.*

# BEST FOOD SHOPS

**SANDWICHES:** ◆ **Modica Market.** *Seaside, FL 32459; tel. 904-231-1214. Open daily. On the east side of Central Sq.*

**SEAFOOD:** ◆ **Goatfeathers Seafood Market.** *Rte. 30A, Santa Rosa Beach, FL 32459; tel. 904-267-2627. Open Thu.-Tue. On Rte. 30A west, of Grayton Beach.*

**FRESH PRODUCE:** ◆ **Modica Market.** *Seaside, FL 32459; tel. 904-231-1214. Open daily. On the east side of Central Sq.*

**BAKERY:** ◆ **Modica Market.** *Seaside, FL 32459; tel. 904-231-1214. Open daily. On the east side of Central Sq.*

**ICE CREAM:** ◆ **Brenda's Ice Cream & Yogurt.** *Rte. 30A, Blue Mountain Beach, FL 32459; tel. 904-267-1630. Open daily. 2 mi. west of Grayton Beach village on Rte. 30A.*

**BEVERAGES:** ◆ **Modica Market.** *Seaside, FL 32459; tel. 904-231-1214. Open daily. On the east side of Central Sq.*

**WINE:** ◆ **Modica Market.** *Seaside, FL 32459; tel. 904-231-1214. Open daily. On the east side of Central Sq.*

# SPORTS
## FISHING

Fishermen have a choice of Gulf, bay, or fresh-water lakes. When fishing in brackish water, you can catch both fresh and saltwater species, so you must have both types of licenses. To procure a license in advance, call the Walton County Tax Collector's Office at 904-892-8121. Licenses are also available at convenience stores along Highway 98. (For fishing charters and party boats, *see* Chapter 3, Destin.)

## BOATING

◆ **Cabana Man.** Rents Hobie Cats, kayaks, aqua-cycles, and Boogie boards. *Seaside, FL 32459; tel. 904-231-5046. Open daily Mar. 1-Nov. 15. Below Bud & Alley's restaurant on Rte. 30A, about 3 mi. east of Rte. 283.*

## SURFING

Although Grayton Beach has always attracted surfers, there is no place to rent surfboards in the immediate area.

## DIVING

Most of the great diving in Western Florida lies east or west of Grayton Beach (*see* Chapter 3, Destin, and Chapter 5, St. Andrews).

## BICYCLING

Traffic in Seaside is often more bicyclists than motorists, since only residents and guests may drive the brick-paved streets.
◆ **Seaside Bicycle Rental.** Rents by the hour, day, week, or month. *Savannah St., Seaside, FL 32459; tel. 904-231-2279. Open daily.*

## GOLF

Most of the area's golfing is found in resorts from Santa Rosa Beach west to Destin (*see* Chapter 3, Destin, for more choices).
◆ **Santa Rosa Golf & Beach Club.** 18 holes and a driving range open to the public. Reservations are required. *Box 3950, Santa Rosa Beach, FL 32459; tel. 904-267-2229. Open daily. Admission. On Rte.*

*30A, west of Grayton Beach.*

◆ **The Southern Golf School.** Offers three- to five-day classes and private lessons. *Santa Rosa Beach, FL 32459; tel. 904-267-3745, 800-889-4126. Open daily. Admission.*

## TENNIS

◆ **Santa Rosa Golf & Beach Club.** Its two courts are open to the public. *Box 3950, Santa Rosa Beach, FL 32459; tel. 904-267-2229. Open daily. Admission. On Rte. 30A, west of Grayton Beach.*

◆ **Seaside.** Guests play free. Others pay a nominal fee to use the resort's six clay and hard courts. *Seaside, FL 32459; tel. 904-231-4224. Open daily. Admission. In the recreation complex, at the north end of Seaside Ave.*

# NATURE

◆ **Grayton Beach State Recreation Area.** To learn all about the dunes and local plant varieties, take the nature trail through this 400-acre park. Check the ranger station for information. Shorebirds and sea turtles nest here, and you'll see dwarfed Southern magnolia trees, sea oats, pines, and scrub bushes. *357 Main Park Rd., Santa Rosa Beach, FL 32459; tel. 904-231-4210. Open daily 8-sunset in summer; 8-5 in winter. Admission. 1 mi. east of Grayton Beach.*

# SAFETY TIPS

The Grayton Beach area is so far off the beaten path that crime is practically nonexistent. But when it occurs, tourists are often targets, so lock your car and be careful, especially at the more-deserted beaches. There are few problems at busy beaches.

# TOURIST INFORMATION

◆ **South Walton Tourist Development Council.** *Box 1248, Santa Rosa Beach, FL 32459; tel. 800-822-6877. Open Mon.-Fri., 8-4:30. Welcome center at intersection of Hwys. 98 and 331, west of Grayton Beach.*

## CHAPTER 5

# St. Andrews

St. Andrews State Recreation Area is Panama City Beach's saving grace, a respite from the myriad amusement parks, eateries, and motels that engulf much of the surrounding area. Besides a beautiful expanse of rolling white dunes, the park offers a variety of natural habitats and a dash of history. At the fishing dock stands an authentic turpentine still, a reminder of bygone days when a turpentine distillery flourished here. Gun platforms by the rock jetty are left over from World War II, when

| | |
|---|---|
| Beauty | A- |
| Swimming | B+ |
| Sand | A |
| Hotels/Inns/B&Bs | B+ |
| House rentals | D |
| Restaurants | B |
| Nightlife | A- |
| Attractions | A+ |
| Shopping | C+ |
| Sports | A+ |
| Nature | A- |

part of the park's 1,260 acres served as a military reservation.

Opened in 1951, the park is a natural treasure. It lies on a peninsula between the Gulf of Mexico and Grand Lagoon, both rich sources of marine life. Birds and other wildlife populate its beaches, pine forests, and inland marshes.

Across a narrow inlet is Shell Island, a spit of land severed in the early 1930s to facilitate boat passage between Panama City and the Gulf. Part of the island is within St. Andrews State Recreation Area. Accessible by boat, either from the park dock or from Panama City Beach (*see* Boating), its unspoiled beauty is a good example of how barrier beaches in Panhandle Florida once looked.

Outside the park gate, Panama City Beach exemplifies today's Panhandle Florida at its gaudiest. Its bright lights and diversions draw people by the thousands during the summer. In spring, it woos the spring-break crowd with good-time bars, wet T-shirt contests, and bungee jumping. Unless you want to be part of all of these festivities, avoid Panama City Beach at that time of year.

For water-sports enthusiasts, however, this is a good place to be anytime. For one thing, the town has a jam-packed selection of diving, fishing, sightseeing, waterskiing, and parasailing charters. For another, the artificial reef program started by Panama City Marine Institute has turned local waters into a prime dive site. Besides natural ledges, scuba divers, and snorkelers can explore everything from airplane wrecks to old bridge rubble.

# GULF BEACHES
## ST. ANDREWS STATE RECREATION AREA

This is a popular park, so plan accordingly. Cars often line up at the gate before it opens in the morning. Along its 1 1/4 miles of Gulf front, it has two beach accesses, and many people flock here to enjoy the uncluttered

| | |
|---|---|
| Beauty | B+ |
| Swimming | A- |
| Sand | A |
| Amenities | A |

view and the water sports. Snorkeling around the jetty, you may see large fish swimming from Gulf to bay. Not surprisingly, this is the park's prime fishing spot. There's a fishing

**HOW TO GET THERE**

◆ From Panama City Airport (20 minutes from Panama City Beach and St. Andrews State Recreation Area), follow Airport Rd. south. Turn right on Rte. 390 and right again on Hwy. 98/Rte. 30. Cross the Hathaway Bridge and turn left on Thomas Dr. Continue across another bridge and, where the road splits, bear left. The entrance to St. Andrews State Recreation Area is a block down the street.

pier at the first public beach access and another one on the bay that has a cleaning station.

Diving certification courses are given at the park, and snorkeling excursions to Shell Island leave from here. The park store sells snorkeling and fishing supplies. There's a boat launch on the lagoon.

If you just want to get away from it all, it's possible to feel isolated from civilization here—provided you don't look over your shoulder at the high-rise sprawl in Panama City Beach. *Off Thomas Dr., at the east end of the beach.*

*Swimming:* Wave action can get rough. A flag posted at the entrance indicates the day's swimming conditions. The rock jetty at the end of the beach offers some protection. Be careful not to get into the channel where currents are strong, especially on an incoming tide. Water temperatures average in the 70s throughout the year.

*Sand:* A wide beach of glaring white Panhandle sand lightly peppered with black. Nice dunes anchored with scrub growth.

*Amenities:* Both beach accesses have rest rooms, showers, picnic shelters, soda machines, and stores (open Memorial Day through Labor Day and some weekends in the off-season). No lifeguard.

*Sports:* Water sports predominate. Stores that rent and sell equipment are less than a mile away outside the park.

*Parking:* Ample. Entry to the park costs $3.25 per car; $1 per pedestrian or cyclist.

## Fishing Pier Beach

Don't look for a sign with this name. Park beaches don't have names, but this designation hopefully will make it easier for you to find the beach. Close to the park entrance and to Panama City Beach's stores and restaurants, it's convenient though not as pretty as the beach by the jetty. It's popular with fishermen, who cast into the Gulf from the pier.

## Jetty Beach

Again, the name is not official. Swimming is calmest between the shoreline and the rock jetty. This is where you catch the shuttle to Shell Island. The beach store has diving gear.

## SHELL ISLAND

This ever-shifting sandbar was sliced from Panama City Beach's eastern end in the 1930s to provide fishermen and boaters with an easy passage to the harbor. The federal government owns the eastern third of the three-mile-long island, which

| Beauty | A |
|---|---|
| Swimming | B+ |
| Sand | A |
| Amenities | NA |

looks across the bay to Tyndall Naval Base, but this area is open to the public. Except for a few privately owned lots, the remainder is part of St. Andrews State Recreation Area.

Passage to the island is by boat only. The state park runs a shuttle, and a half-dozen tour operators and resorts have permission to tie up at docks on the bay side. People come mainly to collect shells, although, despite the island's name, shells aren't as bountiful here as they are on several other barrier islands off the Florida coast.

Birds seek refuge here in great numbers and, on the western part of the island, alligators and deer inhabit forest and ponds. Vegetation gets lower along the dunes in the middle of the island, and the ever-growing eastern end is flat. *Accessible by the state park shuttle, which leaves from beach by the jetty. The shuttle runs every half-hour from 9-5 in summer; 10-3 in the off-season. Cost: $7 for adults; $5 for children. Several tour operators also make the trip.*

*Swimming:* Generally shallow waters and offshore sandbars favor swimmers, but the Gulf can play rough here, depending on tides, time of year, and weather patterns. There's a narrow beach along the bay where the water is always quiet. Stay out of the passes on either end of the island.

*Sand:* Soft and fluffy along most of the wide beach. At the east end, where the island is growing steadily, the sand is packed hard by tide action and is slightly muddy at the fringes. This is where you'll find the most shells.

*Amenities:* A wooden boardwalk crosses the island from the public tour dock. That's it.

*Sports:* The state park shuttle to the island offers a snorkeling option. Snorkeling is best around the rock jetty at the west end of the island.

# HOTELS/INNS/B&Bs

**P**anama City Beach has plenty of inexpensive motels and hotels. Many are huge complexes with entertainment and beach front. Not much solitude here, but lots for children to do.

◆ **Boardwalk Beach Resort** (moderate). A typical Panama City Beach mega-resort, it has four hotels with 626 rooms and suites plus restaurants, bars, a children's program, and an 1,800-foot boardwalk leading to a half-mile beach. Ask for a room with a kitchen ($10-$20 more a night). Rooms in the Gulfwalk and the Beachwalk are priced in the inexpensive range. *9450 Thomas Dr., Panama City Beach, FL 32408; tel. 904-234-3484, 800-224-4853; fax 904-233-4369.*

◆ **Marriott's Bay Point Resort** (moderate). Removed from the hub-bub of Panama City Beach, this is the nicest place to stay in the area. It backs up to St. Andrews Bay and operates a daily shuttle to Shell Island. Its 355 units include suites and villas overlooking the golf courses. Beach-lovers will prefer the main hotel, which offers the best water views. Water sports, 12 soft tennis courts, excellent children's program. *4200 Marriott Dr., Panama City Beach, FL 32411; tel. 904-234-3307, 800-874-7105. From Hwy. 98, turn south on Thomas Dr. Signs direct you to turn left on Magnolia Beach Rd., then right on Delwood Beach Rd.*

◆ **St. Andrews State Recreation Area** (inexpensive). Shaded by slash pine, 175 campsites hug the bay shore. Half of them can be reserved by phone; the rest are rented on a first-come basis. Electricity, water, picnic tables, grills. A campground store, fishing pier, and boat ramp are nearby. *4607 State Park Ln., Panama City Beach, FL 32408; tel. 904-233-5140. Registration open daily 8-sunset.*

# HOUSE RENTALS

**H**omes to rent are scarce in this section of the Panhandle. You'll have better luck with condos, which are far more plentiful.

◆ **St. Andrews Bay Resort Management, Inc.** Rents houses on the beach, along with condominiums and townhouses. *726 Thomas Dr., Panama City Beach, FL 32408; tel. 800-621-2462, 800-621-2426. Open daily.*

# RESTAURANTS

Dining spots are as easy to find as fun parks. Prices are reasonable; seafood ubiquitous. Stand-out restaurants are few.

◆ **Treasure Ship Restaurant** (expensive). Go here for the fun of it. The building is shaped like a huge pirate's ship and overlooks the water. The extensive menu specializes in steaks and seafood. Early-bird menu offers good value. *3605 Thomas Dr., Panama City Beach, FL 32408; tel. 904-234-8881. Open daily for dinner.*

◆ **Harbour House** (moderate). To escape the beach scene for a peaceful lunch, head for this landmark in downtown Panama City. The lunch buffet is legendary, sagging with black-eyed peas, greens, hush puppies, and other Southern delicacies. The dining room looks out on the shrimp fleet. Dinner is much the same but with a menu. *3001A W. Tenth St., Panama City, FL 32401; tel. 904-785-9053. Open daily for breakfast, lunch and dinner. From Hwy. 98 E., turn right on Beck Ave. and follow the signs.*

# NIGHTLIFE

Opportunities to dance and party the night away are abundant. There are many places that are geared toward the youthful.

◆ **Ocean Opry Music & Comedy Show.** In a theater setting, a cast of 17 does comedy and music. *8400 Front Beach Rd., Panama City Beach, FL 32408; tel. 904-234-5464. Open Mon.-Sat. Admission.*

◆ **Pineapple Willie's.** Features rock and reggae bands, with dancing and famous Jack Daniels ribs. *9875 S. Thomas Dr., Panama City Beach, FL 32408; tel. 904-235-0928.*

# ATTRACTIONS

Before Disney World, Panama City Beach was the amusement-park capital of Florida. During summer, the options are endless. Some close in the off-season.

◆ **Coastal Helicopter Charters.** See the sights from above. *12106 Front Beach Rd., Panama City Beach, FL 32407; tel. 904-234-8643. Open daily in summer. Closed in off-season. Admission.*

◆ **Emerald Falls Raceway and Fantasy Golf.** Fun for the kids without the overkill of Miracle Strip. Especially nice for preschoolers, with rides, race carts, and putt-putt golf for all ages. *8602 Thomas Dr., Panama City Beach, FL 32408; tel. 904-234-1049. Open daily 10 a.m.-11 p.m. in summer. Hours vary in off-season. Admission.*

◆ **Gulf World.** Besides the usual marine-park gigs, it offers scuba demonstrations, a shark tank, and a tropical garden with flamingoes and peacocks. *15412 Front Beach Rd., Panama City Beach, FL 32413; tel. 904-234-5271. Hours vary by season. Call for times. Admission.*

◆ **Miracle Strip Amusement Park.** Here's where the town's family fun-time reputation began. An all-day affair with more than 30 rides, attractions, and live shows spread over nine acres. The brave head for the 2,000-foot roller coaster or the Sea Dragon. *12000 Front Beach Rd., Panama City Beach, FL 32407; tel. 904-234-5810, 800-538-7395. Open daily mid-Mar. to mid.-Aug.; Sat.-Sun. mid-Aug. to Labor Day. Hours vary. Closed after Labor Day. Admission.*

◆ **Museum of Man in the Sea.** Traces the history of underwater adventure from 1690, including diving bells and modern scuba gear. Treasures from shipwrecks around Florida are on loan. *17314 Back Beach Rd., Panama City Beach, FL 32413; tel. 904-235-4101. Open daily 9-5. Admission.*

◆ **Shipwreck Island.** From the gentle excitement of Tadpole Hole and Kid Car Wash, to the high-speed White Water Tube, this water theme park thrills all ages. Lifeguards supervise. *12000 Front Beach Rd., Panama City Beach, FL 32407; tel. 904-234-0368, 800-538-7395. Open daily Apr.-Labor Day. Admission. On Hwy. 98.*

◆ **Zoo World.** Endangered and other rare creatures are among the 350 animals at this entertainment/education facility. Kids enjoy the petting zoo, and the aviary is a colorful favorite. *9008 Front Beach Rd., Panama City Beach, FL 32407; tel. 904-230-0096. Open daily 9-sunset. Admission. On Hwy. 98.*

# SHOPPING

If you're in the market for air-brushed T-shirts, you're in luck. Beach and surf shops are plentiful.

◆ **African Curio Shoppe & Clothing Boutique.** Jewelry, inexpensive imported art, wood carvings, handwoven items, leather bags, and clothing. *8730 Thomas Dr., Panama City Beach, FL 32408; tel. 904-235-1288. Open daily 10-6.*

◆ **Alvin's Island-Magic Mountain Store.** Part entertainment, part souvenir supermarket, it has aquariums, gator-feeding shows, and tropical birds to entertain the kids while you pick up T-shirts, shells, and tacky gifts. *12010 Front Beach Rd., Panama City Beach, FL 32407; tel. 904-234-3048. Open daily. Near Miracle Strip Amusement Park.*

# BEST FOOD SHOPS

**SANDWICHES:** ◆ **Jr. Food Store.** *4909 Thomas Dr., Panama City Beach, FL 32408; tel. 904-235-3248. Open daily.*

**SEAFOOD:** ◆ **Treasure Island Seafood Market.** *Treasure Island Marina, 3603 Thomas Dr., Panama City Beach, FL 32408; tel. 904-234-8942. Open daily.*

**BAKERY:** ◆ **Donut Shop.** *13624 Front Beach Rd., Panama City Beach, FL 32407; tel. 904-234-1771. Open daily.*

**ICE CREAM:** ◆ **St. Andrews State Recreation Area Camp Store.** *4415 Thomas Dr., Panama City, FL 32408; tel. 904-233-5140. Open daily.*

**BEVERAGES:** ◆ **St. Andrews State Recreation Area Camp Store.** *4415 Thomas Dr., Panama City, FL 32408; tel. 904-233-5140. Open daily.*

**WINE:** ◆ **Newby's Liquor.** *4103 Thomas Dr., Panama City Beach, FL 32408; tel. 904-234-6203. Open daily.*

# SPORTS
## FISHING

St. Andrews State Recreation Area has several vantage points for anglers. For large fish, such as grouper and Spanish mackerel, cast from the jetties. For others, try the piers on the Gulf and in Grand Lagoon.

◆ **Half Hitch Tackle.** Full-service fishing supplier, with license sales and rod-and-reel rentals and service. *2206 Thomas Dr., Panama City Beach, FL 32408; tel. 904-234-2621. Open daily.*

◆ **Treasure Island Seafood Market.** Sells bait, cleans fish, and stores your catch. *Treasure Island Marina, 3603 Thomas Dr., Panama City Beach, FL 32408; tel. 904-234-8942. Open daily.*

◆ **Zodiac Charter Fleet.** Charters for half- and full-day fishing trips. *Box 4302, Panama City, FL 32401; tel. 904-763-7249. Open daily. At Treasure Island Marina, 3605 Thomas Dr.*

## BOATING

◆ **Adventure Sailing Cruises.** Sailing cruises, sailboat rentals, snorkeling excursions. *Treasure Island Marina, 3605 Thomas Dr., Panama City Beach, FL 32408; tel. 904-233-5499. Open daily May-Sep.*

◆ **Glass Bottom Boat Tours.** A family well-versed in local waters runs shell-collecting tours to Shell Island and educational excursions that enable passengers to examine sea life pulled in by crab trap. Tip: The glass bottom cruise is best with an inbound tide. *Treasure Island Marina, 3605 Thomas Dr., Panama City Beach, FL 32408; tel. 904-234-8944. Tours operate year-round.*

◆ **Ragin Rentals.** Rents boats and arranges snorkeling and fishing charters. *5325 N. Lagoon Dr., Panama City Beach, FL 32408; tel. 904-234-6775. Open daily. West of Thomas Dr. and north of the lagoon bridge.*

◆ **The Island Queen.** Climb aboard a paddle-wheel riverboat for an unusual excursion to Shell Island. *Marriott's Bay Point Resort, 4200 Marriott Dr., Panama City Beach, FL 32411; tel. 904-234-3307. Open Tue.-Sun., weather permitting. From the northern extension of Thomas Dr., turn west on Magnolia Beach Rd. and follow the signs for Marriott's Bay Point Resort. Turn right on Delwood Beach Rd. and continue 1 mi. to Jan Cooley Rd. Turn right and continue to Marriott gate. Ticket sales at Teddy's Gift Shop behind the hotel.*

## DIVING

Limestone ledges, artificial reefs, and clean water attract divers in the know.

◆ **Hydrospace Dive Shop.** Sign up for snorkel trips, scuba dives, and diving courses. *3605-A Thomas Dr., Panama City Beach, FL 32407; tel. 904-234-9463, 800-874-3483. Open daily.*

◆ **Panama City Dive Center.** Full-service shop with equipment sales and rentals; snorkel and dive charters. *4823 Thomas Dr.,*

*Panama City Beach, FL 32408; tel. 904-235-3390. Open daily.*

## BICYCLING

Best bicycling is within St. Andrews State Recreation Area.
◆ **Gator Race Track.** Rents bikes. *10333 W. Alt. Hwy. 98, Panama City Beach, FL 32407; tel. 904-234-1425. Open daily.*

## GOLF

◆ **Marriott's Bay Point Resort.** Two top-rated courses. *4200 Marriott Dr., Panama City Beach, FL 32411; tel. 904-234-3307. Open daily. Admission. (For directions, see Hotels/Inns/B&Bs.)*
◆ **Signal Hill Golf Course.** 18 holes on a public course. Call ahead for tee times. *9615 N. Thomas Dr., Panama City Beach, FL 32408; tel. 904-234-5051. Open daily. Admission.*

## TENNIS

◆ **Frank Brown Park.** Two courts. *16200 Back Beach Rd., Panama City Beach, FL 32413; tel. 904-233-5040. Open daily. On Bypass Hwy. 98, east of Hwy. 79.*

# NATURE

◆ **St. Andrews State Recreation Area.** Trails lead to pine forest and marshes, home to alligators and wading birds. *4607 State Park Ln., Panama City Beach, FL 32408; tel. 904-233-5140. Open daily 8-sunset. Admission.*

# SAFETY TIPS

Avoid visiting the area during spring break. Roads are jammed with cars by day and staggering students by night.

# TOURIST INFORMATION

◆ **Panama City Beach Convention & Visitors Bureau.** *Box 9473, Panama City Beach, FL 32417; tel. 904-233-6503, 800-722-3224; fax 904-233-5072. Office open Mon.-Fri. 8-5. Visitors center is at 12015 Front Beach Rd.*

## CHAPTER 6

# St. Joseph Peninsula

f you're looking for towering sand dunes and utter quiet on your beach vacation, this is the place. Tucked away far from Panama City Beach's madding crowds (but close enough to take day trips with the kids), St. Joseph Peninsula and its environs are delightfully rural and close to nature.

| | |
|---|---|
| Beauty | A+ |
| Swimming | A |
| Sand | A |
| Hotels/Inns/B&Bs | B- |
| House rentals | A- |
| Restaurants | C |
| Nightlife | C- |
| Attractions | C |
| Shopping | D- |
| Sports | B+ |
| Nature | A+ |

Ironically, in an earlier time, this was one of the state's fastest growing areas. Then, in 1841, twin disasters struck. A sailing ship from the West Indies introduced yellow fever to the area. It spread quickly, and the epidemic, combined with a powerful hurricane, wiped the original settlement of St. Joseph off the map.

The first Cape San Blas lighthouse, built in 1847, made St. Joseph Peninsula an important Civil War site. Salt was processed nearby from the sea to supply the Confederate army. Since then, three more lighthouses have been constructed to replace those swallowed by the sea as the narrow peninsula shifted.

Today, the 22-mile crook of land with its ivory colored sands offers beachgoers exciting vistas and natural habitats capped by the 2,500-acre St. Joseph Peninsula State Park. Driving from the mainland, you'll find a fragile stretch of sand so narrow that you can see both the Gulf of Mexico and St. Joseph Bay from the road nearly all the time. Scrubby vegetation pokes through the high dunes.

The casually organized community on the peninsula is

known as Cape San Blas (*SAN-blass*), for the chin of land jutting into the Gulf at the southern end. Most residents are seasonal. The community subsists on tourism, but it's low key. There's only one restaurant, three convenience stores, and no fancy resorts. Lodging, other than campsites at the state park, consists mainly of cabins and cottages, though some of the houses for rent are luxurious.

You won't find everything you need here, and that's part of the charm. A vacation on the peninsula requires that you get out and explore the wilderness and fishing towns around it. Port St. Joe is closest. As if to make up for its smelly paper factories, it offers an unusual range of water activities, including world-class wreck diving. The hulk of the *Empire Mica*, a British tanker torpedoed in World War II, is one of the best underwater sights in the Panhandle. You can also harvest your own scallops here. (It's one of the few places in Florida where the public can do so, thanks to plentiful supplies.)

Visitors often venture as far as Panama City to the west and Apalachicola to the east for dining and entertainment, but they return gratefully to the eerie silence of Cape San Blas. Here, they can lose touch with civilization and submerge themselves in a world that's home to hawks, peregrine falcons, foxes, and armadillos. Come fall, the beach may be covered with migrating monarch butterflies. Beach time is a quiet affair that allows you to commune with the cosmos, dig your toes into soft, fine sand, and take occasional dips in water that maintains a temperature range of between 64 and 83 degrees.

## HOW TO GET THERE

◆ **From Panama City Regional Airport (an hour from St. Joseph Peninsula State Park), take Airport Rd. to Hwy. 98 and turn left. Follow Hwy. 98 east of Port St. Joe to Rte. C-30 (about 40 mi.). Turn right and follow signs for St. Joseph Peninsula State Park. They'll direct you to turn right on Rte. 30E to Cape San Blas.**

# GULF BEACHES
## CAPE SAN BLAS

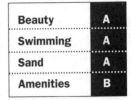

| | |
|---|---|
| Beauty | A |
| Swimming | A |
| Sand | A |
| Amenities | B |

Cape San Blas is nothing but sand, so the beach is rarely more than a few steps away. Tall dunes rise from the wide beach apron. Recent storms bit some of them off and spit them out on other parts of the peninsula. Salinas Park provides visitors with a pleasant place to picnic, walk on the beach, and swim.

*Swimming:* The clear, green water is calm, and the bottom gradually sloping.

*Sand:* A tad tanner than the superlative beaches to the west, the peninsula's sands spread wide and luxuriously fine, with scatterings of coquinas and other small shells at water's edge. The beach is especially wide and flat at the park.

*Amenities:* Picnic tables and a nice playground. Boardwalks lead to the beach and to a breezy gazebo at the top of one dune. No lifeguards.

*Sports:* No nearby concessions.

*Parking:* Small sand lots that fill up in summer.

### Salinas Park

This is a great little beach park, but you may have to share it with the mosquitoes if the wind is off the bay. Also, beware of sand spurs, burry seed pods that hurt when you step on them. The beach is wide here and hard-packed near the water. You'll see a lot of ghost crabs and their holes. *On Rte. 30E, near the intersection of Rte. 30.*

### ST. JOSEPH PENINSULA STATE PARK

| | |
|---|---|
| Beauty | A+ |
| Swimming | A+ |
| Sand | A |
| Amenities | B+ |

The view from the boardwalk tells you that you've come to the right place. Tall dunes make you feel hidden from the world, and the fine sand seems to stretch endlessly in either direction. Except for an occasional jet from the local Air Force base, there's no hint of civilization. *On St. Joseph Peninsula, at the end of Rte. 30E.*

*Swimming:* Gently sloping sand and refreshingly cool water with small, playful breakers.

*Sand:* Blond sands heap into ten-foot dunes. The beach varies in width and becomes impassable in some spots at high tide.

*Amenities:* Rest rooms and showers are off the boardwalk. Across the road is a park store, picnic shelters, and a playground. Not far outside the park entrance, there's a restaurant and a general store. No lifeguards.

*Sports:* The park boat basin has canoe rentals and a boat ramp. There's surf-casting in the Gulf and fishing in St. Joseph Bay. Hikers can take to the long beaches or explore inland on nature trails.

*Parking:* Ample space at the boat basin.

# HOTELS/INNS/B&Bs

Until recently, Cape San Blas's lodging consisted of campsites and cabins. Now, residential and resort communities offer other accommodations at very reasonable rates.

◆ **Cape Cottages** (inexpensive). Nestled among the dunes near St. Joseph Park, the cottages have one or two bedrooms and a kitchen. Linens are extra. A secluded beach is a short walk away. Convenience store and laundry facilities. Cottages 1 and 2 have the best Gulf views. *Star Rte. 1, Box 351, Port St. Joe, FL 32456; tel. 904-229-8775, 800-556-1322. Stop at the Cape Tradin' Post on Rte. 30E to check in (see* Shopping).

◆ **Old Salt Works Cabins** (inexpensive). A Civil War historic site and museum add interest to these pleasant, privately owned cabins, which front either Gulf or bay. In Fort Crooked Tree, children can play with mannequins in Civil War dress. *Box 526, Port St. Joe, FL 32456; tel. 904-229-6097. On the bay side shortly after you turn onto the Cape on Rte. 30E.*

◆ **St. Joseph Peninsula State Park** (inexpensive). Besides 119 tent and RV sites, there are eight furnished town-house-style cabins that are clearly not your average rustic state-park lodging. Cabins sleep up to seven. Each has a fireplace, screened porch, and boardwalk to the bay. Maximum stay: 14 nights. Guests are asked to bring extra towels. Reserve well in advance. *Star Rte. 1, Box 200, Port St. Joe, FL 32456; tel. 904-227-1327.*

*Check in at the park 8-sunset. On St. Joseph Peninsula, at the end of Rte. 30E.*

# HOUSE RENTALS

Cape San Blas has a nice selection of rental houses and townhouses. Weekly rates run from $500 for a cottage to $1,650 for a deluxe, multibedroom home. Linens are extra.

◆ **Anchor Realty & Mortgage Co.** *Star Rte. 1, Box 357, Port St. Joe, FL 32456; tel. 904-229-2770, 800-624-3964; fax 904-927-2735. Open daily.*

◆ **Cape San Blas Realty.** *HC1, Box 403, Rte. 30E, Cape San Blas, Port St. Joe, FL 32456; tel. 904-229-6916. Open daily.*

# RESTAURANTS

◆ **Toucan's** (moderate). A bit out of the way (25 minutes from St. Joseph Peninsula), but it's one of the best places in the vicinity. Besides, it has a beach, so go for lunch and some sun. Extensive menu emphasizes seafood. Have oysters raw, steamed, or baked eight different ways. Bourbon Street snapper (baked in Cajun seasonings) and seafood mustafa (shrimp, lobster, or blue crab with vegetables and a light cream sauce) are winners. *812 Hwy. 98, Box 13772, Mexico Beach, FL 32410; tel. 904-648-3010; fax 904-648-8129. Open daily for lunch and dinner. Breakfast served in summer. About 12 mi. west of the Rte. 30 turn-off.*

◆ **Cape Cafe** (inexpensive). The peninsula's only restaurant, it serves deli-type cuisine for lunch and local seafood for dinner. The shrimp specialties are best. Reservations required for dinner. *Rte. 30E, Cape San Blas, FL 32456; tel. 904-229-8688. Open daily in summer for breakfast, lunch, and dinner. Hours vary in the off-season.*

◆ **Indian Pass Raw Bar** (inexpensive). Housed in an old roadside general store, this place is famous for its gumbo, oysters, steamed shrimp, clams, crawfish, and local color. No fried food. *Rte. 30B, Port St. Joe, FL 32456; tel. 904-227-1670. Open daily for lunch and dinner. On Rte. 30B, 2 mi. east of the 30E turn-off to Cape San Blas.*

◆ **J. Patrick's Restaurant** (inexpensive). A favorite of Port St. Joe business folk and locals, it serves sandwiches, salads, seafood, and steaks in a casual setting. The all-you-can-eat hot bar is a great buy for lunch. *412 Reid Ave., Port St. Joe, FL 32456; tel. 904-227-7400. Open Mon.-Fri. for breakfast and lunch; for dinner, by reservation, for parties of 10 or more. Sunday brunch. From Hwy. 98, turn north on Fifth St. and left on Reid Ave.*

# NIGHTLIFE

Not a lot happens at night in these parts, so try Mexico Beach, some 25 minutes away, if you want to find a greater variety of things to do, including live entertainment, especially on weekends.

◆ **Jam's Sports Bar & Grill.** A classy place with pool and dart tournaments, happy-hour specials, sports TV, dance lessons, jam sessions, and karaoke. *Hwy. 98, Mexico Beach, FL 32410; tel. 904-648-4464. Open daily.*

# SHOPPING

◆ **Cape Tradin' Post.** This and two other convenience stores provide the only shopping on the peninsula. Here you'll find groceries, beach necessities, toys, and T-shirts. *Rte. 30E, Cape San Blas, Port St. Joe, FL 32456; tel. 904-229-8775. Open daily.*

# BEST FOOD SHOPS

**SANDWICHES:** ◆ **Cape Cafe.** *Rte. 30E, Cape San Blas, FL 32456; tel. 904-229-8688. Open daily in summer; hours vary off season.*

**SEAFOOD:** ◆ **Raffield's Seafood Market.** *Hwy. 98, Port St. Joe, FL 32456; tel. 904-227-7220. Open daily.*

**FRESH PRODUCE:** ◆ **Saveway.** *510 Fifth St., Port St. Joe, FL 32456; tel. 904-229-8398. Open daily. Turn north on Fifth St. off Hwy. 98.*

**BAKERY:** ◆ **Flowers Baking Co.** *Jones Homestead, Port St. Joe, FL 32456; tel. 904-229-8956.*

**ICE CREAM:** ◆ **Freckles Yogurt Shop.** *Hwy. 98, Mexico Beach, FL 32410; tel. 904-648-4443. Closed Tue.*

**BEVERAGES:** ◆ **Cape Tradin' Post.** *Rte. 30E, Cape San Blas, Port*

*St. Joe, FL 32456; tel. 904-229-8775. Open daily.*
**WINE:** ◆ **Pics Food Store.** *Rte. 30E, Cape San Blas, Port St. Joe, FL 32456; tel. 904-227-1897. Open daily.*

# SPORTS
## FISHING
One of the few places in Florida where the public may harvest scallops (season: July through August), St. Joseph Bay has lots of good fishing. To try deeper waters, you can catch a boat out of Mexico Beach or Port St. Joe.

◆ **Full Line Tackle Shop.** Fresh and frozen bait; tackle for fresh and salt-water fishing. *306 Reid Ave., Port St. Joe, FL 32456; tel. 904-229-8933. Open daily. From Hwy. 98, turn north on Fifth St. Turn left on Reid Ave.*

◆ **Genesis Fish & Dive Chartering.** Sign on for either fishing or diving here. *100 Third St., Port St. Joe, FL 32456; tel. 904-227-3474. Open daily.*

◆ **Pics Food Store.** Sells fishing and scalloping supplies and licenses. *Rte. 30E, Cape San Blas, Port St. Joe, FL 32456; tel. 904-227-1897. Open daily.*

## BOATING
St. Joseph Peninsula State Park has a public boat ramp. It also rents canoes for use in the park.

◆ **St. Joe Boat Rentals.** Rents 14-foot powerboats and pontoon boats. *Simmons Bayou, Port St. Joe, FL 32456; tel. 904-229-6585. Open daily. From Rte. 30E, turn left on C-30 and go 6 mi.*

## DIVING
These waters give divers plenty to explore. There are a dozen or so wrecks offshore, and lots of colorful fish hang out around the brick base of a former lighthouse at Cape San Blas.

◆ **Captain Black's Dive Shop.** Arranges dive charters and teaches certification courses. *Hwy. 98, Port St. Joe, FL 32456; tel. 904-229-6330. Open daily.*

## BICYCLING
The quiet roads of Cape San Blas are ideal for biking, but bring your own. There are no bike rentals in the vicinity.

## GOLF

In downtown Port St. Joe, at Eighth Street and Garrison Avenue, there's a rustic nine-hole golf course that's free to the public. Bring your own clubs.

◆ **St. Joseph's Bay Country Club.** 18 holes open to nonmembers. *Box 993, Port St. Joe, FL 32456; tel. 904-227-1751. Open daily. Admission. On Rte. 30 east of Port St. Joe.*

## TENNIS

Cape San Blas has no public tennis courts, but there are three in Port St. Joe: one in Frank Pate Park on Highway 98 at Fifth Street, and two on Eighth Street.

# HISTORY

◆ **Constitution Convention Museum.** In a park setting, a monument and museum commemorate Florida's first state Constitutional Convention in 1838 and relate other facets of local history. *200 Allen Memorial Way, Port St. Joe, FL 32456; tel. 904-229-8029. Open Wed.-Sun. 9-5. Admission. On Hwy. 98 east of Port St. Joe.*

◆ **St. Joseph Cemetery.** While visiting the museum above, stop by this site, which holds the remains of the area's first settlers. *Garrison Ave., Port St. Joe, FL. Open daily. From Hwy. 98 in Port St. Joe, turn north on Fifth St. and right on Garrison.*

# NATURE

◆ **St. Vincent Island National Wildlife Refuge.** Once private, the 12,358-acre island has a blend of native and exotic wildlife. Asian Sambar deer co-exist with indigenous white-tailed deer. The fauna and 14 miles of beach attract day-trippers. *Box 447, Apalachicola, FL 32329; tel. 904-653-8808. Accessible only by boat.*

# TOURIST INFORMATION

◆ **Gulf County Chamber of Commerce.** *Box 964, Port St. Joe, FL 32456; tel. 904-227-1223. Open Mon.-Fri. 8-5. Office is at 301 Fifth St. From Hwy. 98, turn north on Fifth.*

## CHAPTER 7

# St. George Island

**S**t. George Island, along with nearby Dog Island, marks the eastern boundary of the Florida Panhandle's great, white beaches. The whiteness, determined largely by the quartz content of the sand, is actually flecked with tan on St. George. This shading becomes even more pronounced on beaches to the south, where the sand is produced mainly from shells. Very much part of the Deep South culture, rural St. George is one of the quietest and least known beach destinations along the Panhandle. Indeed, except for

| | |
|---|---|
| **Beauty** | A |
| **Swimming** | A |
| **Sand** | A |
| **Hotels/Inns/B&Bs** | B- |
| **House rentals** | A+ |
| **Restaurants** | B+ |
| **Nightlife** | C- |
| **Attractions** | B |
| **Shopping** | B+ |
| **Sports** | B- |
| **Nature** | A |

the lone flashing light in the town of Apalachicola, you won't find a traffic light in all of Franklin County.

Life on St. George and in most of the surrounding area revolves around the abundant waters of Apalachicola Bay, which is Florida's largest producer of seafood. In particular, the area is known for its Apalachicola Bay oysters, but its shrimp, blue crab, and a number of saltwater fish are also appreciated by connoisseurs and fisherfolk alike.

Long and slender, St. George has been little touched by civilization since the Creek tribe resided there 1,000 years ago. But it underwent a major transformation in 1954 when the Army Corps of Engineers cut a channel through the island to accommodate local fisheries. Thus, today, there are two islands: 27-mile-long St. George and, to the west, Little

St. George, which can be reached only by boat.

Vacationers in search of a beautiful beach have gradually caught on to St. George. The tourist season begins in late spring and peaks in summer. Afternoon rains are the norm for the summer. Temperatures remain cool, averaging around 81 degrees during the hottest months. In winter, they dip into the 50s.

Development of St. George Island took hold in the 1950s, when realtors from Tallahassee began selling lots. In 1963, the state purchased seven miles of land at St. George's east end, plus the entirety of Little St. George, for a state park. Construction on a bridge commenced two years later, but it wasn't until 1980 that St. George Island State Park opened.

Even today, there are just a handful of commercial enterprises on the island: a few shops, stores that sell fishing gear, a motel, an inn, and several seafood restaurants. Beach-going and fishing are the things to do on St. George. The gold-tinted sands stretch from one end of the island to the other. Fishing is exceptional right from land, both on the Gulf and in the bay.

For other things, visitors don't have to go far, however. The town of Apalachicola, less than 20 minutes away, beckons with its parks, restaurants, and historic buildings, many of which contain art galleries and shops.

## HOW TO GET THERE

◆ From Tallahassee Regional Airport (two hours from St. George Island), turn right on Capital Circle S.W. (Rte. 263) and continue about 3 1/2 mi. Turn right (south) on Hwy. 319 and drive 32 mi. to where it merges with Hwy. 98 in Medart. Continue south on Hwy. 98 to Ochlockonee Bay, then west to Eastpoint (another 30 mi.). In Eastpoint, turn left on Island Dr. (watch for signs to St. George Island) and continue across the Franklin Bridge to the island.

# GULF BEACHES
## ST. GEORGE ISLAND

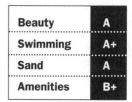

| | |
|---|---|
| Beauty | A |
| Swimming | A+ |
| Sand | A |
| Amenities | B+ |

With mainly single-family homes dotting the western half of the island, there is little to mar the view on St. George, and it's even better inside the state park. There, the sands stretch for seven miles, making it the longest beachfront of any Florida state park. It's a joy for any lover of nature and seclusion. You see nothing but sea grass, rolling dunes, and, in the distance, pines. These unscathed sands are known for excellent surf fishing.

*Swimming:* Thanks to an offshore sandbar, St. George Island's beach provides a safe swimming environment, free of the rip currents that occur off other Panhandle beaches. The bottom has a slight slope at the state park, and gets steeper to the west. Water temperatures range from the 60s to the 80s throughout the year.

*Sand:* Ground minerals give the powdered-quartz sand a golden cast that is often enhanced by a colorful mosaic of crushed shell. Soft and fine, the sand builds into high dunes on either side of the public beach.

*Amenities:* The public beach is near restaurants, convenience marts, and other shops. At the state park accesses, there are rest rooms, showers, food concessions, sheltered picnic areas, and dune walkovers. No lifeguard.

*Sports:* Fishing is number one, especially in the state park. Sea kayaking is becoming popular there, but you have to bring your own. A 2 1/2-mile hiking trail lets you explore local flora and fauna. There are a couple of volleyball nets at the public beach.

*Parking:* The public beach has about 20 angled spaces on the road, which fill up quickly. You can park at the nearby restaurant if you plan to lunch there, but that, too, gets crowded. At the state park, two paved lots with a total of 400 spaces provide ample parking. Entry to the park costs $3.25 per car; $1 per cyclist or hiker.

## Public Beach

There's no sign saying "Public Beach"—but that's what it's called by everyone who goes there. Popular with the school crowd because of its volleyball and proximity to food and drink, it is not as pristine as the state park. However, the surrounding buildings are not as intrusive as the high-rises at some Florida beaches, making this a good compromise for people in search of a nice beach with extensive amenities nearby. *At the end of Franklin Bridge Rd.*

## St. George Island State Park

There are several footbridges over the dunes to the beach, but only two areas that have parking and facilities. East of the last access, a four-wheel-drive road takes fishermen to the pass, where they cast for big fish entering from the Gulf. Campsites are available, but must be reserved in advance. *Open daily 8-sunset. From the Franklin Bridge, turn left on E. Gulf Blvd. and drive 3 1/2 mi. to the park entrance.*

## LITTLE ST. GEORGE ISLAND

All that Little St. George can offer visitors is a seemingly endless stretch of deserted beach and a lighthouse. For plenty of beach-lovers, that's enough. The lighthouse, which will soon be decommissioned, is slowly sliding into the sea. The island is maintained by

| | |
|---|---|
| Beauty | A+ |
| Swimming | A+ |
| Sand | A |
| Amenities | D- |

the state as part of St. George Island Park. Camping is allowed by special permit. *West of St. George Island. Accessible only by boat. Charters out of Apalachicola go there (see* Boating*).*
*Swimming:* Calm, clear shallow waters.
*Sand:* Fine, golden beaches cresting in dunes.
*Amenities:* None.
*Sports:* Fishing is good, especially at the cut on the west end.

# HOTELS/INNS/B&Bs

◆ **Coombs House Inn** (moderate). Elegant drapery, fireplaces, dark wood, and antiques adorn this restored 1905 Victorian mansion in Apalachicola's historic district. Each of the ten rooms has its own bath and TV. For a treat, request the Coombs Suite (room 8), which has a king-sized, four-poster bed and a Jacuzzi. *80 Sixth St., Apalachicola, FL 32320; tel. 904-653-9199. In Apalachicola, take Hwy. 98 west through the downtown area to Sixth St.*

◆ **Gibson Inn** (inexpensive). Southern hospitality lives! Ensconced in a three-story, Florida-style building with wrap-around porches upstairs and down, this gracious inn makes you feel at home. Each of its 31 rooms gets its own personality from antique furnishings and period wallpaper. Private baths, TVs. Second-floor rooms are best because they open onto the porch. *57 Market St., Apalachicola, FL 32329; tel. 904-653-2191. At the Apalachicola bridge.*

◆ **St. George Inn** (inexpensive). A Victorian replica, this nine-year-old structure greets island visitors with Florida-style grandeur: white clapboard, blue shutters, and a tin roof. All eight rooms look onto either the bay or Gulf. You might prefer a view of the wooded bay, especially from room B. Rooms open onto the second-story porch through French doors. All are spacious and homey, with wood paneling, private baths, and down comforters. *Franklin Blvd., St. George Island, FL 32328; tel. 904-927-2903.*

◆ **St. George Island State Park** (inexpensive). Sixty campsites are available by reservation. *HCR Box 62, St. George Island, FL 32328; tel. 904-927-2111. From the Franklin Bridge, follow Franklin Blvd. to Gulf Beach Dr. Turn left and drive to the east end of the island.*

# HOUSE RENTALS

**M**ore than 750 homes on St. George Island are for rent. The modest ones run about $400 a week. Grand, beachfront homes in St. George Plantation fetch up to $3,000. In season and over holidays, a one-week minimum stay is required. Rates are highest from late May to September. Reserve early for those months.

◆ **Accommodations St. George.** *118-120 Gulf Beach Dr. W., HCR Box 108, St. George Island, FL 32328; tel. 904-927-2666, 800-332-5196. Open daily.*

◆ **Anchor Realty and Mortgage Co.** *212 Franklin Blvd., St. George Island, FL 32328; tel. 800-824-0416. Open daily.*

# RESTAURANTS

Apalachicola Bay oysters are the pride of local fisheries and are known the world over for their succulence. Upriver pollution poses a danger to the industry, however. Restaurants carry a warning against eating raw oysters if you have certain health problems. Cooked oysters will not harm you, unless you're allergic to them. Fishermen also bring just-caught shrimp, blue crabs, amberjack, scallops, and bulldozer lobster to restaurant tables. If you're doing your own cooking, you can find fresh seafood on the island or at the docks in Apalachicola and Eastpoint.

◆ **Gibson Inn** (expensive). Folks drive two hours or more to enjoy good food and Old South graciousness. Oysters and seafood are prepared in styles from fish-house to continental. *57 Market St., Apalachicola, FL 32329; tel. 904-653-2191. Open daily for lunch and dinner. At the Apalachicola bridge.*

◆ **Oyster Cove Seafood Bar & Grill** (expensive). With its soothing view of the bay and fresh seafood prepared either Cajun or Greek style, it offers some of the island's best dining. Fresh catches can be ordered grilled, blackened, fried, or in special sauces. The Newburg style is a light, tasty version of creamy white sauce studded with shrimp and scallops. Terrific! *E. Pine St. and E. Second St., HCR Box 199, St. George Island, FL 32328-9705; tel. 904-927-2600, 904-927-2829. Open daily for dinner. Take a left immediately after coming over the Franklin Bridge.*

◆ **St. George Inn** (moderate). Three intimate dining rooms dressed in royal blue linen serve local delicacies: amberjack, shrimp, flounder, and scallops. Its specialty is stuffed flounder. Fried food available only on request. *Franklin Blvd., St. George Island, FL 32328; tel. 904-927-2903. Open Tue.-Sun. for dinner.*

◆ **Happy Pelican** (inexpensive). The kind of place where locals hang out, and they have a good reason: simple, mainly fried seafood from area waters. You can eat inside in unpretentious surroundings where crab traps hang from the ceiling, or outdoors at picnic tables under umbrellas. For a great lunch, try an oysterburger. The homemade egg rolls come highly recommended, too. *W. Pine Ave., St. George Island, FL 32328; tel. 904-927-9826. Open daily for lunch and dinner. From Franklin Blvd., drive west on Pine Ave.*

# NIGHTLIFE

**D**on't come to St. George looking for swinging night scenes and cultural overload. On the island, there's only one place known for its nightlife:

◆ **Harry A's.** A neighborhood bar with a big-screen TV, a pool table, and live country and rock bands. *10 Bayshore Dr., St. George Island, FL 32328; tel. 904-927-9810. Open daily. Turn west on the first street after the bridge.*

# SHOPPING

◆ **Charlotte's Web.** A whimsical blend of stationery, dolls, antiques, and handcrafts for the home. *45 Market St., Apalachicola, FL 32320; tel. 904-653-9000. Open Tue.-Fri. Across from the Gibson Inn.*

◆ **Long Dream Gallery.** Kristin Anderson sells her silver, gold, and champlevé enamel jewelry here, and displays the work of other artists in stained glass, paint, and pottery. *32 Ave. D, Suite 201, Apalachicola, FL 32329; tel. 904-653-2249. Open only by appointment. Off Hwy. 98 near the Gibson Inn.*

◆ **Palmyra Gallery.** A treasure trove of handcrafted quilts, jewelry, ceramics, wood items, and tropical art. *25 Ave. D, Apalachicola, FL 32320; tel. 904-653-9090. Open Mon.-Sat. From the Apalachicola bridge, take a right off Hwy. 98 onto Ave. D.*

◆ **Peddlers' Cove.** A collection of shops selling antiques, collectibles, T-shirts, caps, and other souvenirs. *77 Commerce St., Apalachicola, FL 32320; tel. 904-653-8877. Open Mon.-Sat. One block north of Hwy. 98 in the historic district.*

◆ **Riverlily.** Calling itself "a shop for your senses," this New Age place carries aromatic items such as massage oils, potpourri, and soaps, plus greeting cards and one-of-a-kind dresses. *78*

*Commerce St., Apalachicola, FL 32320; tel. 904-653-2600. Open Mon.-Sat. One block north of Hwy. 98 in the historic district.*
◆ **Two Gulls.** One of the island's nicer shops, with beach-oriented gifts, cards, and objets d'art. *W. Pine Ave., St. George Island, FL 32328; tel. 904-927-2044. Open daily.*

# BEST FOOD SHOPS

**SANDWICHES:** ◆ **Jr. Food Store & Deli.** *Franklin Blvd., St. George Island, FL 32328; tel. 904-927-2311. Open daily.*
**SEAFOOD:** ◆ **Sharon's Place.** *Hwy. 98, Eastpoint, FL 32328; tel. 904-670-8646. Open Tue.-Sun.*
**FRESH PRODUCE:** ◆ **Market Place.** *148 E. Pine Ave., St. George Island, FL 32328; tel. 904-927-2808. Open daily.*
**ICE CREAM:** ◆ **Dolores' Sweet Shoppe.** *17 Ave. E., Apalachicola, FL 32320; tel. 904-653-9081. Open Mon.-Fri.*
**BEVERAGES:** ◆ **Jr. Food Store & Deli.** *Franklin Blvd., St. George Island, FL 32328; tel. 904-927-2311. Open daily.*
**WINE:** ◆ **Mini, Too Convenience & Package Liquors.** *W. Gorrie Dr., St. George Island; tel. 904-927-2272. Open daily. From Franklin Blvd., turn west on Gorrie Dr.*

# SPORTS
## FISHING

Fishing is one of the main reasons people come to St. George Island. Locals brag that in winter you can bag huge redfish (a prized game food fish not sold commercially) in minutes right off the beach. Other local catches include sheepshead, mackerel, and cobia. Best spots include Bob Sikes Cut at the eastern point of St. George Island State Park and, on the mainland, the Lafayette Park fishing pier in Apalachicola.
◆ **Bay City Lodge.** Call here about charter fishing trips. *Apalachicola, FL 32320; tel. 904-653-9294. Open daily.*
◆ **Fisherman's Headquarters.** Sells bait, tackle, and fishing licenses. Rents rods and reels, and runs fishing charters.
*W. Bayshore Dr., St. George Island, FL 32328; tel. 904-927-9817. Open daily.*

◆ **Jeanni's Journeys.** Booking agent for local fishing charters. *E. Pine St., St. George Island, FL 32328; tel. 904-927-3259. Open daily.*

## BOATING

You can find boat ramps in St. George Island State Park at the youth camp and east slough areas, and at Lafayette and Battery parks in Apalachicola.

◆ *Apalachicola Belle.* This 30-passenger river boat takes sunset and sightseeing cruises into the bay or along the Apalachicola River. In summer, it shuttles to Little St. George Island. *Apalachicola, FL 32320; tel. 904-653-2732. Call for schedule.*

◆ *Governor Stone.* Two-hour sails aboard this National Historic Landmark vessel, a 63-foot, two-masted 1877 schooner. *Apalachicola Maritime Museum, Box 625, Apalachicola, FL 32329; tel. 904-653-8708. Open daily.Call for reservations and directions.*

◆ *Jeanni's Journeys.* Sailing school, canoeing, sightseeing and photographic cruises. Children's environmental excursions. *E. Pine St., St. George Island, FL 32328; tel. 904-927-3259. Open daily.*

## BICYCLING

◆ **Fisherman's Headquarters.** Rents bikes. *W. Bayshore Dr., St. George Island, FL; tel. 904-927-9817. Open daily.*

◆ **Island Bike Rentals.** Delivers bicycles right to your doorstep. *216 W. Gorrie Dr., St. George Island, FL 32328; tel. 904-927-3544. Open daily.*

## GOLF

◆ **St. Joseph Bay Country Club.** The nearest golf course, it has 18 holes. *Box 993, Port St. Joe, FL 32456; tel. 904-227-1751. Open daily. About 45 min. west of St. George Island on Rte. C-30, off Hwy. 98 before the town of Port St. Joe.*

## TENNIS

A couple of the housing complexes have tennis courts for residents and guests. There is a public court in Apalachicola at Seventh Street and Avenue D.

# HISTORY

There are more than 50 sites within the National Historic District of the city of Apalachicola (an Indian word for "Land Beyond" or "Friendly People"). The city was developed in the early 1800s as a cotton port; its waterfront was lined with brick warehouses, many of which are still there. It boasts more pre-Civil War sites than anywhere else in Florida.

◆ **Cape St. George Lighthouse.** Built in 1833 to guide Gulf traffic into Apalachicola Bay, it's been replaced twice, the last time in 1852. It is soon to be retired. *Little St. George Island. Accessible only by boat.*

◆ **John Gorrie State Museum.** A tribute to the physician who, in trying to develop a method for making yellow fever patients more comfortable, invented a forerunner of today's air conditioner. A replica of the 1851 ice-making machine is on display. *Box 267, Apalachicola, FL 32320; tel. 904-653-9347. Open Wed.-Sun. 9-5. Admission. One block off Hwy. 98 on Sixth St.*

# NATURE

◆ **St. George Island State Park.** Within its 1,962 acres, the park has 16 distinct biological communities, from its celebrated maritime environment of dunes and scrub, to rush-fringed marshes, a stand of slash pine, and freshwater ponds. Bald eagles, osprey, and 400 other species of birds seek refuge here. In summer, loggerhead and green sea turtles nest along the beach. *HCR Box 62, St. George Island, FL 32328; tel. 904-927-2111. Open daily. Admission. At the east end of the island on E. Gulf Dr.*

# SAFETY TIPS

You won't feel safer anywhere in Florida. The only natural hazard may be in eating raw oysters if you have health problems.

# TOURIST INFORMATION

◆ **Apalachicola Bay Chamber of Commerce.** *84 Market St., Apalachicola, FL 32320; tel. 904-653-9419; fax 904-653-8219. Open Mon.-Fri. 9:30-4; Sat. 10-3.*

## CHAPTER 8

# Caladesi/Honeymoon

**F**or secluded beauty, it's difficult to surpass the two unspoiled islands off the coast of Dunedin. Battered by hurricanes and threatened by real estate developers, Caladesi and Honeymoon have survived to offer beach lovers a variety of experiences. Both islands are state parks, open from 8 a.m. to sunset, so plan accordingly. There is no camping.

If the two beaches share some of the same virtues, it's understandable, since they started out as one island. Shown on earliest maps as Sand Island, it appears later as Hog Island, denoting the presence of a hog farm.

| | |
|---|---|
| Beauty | A |
| Swimming | A- |
| Sand | B |
| Hotels/Inns/B&Bs | C+ |
| House rentals | D |
| Restaurants | B- |
| Nightlife | C |
| Attractions | B- |
| Shopping | B- |
| Sports | B- |
| Nature | A+ |

One hurricane wiped out the hogs in 1918 and another, in 1921, split the island in two. A few years later, an entrepreneur built thatch-roofed cottages for newlyweds on the northern segment, inspiring the name Honeymoon Island.

There was no link to the mainland until 1964 when developers, contemplating a large resort, built the causeway to Honeymoon. At that point, the state of Florida recognized the importance of the barrier islands and bought both Honeymoon and Caladesi. Caladesi Island State Park opened in 1972, and Honeymoon Island State Recreation Area followed a decade later. Today, the only sign of development is a condo community on Honeymoon that, fortunately, is far from the beach.

Weather continues to change the face of the islands. Another hurricane bit two small islands off the south end of Caladesi in

1985, and winds and waves have left Honeymoon with a rocky beach that's not conducive to swimming or sunbathing. Beachgoers seeking a beautiful stretch of sun-drenched sand take the ferry to Caladesi.

# GULF BEACHES

## HONEYMOON ISLAND

You won't find lush, playful beaches at ruggedly handsome Honeymoon Island State Recreation Area. It's more about nature here, along with barrier-island ecology and geology. Of the four beach areas in the park, swimming is recommended at only one. The park is open from 8 a.m. until sunset.

| | |
|---|---|
| Beauty | B+ |
| Swimming | C |
| Sand | C- |
| Amenities | A- |

### HOW TO GET THERE

◆ From Tampa International Airport (30 minutes from Honeymoon Island), take Rte. 60, crossing Tampa Bay on Courtney Campbell Causeway. Entering Clearwater, this turns into Gulf-to-Bay Blvd., then Cleveland St. Turn right onto Fort Harrison Ave. (Alt. Hwy. 19) and drive north 6 mi. through Dunedin. Turn left on Causeway Blvd. and cross St. Joseph Sound on the Dunedin Causeway to reach Honeymoon Island State Recreation Area (entry fee: $3.25 per car).

◆ Caladesi Island is accessible from two points, but only by boat (there are no roads or bike paths on the island). From Drew St. dock in downtown Clearwater, hourly ferry service costs $4.95 for adults and $3 for children (operates Tue.-Sun.; tel. 813-442-7433). From Honeymoon Island, the ferry costs $4 for adults; $2.50 for children (operates daily; tel. 813-734-5263).

Honeymoon has its own natural beauty, however. A stand of pines hosts ospreys and owls. Shorebirds nest along the beach. Pit vipers and diamondback rattlers live in the park's uplands, but are rarely seen. A nature trail, which takes more than an hour to complete, introduces hikers to four types of barrier-island ecology.

*Swimming:* Water temperatures are slightly cooler here than at Clearwater or Pass-A-Grille to the south. Avid swimmers may be disappointed: There's only a small stretch off South Beach where currents and boat traffic don't make swimming dangerous. The bottom is rocky.

*Sand:* Although the state periodically rebuilds the island's Gulf-front beaches, the sand still washes away, leaving a shoreline that's mostly rocks. The southern access has the best beachfront: fewer rocks and a yellowish, coarse sand cover. The southern tip, a bit of a walk from the main parking lot, is sandiest. Shells are fairly abundant.

*Amenities:* Rest rooms, showers, picnic areas, grills, playground, bike racks, and food and beach-supply concessions. From January through April, the park hosts environmental story telling sessions. Lifeguard on duty at South Beach from Memorial Day to Labor Day, and on weekends thereafter.

*Sports:* Volleyball nets at the picnic area. No water-sport rentals. Good fishing at the causeway.

*Parking:* All but one of the four lots are paved. RVs can park at the one south of the picnic area.

## South Beach

Of the park's four waterfront accesses, South Beach has the best swimming and facilities. Studded with rocks in places, it wraps around the tip of the island. Shell collectors will find this beach rewarding.

## Causeway Beach

This is a prime spot for fishermen. A sailboat rental and charter operation is located on the approach to the park. A food-concession truck often shows up here, and there's a portable toilet. *On the causeway to Honeymoon Island.*

## CALADESI ISLAND STATE PARK

For dedicated beachgoers, Caladesi is a dream destination. Edged in sea grass and palmettos, the wide strand is three miles long, so you can enjoy relative seclusion. Also, because there are no roads or bike paths on the island, it is quiet.

| | |
|---|---|
| Beauty | A+ |
| Swimming | A+ |
| Sand | A· |
| Amenities | B+ |

Upon landing at the marina docks, you can see most of the buildings on the island: the park ranger's office, picnic shelters, and a snack-and-souvenir concession. Behind the buildings, a boardwalk leads to the beach and an upland nature trail. The trail takes about 1 1/2 hours. Wear sturdy shoes if you plan to hike it, because the soft sand is harder on feet than you might imagine.

The ferry to Caladesi from Honeymoon Island leaves every hour on the hour, beginning at 10. (On busy weekends, it runs every half hour.) Passengers are assigned a four-hour return time, but you can catch an earlier ferry back if room permits. Last trip leaves Honeymoon at 4, and day visitors must be off the island before sundown.

This rule does not apply to overnighters who come to Caladesi by private boat, however (fee: $3.25 per boatload of up to eight people). Overnight docking is permitted, but you must dock before sundown.
*Swimming:* Caladesi is protected by Honeymoon Island to the north, making the water calm as a lagoon. The gradual slope of the beach and the water's shimmering clarity also appeal to swimmers.
*Sand:* As cushy as a down comforter, and fine enough to flow through an hourglass. Small shells may be found at water's edge, along with seaweed, which lends a slight pungency to the air.
*Amenities:* Bathhouses with rest rooms and showers, snack bar, playground, picnic areas with grills. Beach chairs and umbrellas for rent. Lifeguards on duty during the summer.
*Sports:* Best fishing is off the docks in the marina. No water-sport rentals.

# HOTELS/INNS/B&Bs

Honeymoon and Caladesi islands have no camping facilities or other accommodations, except for boat docks. The nearest hotels are on the mainland in Dunedin.

◆ **Best Western Jamaica Inn** (moderate). Situated at the marina, it offers 55 bedrooms and efficiencies with individual patios and pleasant decor. The efficiencies are worth the $10 extra a night. Try to get one on the harbor front. Restaurant. Access to fishing dock.*150 Marina Plaza, Dunedin, FL 34698; tel. 813-733-4121, 800-447-4728; fax 813-736-4365. At the Dunedin Municipal Marina.*

◆ **Inn on the Bay** (moderate). "Inn" is a misnomer for this multi-floored hotel with 41 units, but the service is friendly enough to redeem it. The bay location makes it special, and its tiki bar is a popular spot. Rooms and suites are modern, clean, and pleasantly decorated. All have kitchenettes and balconies. Those with bay views are nicest. Continental breakfast and bikes are included. Fishing dock and heated swimming pool.*1420 Bayshore Blvd., Dunedin, FL 34698; tel. 813-734-7689, 800-759-5045; fax 813-734-0972. On Alt. Hwy. 19, about 2 mi. south of Dunedin Causeway Blvd.*

# HOUSE RENTALS

Most people in the Dunedin area who rent their homes require at least a three-month stay at about $1,000 a month.
◆ **Executive Inc.** *132 Island Way, Clearwater Beach, FL 34630; tel. 813-461-6000, 800-940-3932. Open daily.*

# RESTAURANTS

◆ **Jesse's Seafood House** (expensive). Overlooking a yacht-filled marina, Jesse's sports a nautical atmosphere with lots of brass and dark wood, and good views over the water. The seafood is prepared in classic manner: broiled, steamed, or fried. The best is Jesse's Favorite Combination: broiled Danish lobster, steamed snow crab legs, and broiled shrimp scampi. The menu also offers pasta, steak, chicken, and sandwiches. *345 Causeway Blvd., Dunedin, FL 34698; tel. 813-736-2611. Open daily for lunch and dinner. On the mainland side of the causeway to Honeymoon Island.*

◆ **Molly Goodhead's Raw Bar & Seafood** (moderate). Offbeat is the rule here. Eat on the porch or in the wackily decorated bar/dining room. Sandwiches and seafood platters are served all day. Grouper right off the boat is a specialty. For a culinary twist, try the grouper reuben. *400 Orange St., Ozona, FL 34660; tel. 813-786-6255. Open daily for lunch and dinner; Sat.-Sun. for breakfast. From Alt. Hwy. 19, about 2 mi. north of the Dunedin Causeway, turn right on Tampa Ave. in Ozona, then right on Orange Ave.*

◆ **El Zarape** (inexpensive). Some of the most authentic Mexican food this side of the Rio Grande. Decorated with serape table coverings, pinatas, and colorful murals, this modest eatery serves Tex-Mex standards. Then, for the adventurous, it has such delights as *nopales* (Mexican cactus) *con huevo* and *lengua* (tongue) *en mole.* Even the burritos, refried beans, and rice taste home-cooked. El Zarape is also famous for its frozen cocktails. *2020 Bayshore Blvd., Dunedin, FL 34698; tel. 813-736-6286. Open daily 11-10. On Alt. Hwy. 19, about 1 1/2 mi. south of the Dunedin Causeway.*

# NIGHTLIFE

◆ **Flanagan's Hunt Irish Pub.** Dunedin's antecedents are mainly Scottish, but live Irish music draws applause here. *465 Main St., Dunedin, FL 34698; tel. 813-736-4994. Live music Wed.-Sun. nights.*

# ATTRACTIONS

◆ **Grant's Field.** Spring training ground for the Toronto Blue Jays. *311 Douglas Ave., Dunedin, FL 34698; tel. 813-733-9302. Exhibition games Mar.-early Apr. Admission.*

# SHOPPING

There are shopping centers at the intersection of Causeway Boulevard and Alternate Highway 19, but the most unusual shopping is found in Dunedin's historic Main Street district. Antique shops, many in restored homes, have helped establish Dunedin as an antiques center. The city hosts an antiques fair every spring.

◆ **Beehive Antiques.** In a lovely location, it displays antiques of all sorts, from toys to furniture. *214 E. Tarpon Ave., Tarpon Springs, FL 34689; tel. 813-942-8840. Open daily. Drive 9 mi.*

*north on Alt. Hwy. 19 to Tarpon Springs.*

◆ **The Old Feed Store Antiques.** More like a museum than a store, it exhibits antiques in period settings. The building is huge and full of collectibles, including quilts, one of Dunedin's specialties.*735 Railroad Ave., Dunedin, FL 34698; tel. 813-734-4705. Open Tue.-Sat. 10-4; Sun. noon-4. On a side street off Main St., in the historic district.*

# BEST FOOD SHOPS

**SANDWICHES:** ◆ **Marguerite's Deli.** *420 Patricia Ave., Dunedin, FL 34698; tel. 813-736-2494. Open daily.*

**SEAFOOD:** ◆ **Dunedin Fish Co.** *51 Main St., Dunedin, FL 34698; tel. 813-733-2542. Open daily.*

**FRESH PRODUCE:** ◆ **Publix.** *902 Curlew Rd., Dunedin, FL 34698; tel. 813-733-4173. Open daily. At the intersection of Alt. Hwy. 19 and the approach to the Dunedin Causeway.*

**BAKERY:** ◆ **Briden's Bakery.** *916B Patricia Ave., Dunedin, FL 34698; tel. 813-733-1349. Open daily.*

**ICE CREAM:** ◆ **Beach Deli & Ice Cream.** *573 Causeway Blvd., Dunedin, FL 34698; tel. 813-736-4177. Open daily. On the approach to the Dunedin Causeway.*

**WINE:** ◆ **Creative Spirits.** *537 Douglas Ave., Dunedin, FL 34698; tel. 813-736-0885. Open daily.*

# SPORTS

## FISHING

Many fishermen cast from the bridges of the Dunedin Causeway, and others take boats along the shores of the islands and far out in the Gulf.

◆ **Dunedin Municipal Marina.** Headquarters for fishing charters going to local waters and deep seas. There also is a fishing pier here. *51 Main St., Dunedin, FL 34698; tel. 813-738-1909. Open daily.*

◆ **Island Bait & Tackle.** Sells fishing gear and licenses. *290 Causeway Blvd., Dunedin, FL 34698; tel. 813-733-1854. Open daily. On the approach to the Dunedin Causeway, in a strip mall on the north side of the street.*

## BOATING

A mobile concession rents sailboats and conducts sailboat charters on the causeway to Honeymoon Island. Caladesi Island has
a 99-slip marina on the bay side. Overnight docking permitted
if you register before sundown. Boats are accepted on a first-
come, first-served basis.

◆ **VIP Rentals.** *Marker One Marina, 334 Causeway Blvd.,
Dunedin, FL 34698; tel. 813-734-5969. Open daily. On the
approach to the Dunedin Causeway.*

## BICYCLING

Although Honeymoon Island has no bike paths, its lightly traveled, one-way roads take cyclists easily through the pristine
environment. There are bike racks at beach entrances. The
Pinellas Trail, a biking and jogging path that runs 47 miles from
Tarpon Springs to St. Petersburg, follows Alternate Highway 19
through the Dunedin area. (For bike-trail information, call the
Pinellas County Planning Department at 813-464-4751.)

◆ **Pirate's Cove Marina.** Has bicycles for rent. *2400 Bayshore
Blvd., Dunedin, FL 34698; tel. 813-733-1102. Open daily. On Alt.
Hwy. 19, south of downtown Dunedin.*

## GOLF

◆ **St. Andrews Links.** In addition to the golf course, there's a light-
ed driving range, a pro shop, and a restaurant. *620 Palm Blvd.,
Dunedin, FL 34698; tel. 813-733-5061. Open daily. Admission. On
Alt. Hwy. 19, one block south of Causeway Blvd.*

## TENNIS

Tennis courts in Dunedin are open to the public only at certain
times. A non-resident I.D. may be obtained for $2 from the
Community Center, which is open weekdays at the address
below.

◆ **Highlander Tennis Courts.** Four lighted courts, picnic shelters.
*1141 Michigan Blvd., Dunedin, FL 34698; tel. 813-738-1888.
Open daily. Admission. About 1 mi. south of the Dunedin Causeway
on Alt. Hwy. 19, turn left on Michigan Blvd. and drive east for about
1/2 mi.*

# HISTORY

The city of Dunedin has designed a walking tour around a 15-block historic district in the vicinity of Main Street and Alternate Highway 19. Check with the Chamber of Commerce for a brochure.

◆ **Dunedin Historical Museum.** Housed in an old train depot, this unusual museum contains artifacts and photos that recall events in the town's history. One room is devoted to railroad memorabilia. Another display depicts the life of Caladesi Island's only settler, and an album describes how the Army's amphibious tank was invented in Dunedin. *349 Main St., Dunedin, FL 34698; tel. 813-736-1176. Open Tue.-Sat. 10 a.m.-1. p.m. Admission.*

# NATURE

◆ **Hammock Park.** Seventy-five acres provide a habitat for wildlife, which may be seen from an observation deck and along nature trails. Picnic shelters and playground. The center conducts nature walks and programs. *903 Michigan Blvd., Dunedin, FL 33968; tel. 813-738-1905. Open daily during daylight hours. From Alt. Hwy. 19, go east 4 blocks on Mira Vista Dr. (about halfway between the Dunedin Causeway and Main St.) to San Mateo Dr.*

# SAFETY TIPS

Entrance fees to Caladesi and Honeymoon islands keep the incidence of crime low, but don't let your guard down completely. Put valuables in the trunk or out of sight and lock your car, especially when parking for the day to leave for Caladesi.

# TOURIST INFORMATION

◆ **Dunedin Chamber of Commerce.** *301 Main St., Dunedin, FL 34698; tel. 813-733-3197; fax 813-734-8942. Open Sun.-Fri 8:30-4:30.*
◆ **Honeymoon Island State Recreation Area.** *Gulf Islands Geopark, 1 Causeway Blvd., Dunedin, FL 34698; tel. 813-469-5942. No visitors center.*

## CHAPTER 9

# Clearwater

**J**ust a mile across the water from the bustling city of Clearwater is a wonderfully wide beach that's at once happy-go-lucky and somewhat reserved. The southern end of Clearwater Beach is a resort playground, but the north retains a residential quiet that has eluded over-development despite a steady influx of beachgoers.

| | |
|---|---|
| Beauty | B+ |
| Swimming | A |
| Sand | A- |
| Hotels/Inns/B&Bs | A |
| House rentals | A- |
| Restaurants | A |
| Nightlife | A |
| Attractions | A- |
| Shopping | B+ |
| Sports | A |
| Nature | B |

Besides surf and sand, the beach is known as a hotbed of beach volleyball. Many of the beaches have permanent nets, and major tournaments are held here.

The Timucuan Indians were the first to call the area Clear Water, or Pocotopaug in their vernacular. Early settlers adopted the name for the harbor that separates the island from the mainland, and later for the settlement that today is the city of Clearwater.

The island's first major developer named his subdivision Mandalay, after Rudyard Kipling's poem. In 1924, the community's name officially changed to Clearwater Beach, but little else changed through the 1940s, except for the building of Memorial Causeway, which replaced a rickety 1916 wooden model.

Today, Clearwater hosts a number of festivals, including the Fun 'n' Sun Festival, which includes parades, a boat regatta, and music and sports competitions in the last two weeks of April. In the second week of November, there's the annual Kahlua Cup International Yacht Races, which draws competitors from around the world.

# GULF BEACHES
## CLEARWATER AREA

Clearwater's wonderful beaches stretch along the Gulf for about three miles, attracting sun-lovers and water-sports enthusiasts. It's a great spot for swimmers of all abilities. The silky, sink-your-toes-in sand falls short of an A grade because

| | |
|---|---|
| Beauty | B |
| Swimming | A |
| Sand | A- |
| Amenities | A+ |

careless beachers drop cigarette butts and garbage where they please. This gets cleaned up on a regular basis, however.

*Swimming:* Conditions are great all along the island: There's a shallow shelf, a sandy bottom, and warm, calm waters. Water temperatures vary between 63 and 85 degrees.

*Sand:* Fine-grained and abundant.

*Amenities:* All major beaches have rest rooms, outdoor showers, food and beachwear concessions, and water-sports rentals. Lifeguards on duty at Pier 60 Beach and South Gulfview.

*Sports:* The long pier attracts fishermen. Small water-sports vessels and equipment can be rented at Pier 60 and South Gulfview. And don't forget your volleyball.

*Parking:* Lots are large and require fees either by a gate system or parking meters. Rates range from 25 cents for 15 minutes to $7 a day. At the north end of the island, many of the beach areas are reachable only by walking.

### Pier 60 Beach

The pier is the center of many beach activities. Swimming conditions are good, but swimming is not allowed under the

## HOW TO GET THERE

◆ From Tampa International Airport (30 minutes from Clearwater Beach), take Rte. 60, crossing Tampa Bay on Courtney Campbell Causeway. This turns into Gulf-To-Bay Blvd., then Cleveland St., and finally Memorial Causeway, which crosses Clearwater Harbor to Clearwater Beach.

pier. In the evenings, the city sponsors a sunset event known as the Buskerfest featuring local performers. They draw large crowds, but there's plenty of room because the beach is extremely wide. The parking lot accommodates RVs and other oversized vehicles. *At the junction of Causeway Blvd. (Rte. 60) and Gulfview Blvd.*

## South Gulfview Beach

Actually an extension of the pier beach, it has a separate parking lot and is closer to shops and other commercial development. *On Gulfview Blvd., near the intersection of Hamden Dr.*

## Passive Beach Area

This stretch of fluffy sand is quieter and cleaner than around Pier 60. The wide beach is edged by tall dunes. A park across the street has a playground and other recreation facilities. Restaurants at either end of the beach cater to the hungry. "Passive" refers to the absence of beach-sports rentals. It has stationary volleyball nets, however. *From Mandalay Ave., go west on Rockaway St. or Bay Esplanade.*

## SAND KEY PARK

To the south of Clearwater Beach lies Sand Key, another barrier island that has felt the pressure of development but, fortunately, has one well-preserved area at its northern tip. An oasis among skyscrapers, 65-acre Sand Key Park is thoughtfully laid

| | |
|---|---|
| Beauty | A |
| Swimming | A- |
| Sand | B+ |
| Amenities | A |

out and well-maintained. There are sizable dunes and lots of cabbage palms and other native vegetation. *Take the Clearwater Pass Bridge (75-cent toll) to the park.*

*Swimming:* The bottom, sandy with a gradual incline, makes this beach very swimmer-friendly.

*Sand:* Fine to coarse, with some shells at water's edge. The beach is wide, flat, and well-maintained.

*Amenities:* Rest rooms, outdoor showers, water fountains, and chair rentals are at the beach. A green area some yards from the beach has picnic shelters, rest rooms, and a playground. Lifeguard on duty.

*Sports:* You can rent beach and sports equipment here or next door at the Sheraton Sand Key Resort. Skating and biking are forbidden in the parking lot.

*Parking:* Room for 800 cars. Cost: 25 cents for 20 minutes; maximum, 4 hours.

# HOTELS/INNS/B&Bs

◆ **Belleview Mido Resort Hotel** (very expensive). The grande dame of Florida's West Coast, the Belleview is one of the few surviving wooden hotels in the state. Built in the 1890s, it retains much of its stately bearing. A sprawling structure with wide verandas, it has 310 rooms. New additions include a lobby extension, a spa, and a swimming pool with waterfalls. *25 Belleview Blvd., Box 2317, Clearwater, FL 34617; tel. 813-442-6171, 800-237-8947; fax 813-441-4173. From Rte. 60, turn left on Fort Harrison Ave. and head south to Belleview Blvd. Turn right on Belleview to reach the entry gate.*

◆ **Radisson Suites Resort at Sand Key** (very expensive). Across the street from Sand Key Park, it towers over the Intracoastal Waterway with 220 two-room suites. There's a waterfall swimming pool, a spa, a children's program, and nearby shopping. Great for families: Some suites are child-proofed. All have a balcony, two TVs, a micro bar, and a microwave. Free trolley takes guests to the beach. *1201 Gulf Blvd., Clearwater Beach, FL 34630; tel. 813-596-1100, 800-333-3333.*

◆ **Clearwater Beach Hotel** (expensive). A stately hotel that wears its age graciously. One of the island's first hotels, it has built on its success with 150 hotel rooms and suites right on the beach. Common areas have the feel of a grand old hotel, with cut glass, lots of wood, and classical music playing. *500 Mandalay Ave., Clearwater Beach, FL 34630; tel. 813-441-2425, 800-292-2295; fax 813-449-2083. Just north of the causeway road.*

◆ **Sea Stone Resort** (moderate). This complex is sheltered from beach frenzy because it's on the harbor rather than the Gulf. It's a Best Western, but family-run for many generations. The swimming pool and Jacuzzi look onto the marina. A restaurant, lounge, and water-sports rentals complete the amenities. Some suites have private balconies; some shared. *445 Hamden Dr., Clearwater Beach, FL 34630; tel. 813-441-1722; fax 813-461-1680. Take Hamden Dr. off Gulfview Blvd. Go to Sea Stone Suites to register.*

# HOUSE RENTALS

**H**ouse rentals on Clearwater Beach and Sand Key are plentiful. Minimum required stay is usually a month. Rents range from $3,000 to $6,000 a month.

◆ **Executive Inc.** *132 Island Way, Clearwater Beach, FL 34630; tel. 813-461-6000, 800-940-3932.*

# RESTAURANTS

**R**estaurants in Clearwater Beach are among the most reasonably priced along Florida's West Coast. Local seafood, especially shrimp, grouper, and stone crab, are plentiful. Sand Key is the region's fishing headquarters, so you can be sure that local seafood ordered there is as fresh as you're going to get.

◆ **Lobster Pot** (expensive). Ramshackle on the outside, this local favorite features cuisine that's more diverse than you'd suspect. Lobster from around the world joins grouper as house specialties. *17814 Gulf Blvd., Redington Shores, FL 33708; tel. 813-391-8592. Open daily for dinner. About 10 mi. south of Sand Key Park.*

◆ **Bob Heilman's Beachcomber** (moderate). The Beachcomber reigns supreme on Clearwater Beach by preparing its prime products with care. People dress up to come here, and they come in flocks. The kitchen excels at American cuisine with a flair for creativity, yet it still offers the down-home favorite that first gained it popularity: back-to-the-farm chicken with all the fixings. *447 Mandalay Ave., Clearwater Beach, FL 34630; tel. 813-442-4144. Open daily for lunch and dinner.*

◆ **Frenchy's Rockaway Grill** (inexpensive). You'll see a lot of seafood places with the name Frenchy's in the area. They're all good. This one is a favorite because of its enviable location for viewing sunsets. Lively Caribbean decor. Seafood and meat are done grilled, blackened, or jerked. For an unusual snack, try the blackened fish tacos. *7 Rockaway St., Clearwater Beach, FL 34630; tel. 813-446-4844. Open daily for lunch and dinner. Off Gulfview Blvd.*

◆ **Seafood & Sunsets at Julie's** (inexpensive). Tiny dining rooms in a tiny, charming house make you feel a bit like Alice in Wonderland. But this home-turned-restaurant gives you what its name promises: the best of the island's sunsets and seafood. Sit on the front porch or upstairs and enjoy mahimahi, shrimp, scallops, grouper, conch, lobster, stone crab, and Alaskan snow crab. Seafood platters let you have two items if you can't decide on one. *351 S. Gulfview Blvd., Clearwater Beach, FL 34630; tel. 813-441-2548. Open daily for lunch and dinner. Across from the main public beach.*

# NIGHTLIFE

Clearwater Beach stages a Sunset Buskerfest featuring local performance artists at Pier 60 Monday through Thursday evenings in season. Festivities begin two hours before sunset. More traditional nighttime activities are listed below.

◆ **Bill Irle Early Bird Dinner Theatre.** For early diners, musicals and dramas take the stage. *1411 N. Fort Harrison Ave., Clearwater, FL 34615; tel. 813-446-5898. Open Thu.-Sun. From Memorial Causeway, take a left on Fort Harrison Ave. (Alt. Hwy. 19).*

◆ **Empress Cruise Lines.** The *Crown Princess* is one of several gambling cruisers based in the area. It features buffet dining, live music, and skeet shooting. *198 Seminole St., Clearwater, FL 34616; tel. 813-895-3325. Departs twice daily from Clearwater Bay Marina; off Alt. Hwy. 19 about 1 mi. north of Memorial Causeway.*

◆ **The Beach Bar.** Live bands play rock and Top 40 tunes. *454 Mandalay Ave., Clearwater Beach, FL 34630; tel. 813-446-8866. Open nightly.*

# SHOPPING

◆ **Key West Express.** Carries a selection of jewelry, women's clothes, and T-shirts above the standard of the typical beach shop. *484 Mandalay Ave., Clearwater Beach, FL 34630; tel. 813-461-6462. Open daily.*

◆ **Nicholson House.** Objets d'art and furniture and accessories are sold in a charmingly restored home. *913 N. Fort Harrison Ave., Clearwater, FL 34615; tel. 813-447-3055. Open Mon.-Sat. 10-6; Sun. 12-5. From Clearwater Beach, go over Memorial Causeway and turn left on Fort Harrison Ave. (Alt. Hwy. 19).*

◆ **Wish You Were Here.** Specializes in unusual decor, kitchen, and children's items. *483 Mandalay Ave., Clearwater Beach, FL 34630; tel. 813-449-8220. Open daily. At Pelican Walk.*

# BEST FOOD SHOPS

**SANDWICHES:** ◆ **New York Deli & Yogurt Co.** *2551 Drew St., Clearwater, FL 34615; tel. 813-796-7822. Open daily.*

**SEAFOOD:** ◆ **Seafood & Sunsets at Julie's.** *351 S. Gulfview Blvd., Clearwater Beach, FL 34630; tel. 813-441-2548. Open daily. Store is inside the restaurant.*

**FRESH PRODUCE:** ◆ **Little Big Fruit & Vegetable Market.** *1001 S. Fort Harrison Ave., Clearwater, FL 34616; tel. 813-466-2172. Open Mon.-Sat. From Clearwater Beach, go back over Memorial Causeway and turn right on Fort Harrison Ave.*

**BAKERY:** ◆ **Dutch Bakery.** *490 Mandalay Ave., Clearwater Beach, FL 34630; tel. 813-441-2254. Open daily.*

**ICE CREAM:** ◆ **Lappert's Ice Cream.** *387 Mandalay Ave., Clearwater Beach, FL 34630; tel. 813-449-2663. Open daily.*

**BEVERAGES:** ◆ **Pick Kwik Food Store.** *696 S. Gulfview Blvd., Clearwater Beach, FL 34630; tel. 813-443-3089. Open daily.*

**WINE:** ◆ **Drew Spirits.** *1745 Drew St., Clearwater, FL 34615; tel. 813-447-1944. Open Mon.-Sat.*

# SPORTS
## FISHING

The most popular fishing spot is Pier 60 on the beach. It costs from $2.50 to $5.35 to fish there, depending upon your age. A bait and tackle shop sits at the entrance. You can buy fishing licenses there.

◆ **Boating Zone.** Half- and full-day fishing charters near reefs and wrecks. *Clearwater Beach Marina, Box 3246, Clearwater*

*Beach, FL 34630; tel. 813-446-5503. Open daily. At Clearwater Beach Marina, 25 Causeway Blvd.*

◆ **Bonnie's Bait & Tackle.** *1245 S. Fort Harrison Ave., Clearwater, FL 34616; tel. 813-446-2772. Open daily.*

◆ **Clearwater Beach Marina.** Most fishing charters depart from here, including party boats, which cost around $20 for a half day; $35 for a full day. *25 Causeway Blvd., Clearwater Beach, FL 34630; tel. 813-462-6954. Open daily.*

## BOATING

◆ **Admiral Cruises.** Makes daytime sightseeing cruises into Clearwater Harbor and evening dinner-and-dance excursions. *Box 3335, Clearwater Beach, FL 34630; tel. 813-462-2628, 800-444-4814. Daytime cruises Tue.-Sat. Feb. 16-Nov. 30. Evening cruises year-round. At Clearwater Beach Marina, 25 Causeway Blvd.*

◆ **Boating Zone.** *Clearwater Beach Marina, Box 3246, Clearwater Beach, FL 34630; tel. 813-446-5503. Open daily. At Clearwater Beach Marina, 25 Causeway Blvd.*

◆ **Budget Boat Club Rentals.** Rents motorboats 17 to 20 feet long for $20 an hour, based on an eight-hour rental. $200 deposit required. *Clearwater Beach Marina, 25 Causeway Blvd., Clearwater Beach, FL 34630; tel. 813-443-6685. Open daily. At slips 23 and 24.*

◆ **Captain Memo's Pirate Cruise.** A popular party cruise that sets sail in a swashbuckling vessel four times daily. *Clearwater Beach Marina, 25 Causeway Blvd., Dock 3, Clearwater Beach, FL 34630; tel. 813-446-2587. Open daily.*

◆ **Clearwater Ferry Service.** Based in Clearwater Beach Marina, it runs daily shuttles to and from various beach locations. Also offers dolphin-watching cruises and voyages to Caladesi Island, Tarpon Springs' sponge docks, and Sarasota, for shopping. *Box 3335, Clearwater, FL 34630; tel. 813-442-7433. Open Tue.-Sun. Call for information and directions to pick-up points.*

◆ **National Boat Rental.** Rents powerboats 16 to 22 feet long. *17811 Gulf Blvd., Redington Shores, FL 33708; tel. 813-397-5171. Open daily. About 10 mi. south of Sand Key Park at Redington Shores Marina, across from the Lobster Pot restaurant.*

◆ **Zenith Yacht Charters.** *850 Bayway Blvd., Slip 24, Clearwater Beach, FL 34630; tel. 813-442-3273. Open daily.*

## BICYCLING

Clearwater Beach has no bike paths. Road biking is safest at the north end and along residential roads. The roads of Sand Key Park are nice to bike along, but bikes are not allowed in parking lots.

◆ **Transportation Station.** Rents one-speeds, tandems, racers, and mountain bikes plus accessories. *652 Gulfview, Clearwater Beach, FL 34630; tel. 813-443-3188. Open daily. Also at eight resort locations.*

## GOLF

◆ **Clearwater Country Club.** An 18-hole course open to the public. *525 N. Betty Ln., Clearwater, FL 34615; tel. 813-446-9501. Open daily. From Clearwater Beach, go back over Memorial Causeway. Turn left on N. Fort Harrison Ave. (Alt. Hwy. 19) for one long block. Turn right on Drew St. and drive for about 1 1/2 mi. Turn left on Betty Ln.*

## TENNIS

To use Clearwater recreational facilities, you must purchase a nonresident athletic card, which costs $33 for three months. If you're on a short vacation and are an avid tennis player, look for a resort with courts instead.

◆ **Clearwater Beach Recreational Complex.** Has three courts plus other facilities. *69 Bay Esplanade, Clearwater Beach, FL 34630; tel. 813-462-6138. Open Mon.-Sat. Admission. Across the street from the Passive Beach.*

# HISTORY

◆ **Heritage Park.** In a 21-acre park, they've re-created the life of old Pinellas County, including a train depot, barn, and houses. Artisans in period dress demonstrate weaving, spinning, and other crafts. *11909 125th St. N., Largo, FL 34644; tel. 813-582-2123. Open Tue.-Sat. 10-4; Sun. 1-4. From Sand Key Park, take Gulf Blvd. to Indian Rocks Beach. Turn left on Walsingham Rd. (Rte. 688) and drive east to 125th St. in Largo.*

◆ **Indian Rocks Area Historical Museum.** In a charming old home, photos and memorabilia relate the past of Sand Key.

*1507 Bay Palm Blvd., Indian Rocks Beach, FL 34635; tel. 813-593-3861. Open Sat. 1-4, Tue. 9:30-11. From Sand Key Park, go south on Gulf Blvd. Turn left on 16th Ave. Go for two blocks and turn right on Bay Palm Blvd.*

# NATURE

◆ **Clearwater Science Center Aquarium.** Conducts research and rescues injured marine mammals and sea turtles. You can visit the recovering creatures, including Mo, a 320-pound loggerhead turtle. Touch tanks, aquariums, and hands-on exhibits. *249 Windward Passage, Clearwater Beach, FL 34630; tel. 813-447-0980. Open Mon.-Fri. 9-5; Sat. 9-4; Sun. 11-4. Admission. From Clearwater Beach, take Memorial Causeway back to Island Estates. Turn left on Island Way; drive one block. Turn left on Windward Passage.*

◆ **Suncoast Seabird Sanctuary.** Birds on the mend get tender, loving care here. Owls, sandhill cranes, pelicans, cormorants, and others can be visited as they heal. *18328 Gulf Blvd., Indian Shores, FL 34635; tel. 813-391-6211. Open daily 9-dark; one-hour tours Tue. at 2. On Sand Key Island, about 9 mi. south of Sand Key Park.*

# SAFETY TIPS

The bridge between Clearwater Beach and Sand Key is posted with a 25-mph speed limit. Observe it, because it's enforced.

# TOURIST INFORMATION

◆ **Clearwater Beach Chamber of Commerce.** *40 Causeway Blvd., Clearwater Beach, FL 34630; tel. 813-447-9532. Open daily 9-5.*

◆ **St. Petersburg/Clearwater Area Visitors Bureau.** *St. Petersburg ThunderDome, One Stadium Dr., Suite A, St. Petersburg, FL 33705; tel. 813-892-7892. No visitors center.*

## CHAPTER 10

# Pass-A-Grille

At the turn of the century vacationers began flocking to Pass-A-Grille, the birthplace of tourism on the island of Long Key, now known as St. Pete Beach (the name was officially changed from St. Petersburg Beach two years ago). The first hotel, the Bonhomie, was built in Pass-A-Grille in 1901, and others followed quickly. In 1928, the fantasy-pink Don CeSar Hotel opened to such illuminati as Scott and Zelda Fitzgerald, Babe Ruth, and Lou Gehrig.

| | |
|---|---|
| Beauty | B |
| Swimming | B |
| Sand | A- |
| Hotels/Inns/B&Bs | B+ |
| House rentals | A |
| Restaurants | A- |
| Nightlife | A- |
| Attractions | B |
| Shopping | B- |
| Sports | A |
| Nature | B+ |

Once a separate political entity, Pass-A-Grille today is part of the town of St. Pete Beach. Legend says the community, which is at the southern tip of the island, got its name from fishermen who brought their catches ashore to cure over wood fires (thus Pass Aux Grilleurs). Despite being in the  midst of a popular resort area, it retains an old-fashioned charm. Guarded on its northern doorstep by the venerable Don CeSar Resort, the village has a safe, small-town feel that's long gone from other parts of the area. Sea grape hedges line the streets, and building codes have kept high-rise growth in check along the town's lush beachfront. One section of jaunty clapboard homes and artsy shops was decreed a National Historic Site in 1989.

From the marinas on Pass-A-Grille's bayside, it's an easy boat ride to the the outlying islands of Shell Key and Egmont Key, well-known as natural habitats. On Egmont, the remains of a Spanish-American War fort crumble into the sea, and a historic lighthouse sends its beacon to ships entering Tampa Bay.

# GULF BEACHES
## PASS-A-GRILLE

The village of Pass-A-Grille regards 5,200 feet of clean, soft sand as its front yard. The well-kept beach is wide and inviting, and the dunes are being restored carefully with new plantings. Though it is set in a quaint village, pavement and parking

| | |
|---|---|
| Beauty | B- |
| Swimming | A- |
| Sand | A- |
| Amenities | A |

meters come up to the edge of the beach, and over your shoulder you can see high-rises in the more developed part of St. Pete Beach. Fortunately, there is little through traffic, which keeps the noise level low. Best of all, you can count on the sun to shine nearly every day of the year. *On Gulf Way between 1st Ave. and 21st Ave. From Pass-A-Grille Way, turn right on 21st Ave. and follow signs for the beach.*

*Swimming:* Gentle waves and a gradual slope make the beach safe and enjoyable for bathing. Water temperatures vary from a

## HOW TO GET THERE

◆ From Tampa International Airport (about an hour from Pass-A-Grille), take I-275 south, crossing Tampa Bay on the Howard Frankland Bridge. Leave I-275 at exit 4 (Pinellas Bayway) in St. Petersburg. Follow Pinellas Bayway west (50 cents toll). Turn left on Gulf Blvd. (Rte. 699) and drive south toward the Don CeSar Resort. Drive under the ramp leading to the resort and continue along Gulf Blvd., which becomes Pass-A-Grille Way. Turn right on 21st Ave. and follow signs for the beach. At the beach turn left on Gulf Way to find parking. Shell Key and Egmont Key, which can be reached only by boat, lie offshore.

low of 63 degrees in January to a high of 86 in August.
*Sand:* Soft sand that's the texture of talcum powder is specked with bits of shell along a wide apron.
*Amenities:* Pass-A-Grille sands are close to everything in town: restaurants and pubs, a park, a museum, shopping, and places to stay. Rest rooms and a snack bar on the beach. No lifeguards.
*Sports:* There's no place in the immediate area to rent water-sports equipment, so you may want to stop at the rental conces-sion on the beach next to the Don CeSar. Shuffleboard courts are across the street at the city park.
*Parking:* Metered parking places ($1 per hour) run the 20-block length of the beach. More spaces are down side streets, but they fill up on busy days. Parking regulations are strictly enforced. There's no charge after 5 p.m.

## OUTLYING ISLANDS

Accessible only by boat, Shell and Egmont keys are a beachcomber's dream. Swimmers and boaters congregate at Egmont, a nation-al wildlife preserve, especially in the summer. Shell Key attracts nature-lovers and shell collectors.

| | |
|---|---|
| Beauty | A- |
| Swimming | B+ |
| Sand | B+ |
| Amenities | C- |

*Swimming:* Water is clear and calm. The beach on the Gulf side of Egmont drops off rapidly. Shell Key has a better shelf for swimmers.
*Sand:* Both beaches boast fine sand and plentiful shells.
*Amenities:* No rest rooms, snack bars, or lifeguards.
*Sports:* Snorkeling is good on Egmont Key. Some charters pro-vide gear, but it's best to bring your own equipment.

## Shell Key

As its name suggests, the island's lure is its countless shells. To local birds, such as the blackwing skimmer, it offers nesting sites.
*Must go by boat, a 10-minute trip. Shuttle from Merry Pier, 801 Pass-A-Grille Way, Pass-A-Grille; tel. 813-360-1348. Three trips daily.*

## Egmont Key

This is a beautiful stretch of beach, but it's not entirely unspoiled. The steady stream of weekend boaters has taken its toll on Fort Dade, which is marred by grafitti and litter. There is still much to explore, however. The fort's ruins extend into the water and provide nice snorkeling with colorful coral and fish. On land, trails lead to the lighthouse and to underground nests of rare gopher tortoises. *Must go by boat. Docking is at the northeast end near the lighthouse. Charters available from local marinas.*

# HOTELS/INNS/B&Bs

Except for the Don CeSar, Pass-A-Grille's accommodations are small, homey establishments. Guest houses are the norm.

♦ **Don CeSar Beach Resort** (very expensive). "The Don" reigns over the resort scene. It's thoroughly modern despite its flapper-era roots. Rooms are small but tastefully decorated. If you need more elbow room, a suite is your best bet. The Seville Suite is a favorite with numerous celebrities, including President Clinton. Restaurants are top-notch. Among the resort's recent improvements are a children's activity room, a spa with a sauna, a family pool, and a fitness room with a full menu of services. The adult pool boasts an underwater sound system. The Don earns its reputation with great service and many extras. Staff members address guests by name and pass trays of fresh fruit at poolside. There are Italian marble bathrooms and ironing boards in every room. *3400 Gulf Blvd., St. Pete Beach, FL 33706; tel. 813-360-1881, 800-282-1116.*

♦ **The Inn on the Beach** (moderate). A fixture in Pass-A-Grille's historic district, this newly renovated guest house on the beach is up-to-date but still homey. Apartments have tiled floors and kitchenettes. The best of the 12 units is No. 8, which has a beach view, tropical decor, and antique furnishings. *1401 Gulf Way, St. Pete Beach, FL 33706; tel. 813-360-8844.*

# HOUSE RENTALS

A one-month stay is usually required from January through April, unless you can catch a week between renters. In summer, there's a one-week minimum. A two-bedroom rental begins at $1,000 a month plus utilities.

♦ **Dolphin Realty of Pinellas County.** *980 Pasadena Ave. #B, S. Pasadena, FL 33707; tel. 813-384-2700. Open daily.*
♦ **Frank T. Hurley Associates.** *2506 Pass-A-Grille Way, St. Pete Beach, FL 33706; tel. 813-367-1949. Open daily.*

# RESTAURANTS

The tradition of fishermen bringing their catch to Pass-A-Grille continues. You can especially enjoy fresh grouper, a large, meaty fish with a mild taste. Most restaurants welcome casual attire. The best deal in Sunday brunch is the King Charles Ballroom on the fifth floor of the Don CeSar.

♦ **Maritana's Grille** (expensive to very expensive). The Don CeSar's newest restaurant is spectacular with lush plants, palm trees, and tanks filled with tropical fish. The outstanding menu is built around the Don's version of new-Florida cuisine. Try the roasted lobster with lemon and pepper. If you have children, request one of the aquarium tables: They're entertaining and roomy. Reservations are recommended. *3400 Gulf Blvd., St. Pete Beach, FL 33706; tel. 813-360-1881. Open for dinner Mon.-Sat. Closed Sun. At the Don CeSar Resort.*

♦ **Hurricane Restaurant** (moderate). This Pass-A-Grille landmark serves delicious fare in a Victorian building overlooking the beach and the Gulf of Mexico. There's outdoor seating and a spacious downstairs dining room that specializes in grouper fixed many ways. On the second floor, Stormy's has a more limited menu served in a tropical setting. A rooftop bar occupies the third level. *Ninth Ave. and Gulf Way, St. Pete Beach, FL 33706; tel. 813-360-9558. Open daily for breakfast, lunch, and dinner.*

♦ **Wharf Seafood Restaurant** (inexpensive) A friendly local fish house, the Wharf overlooks the Intracoastal Waterway, so you can watch the boats glide by as you stuff yourself with, shrimp, crab cakes, crab claws, and fish. *2001 Pass-A-Grille Way, St. Pete Beach, FL 33706; tel. 813-367-9469. Open daily for lunch and dinner.*

# NIGHTLIFE

**P**ass-A-Grille's nightlife is limited, but there's plenty of good music at The Don's and at Hurricane Restaurant. Other clubs are nearby in St. Pete Beach.

♦ **Hurricane Restaurant.** Known for progressive jazz, this spot also swings with reggae and rock and roll. Bands play in the ground-floor lounge, at Stormy's, and on the rooftop. *Ninth Ave. and Gulf Way, St. Pete Beach, FL 33706; tel. 813-360-9558. Open nightly. Entertainment Tue.-Sun.*

♦ **Beachcomber Bar.** Caribbean music is usually featured at this resort lounge. *3400 Gulf Blvd., St. Pete Beach, FL 33706; tel. 813-360-1881. Open daily. At the Don CeSar Resort.*

♦ **Sunsets'.** Slide those feet across the dance floor here on weekends to the sounds of jazz and contemporary rock music. *3400 Gulf Blvd., St. Pete Beach, FL 33706; tel. 813-360-1881. Open daily. Live music Fri.-Sun. At the Don CeSar Resort.*

♦ **Bali Hai.** The revolving rooftop lounge is great for sunsets, and the music is live. *5250 Gulf Blvd., St. Pete Beach, FL 33706; tel. 813-360-1811. Open Tues.-Sun. At the St. Petersburg Hilton Inn.*

♦ **Coconuts Comedy Club.** Lots of laughs from local and nationally known stand-up comics. *5300 Gulf Blvd., St. Pete Beach, FL 33706; tel. 813-443-5714. Entertainment Fri.-Sat. Seating begins at 7:30. In the lounge of the Holiday Inn.*

♦ **Crackers Bar and Grille.** Live bands play contemporary and reggae music. *5501 Gulf Blvd., St. Pete Beach, FL 33507; tel. 813-360-6961. Open nightly. At Silas Dent's Restaurant.*

# SHOPPING

In the heart of Pass-A-Grille's historic district is a cluster of shops and galleries that sell jewelry, crafts, and artwork.

♦ **Nancy Markoe Gallery.** This gallery of American-made crafts displays pottery, jewelry, wood items, and weaving. *3112 Pass-A-Grille Way, St. Pete Beach, FL 33706; tel. 813-360-0729. Open daily.*

♦ **Pass-A-Grille Art Colony.** Oils, watercolors, and pottery of local and national artists can be purchased here. *107 Eighth Ave., St.*

*Pete Beach, FL 33706; tel. 813-367-5654. Open daily Oct.-Apr.; open Thu. evening and Fri.-Mon. May-Sep.*

♦ **Mountcastle International Trading Co. Ltd.** This shop aims to support artisans residing overseas by selling works from Thailand, Haiti, Peru, Indonesia, and various other countries in the Third World. *107 Eighth Ave., St. Pete Beach, FL 33706; tel. 813-360-4743. Open Mon.-Fri. and Sat. morning.*

♦ **Evander Preston Contemporary Jewelry.** Besides selling jewelry, Evander Preston displays his eclectic art collection, including a 1986 Harley Davidson and some works by former Beatles songwriter John Lennon. *106 Eighth Ave., St. Pete Beach, FL 33706; tel. 813-367-7894. Open daily.*

# BEST FOOD SHOPS

**SANDWICHES:** ♦ **Captain's Food Store Delicatessen.** *6880 Gulf Blvd., St. Pete Beach, FL 33706; tel. 813-367-3637. Open daily.*

**SEAFOOD:** ♦ **Publix Super Market.** *4655 Gulf Blvd., St. Pete Beach, FL 33706; tel. 813-360-7091. Open daily.*

**FRESH PRODUCE:** ♦ **Fruit Stand.** *Gulf Blvd. and 70th Ave., St. Pete Beach, FL 33706. Open daily.*

**BAKERY:** ♦ **La Casa del Pane.** *4393 Gulf Blvd., St. Pete Beach, FL 33706; tel. 813-367-8322. Open Tue.-Sun.*

**ICE CREAM:** ♦ **Uncle Andy's Old Fashioned Ice Cream Parlor.** *3400 Gulf Blvd., St. Pete Beach, FL 33706; tel. 813-360-5618. Open daily. At the Don CeSar Resort.*

**BEVERAGES:** ♦ **Pass-A-Grille Food Mart.** *2000 Pass-A-Grille Way, St. Pete Beach, FL 33706; tel. 813-367-4292. Open daily.*

**WINE:** ♦ **Jack's Liquor.** *3855 Gulf Blvd., St. Pete Beach, FL 33706; tel. 813-367-1150. Open daily.*

# SPORTS
## FISHING

Deep-sea fishing excursions aboard a party boat get you out on the water with little fuss, and they're less expensive than private charters. Operators charge around $25 per person for a half-day, $40 for a full day, including license, bait, equipment, and cleaning.

Some cruise overnight into deeper waters for grouper and snapper.

Private fishing charters take you to nearby waters for snook, cobia, redfish, and sea trout. Half-day trips for two cost around $150 plus tip; full day, $250. Venturing farther out in the Gulf with a charter costs $400 or more per day plus tip.

♦ **Merry Pier.** This is fishing headquarters in Pass-A-Grille. You'll find snacks, beverages, bait, and boat and equipment rentals. Fishing from the pier is free. Deep-sea fishing trips aboard the *Captain Kidd* depart from here. *801 Pass-A-Grille Way, St. Pete Beach, FL 33706; tel. 813-360-6606. Open daily. Take Pass-A-Grille Way to the waterfront.*

## BOATING

Boating is popular in the protected waters of the Intracoastal Waterway. You can rent anything from a personal watercraft (waverunner) to a small fishing boat or a pleasure boat for eight. Prices range from $40 to $400 a day for powerboats. Waverunners cost about $50 an hour.

♦ **Merry Pier.** *801 Pass-A-Grille Way, St. Pete Beach, FL 33706; tel. 813-360-6606. Open daily. Take Pass-A-Grille Way to the waterfront.*

♦ **Captain Dave's Watersports.** Besides renting waverunners and powerboats, Captain Dave will take you parasailing or waterskiing. *6300 Gulf Blvd., St. Pete Beach, FL 33706; tel. 813-360-1998. Open daily.*

## BICYCLING

Pass-a-Grille's quiet roads and side streets, many of them one-way, are popular with bike-riders, but there is no place in the village to rent bikes. Elsewhere, bike rentals start at $12 a day or $40 a week.

♦ **The Beach Cyclist.** *7517 Blind Pass Rd., St. Pete Beach, FL 33706; tel. 813-367-5001. Open daily. At the north end of the island.*

## GOLF

There are no golf courses in the immediate area. The nearest public course is in Largo or in Treasure Island, each about 25 miles north.

## TENNIS

Several parks have free tennis courts open to the public. Some of the lighted courts charge 25 cents per hour.

◆ **Lazarillo Park.** Four lighted courts. *W. De Bazan Ave., Pass-A-Grille. Open daily. In the residential area across from the Don CeSar.*

◆ **Vino Del Mar Park.** Two lighted courts and a playground. *Isle Dr., Vino Del Mar. Open daily. On the residential island of Vino Del Mar off Pass-A-Grille.*

◆ **Hurley Park.** One court with no lights. *15th Ave., Pass-A-Grille. Open daily.*

# HISTORY

A three-block area between Eighth and Tenth Avenues has been designated Historic Pass-A-Grille, and it does conjure up the past. Shops, motels, and restaurants occupy buildings dating from the early 1900s.

◆ **Gulf Beaches Historical Museum.** Housed in a historic church near the beach, it describes the settlement of the Pass-A-Grille area with pictures and artifacts. *115 Tenth Ave., St. Pete Beach, FL 33706; tel. 813-360-2491. Open Thu. and Sat. 10-4; Sun. 1-4.*

◆ **Fort Dade ruins.** During the Spanish-American War, Fort Dade was built on Egmont Key to protect the mouth of Tampa Bay from Spanish invasion. With it came a town of more than 70 buildings and 300 residents. Few traces of the town remain, but the fort's ruins provide sport for explorers and snorkelers. *Northwest end of Egmont Key.*

◆ **Egmont Key Lighthouse.** Egmont's original lighthouse, built in 1848, was the first between St. Marks (near Tallahassee) and Key West. Destroyed by a hurricane that same year, it was replaced with the current one in 1858. During the Civil War, it served as a Union Navy outpost. *Northeast end of Egmont Key. Docking nearby.*

# NATURE

◆ **Egmont Key National Wildlife Refuge.** This comprises the entire two-mile-long island, which is natural habitat for nesting seabirds and gopher tortoises. Rattlesnakes inhabit some of the interior bush and prefer to keep their distance. Open daylight hours. *On Egmont Key. Accessible by boat.*

# TOURIST INFORMATION

♦ **St. Pete Beach Area Chamber of Commerce.** *6900 Gulf Blvd., St. Pete Beach, FL 33706; tel. 813-360-6957. Open Mon.-Fri. 9-5.*

♦ **St. Petersburg/Clearwater Area Visitors Bureau.** *St. Petersburg ThunderDome, 1 Stadium Dr., Ste. A, St. Petersburg, FL 33705; tel. 813-892-7892. No visitors center.*

## CHAPTER 11

# Fort DeSoto

Once a pirate haunt, Mullet Key is where residents of Tampa and St. Petersburg go to escape urban life and enjoy the beauty and history of Fort DeSoto Park. A wildlife sanctuary, the park has become known for its many bird species. Vegetation, though largely indigenous, is meticulously groomed. Besides bird-watching, Fort DeSoto is a great place for fishing, biking, camping, and exploring long stretches of beach. In fact, if you want anything else, you'll probably have to look for it in the island communities just outside the park or

| | |
|---|---|
| Beauty | A |
| Swimming | B- |
| Sand | B |
| Hotels/Inns/B&Bs | C |
| House rentals | C |
| Restaurants | B- |
| Nightlife | D+ |
| Attractions | C+ |
| Shopping | C |
| Sports | B- |
| Nature | A |

in St. Pete Beach, a 20-minute drive north. (*See* Chapter 10, Pass-A-Grille, for information about St. Pete Beach.)

Fort DeSoto Park is a Pinellas County park, and although it welcomes visitors from outside the area, its camping facilities are intended primarily for county residents. Campsite reservations must be made in person, and senior-citizen discounts offered by the National Park Service do not apply.

The park's 900 acres are spread over five islands. The first one that you encounter after entering the park is Madelaine Key, site of the public boat ramp. On St. Christopher Key, there's a well-kept campground. Beaches, fishing piers, and the remains of Fort DeSoto are on Mullet Key, a wishbone-shaped island that is the largest of the five.

During the Civil War, Mullet Key was occupied by the

Union Navy, which used it as a base to control the blockade of Tampa Bay. It was not until the Spanish-American War, however, that construction of Fort DeSoto began. The war ended before work was completed in 1900, and the fort was declared obsolete without ever having fired a shot in combat.

Since Fort DeSoto Park opened in 1963, visitors have enjoyed exploring relics at the fort ruins and in the sands of the park's unspoiled beaches. Although there are seven miles of beach, swimming is restricted to two areas. Many park activities center around the fort, which is at the elbow of Mullet Key, a mile west of the junction of Pinellas Bayway and Anderson Boulevard. There's parking, a gift shop, a snack bar, and a fishing pier that juts 1,000 feet into the Gulf. No alcoholic beverages are allowed in the park.

# BAY BEACH
## EAST BEACH

East Beach, which fronts on Tampa Bay and its ship traffic, gives you a marvelous view of the Skyway Bridge and Egmont Key. The area is generally less crowded than North Beach. Park headquarters is next to the swimming area.

| | |
|---|---|
| Beauty | B+ |
| Swimming | B- |
| Sand | B |
| Amenities | B+ |

## HOW TO GET THERE

◆ From Tampa International Airport (about 45 minutes from Fort DeSoto Park), take I-275 south, crossing Tampa Bay on the Howard Frankland Bridge. Get off at exit 4 (Pinellas Bayway) in St. Petersburg. Follow Pinellas Bayway west and then south as it turns to go across the island of Tierra Verde and into Fort DeSoto Park. (You'll pay a 50-cent toll and a 35-cent park entrance fee.) Inside the park, Pinellas Bayway ends at Anderson Blvd., which is adjacent to beaches.

Fishermen and strollers populate the 500-foot pier that juts into the bay at the beach's western end. Beyond that, there's a sailboat launch on a stretch of beach leading to Fort DeSoto and the Gulf pier. *Take Pinellas Bayway until it ends at Anderson Blvd. The swimming area lies directly to the left.*

*Swimming:* Look for signs prohibiting swimming in some areas because of the danger of strong currents and deep holes.

*Sand:* Coarse, grayish, shell-studded sands are bordered by manicured grounds.

*Amenities:* The well-maintained picnic area has rest rooms, grills, and large shelters. Lifeguards are on duty from Memorial Day through Labor Day.

*Sports:* Other than those for fishing, there are no sport facilities and no places to rent equipment.

*Parking:* Free and ample.

# GULF BEACH
## North Beach

Besides swimming, North Beach, on Mullet Key's gulfside arm, is great for walking, exploring, and bird-watching. The area close to the parking lot is suitable for family outings, while shell collectors tend to walk along the fine sands to

| Beauty | A |
|---|---|
| Swimming | B- |
| Sand | B |
| Amenities | B |

the south and out to barrier sand bars. *From Pinellas Bayway, go right on Anderson Blvd. for 2 mi.*

*Swimming:* Swimming is restricted to a stretch defined by signs that warn of deep holes outside the limits. Take the signs seriously: Gulf currents are tricky. Waters close to the parking lot are protected by sandbars, making them bathtub calm. The bottom is a bit muddy, however. Water temperatures hit a low of 63 degrees in January and peak at 86 in August. Air temperatures range from 70 to 90 degrees throughout the year.

*Sand:* Parts of the beach are extremely wide. Along the water's edge, the sand is sometimes laced with tiny shells that make barefoot walking uncomfortable.

*Amenities:* The beach has rest rooms, showers, picnic shelters, and a playground. Across the road, Arrowhead Picnic Area provides an ideal setting for picnics, and it has a nature trail. Lifeguards on duty from Memorial Day through Labor Day.

*Sports:* No facilities or equipment rentals.

*Parking:* Free and ample.

# HOTELS/INNS/B&Bs

In Fort DeSoto Park, the only accommodations are for campers, but there are hotels, apartments, and many resorts nearby on Tierra Verde and St. Pete Beach (see Chapter 10, Pass-A-Grille). Many require a certain length of stay. If you are planning a vacation for December through April, book well in advance.

♦ **Tierra Verde Yacht & Tennis Resort** (moderate). Built around a yacht basin, this is the community's social center. It has a huge swimming pool, four tennis courts, a Jacuzzi, restaurants, bars, and entertainment. Its 66 apartments, all with kitchenettes and private balconies, accommodate up to six people. *200 Madonna Blvd., Tierra Verde, FL 33715; tel. 813-867-8611, 800-934-0549.*

♦ **Fort DeSoto Park Campground** (inexpensive). This well-equipped campground accommodates tent and RV campers at 233 sites; most are located on the waterfront. It has playgrounds, rest rooms, laundries, a camp store, dump stations for emptying RV toilets, and electricity hookups. Note: Reservations, accompanied by full payment, must be made in person at the park office or at a designated location (call for other addresses). *3500 Pinellas Bayway, Tierra Verde, FL 33715; tel. 813-866-2662.*

# HOUSE RENTALS

In the community of Isla del Sol, there is no minimum stay required. Rentals for homes in the area range from $750 to $905 a week.

♦ **Isla Del Sol Realty.** *6025 Sun Blvd., St. Petersburg, FL 33715; tel. 813-867-1191. Open daily.*

♦ **Re/Max Bayway Islands Realty.** *18 Madonna Blvd., Tierra Verde, FL 33715; tel. 813-867-3100. Open daily.*

# RESTAURANTS

Just outside Fort DeSoto Park, there are a few fine restaurants in Tierra Verde. For a wider variety, ranging from seafood and burgers to fine cuisine, you can drive 15 to 25 minutes toward downtown St. Petersburg or north to the resort area of St. Pete Beach.

♦ **Good Times** (moderate). German and Slavic dishes are the specialty here. Try the Bohemian sauerbraten with lingonberries. Desserts include such rich, Old-World favorites as apple strudel and Black Forest cake. *1130 Pinellas Bayway, Tierra Verde, FL 33715; tel. 813-867-0774. Open Tue.-Sat. for dinner.*

♦ **Billy's Ft. DeSoto Joe's Wharf** (moderate). Fresh seafood, served alongside the marina, makes for a delightful dining experience. The stone crab is great in season (October 15 through May 15), and the early-bird dinners (noon to 6) are attractively priced. *200 Madonna Blvd., Tierra Verde, FL 33715; tel. 813-867-8710. Open daily for lunch and dinner. At Tierra Verde Yacht & Tennis Resort.*

♦ **Skyway Jack's** (inexpensive). A local legend, Skyway Jack's serves generous portions of down-home, Southern dishes. A hit with fishermen, its atmosphere is somewhere between funky and dumpy. Breakfast is a treat, especially the ham hash. *6701 34th St. S., St. Petersburg, FL 33711; tel. 813-866-3217. Open daily for breakfast, lunch, and dinner. Turn left into the parking lot just before the entrance of Maximo Park.*

# NIGHTLIFE

Nightlife at Fort DeSoto Park means a campfire or a moonlit beach walk. After dark, the park is open only to campers. Besides the one local spot listed below, you can venture north to the numerous resorts of St. Pete Beach.

♦ **Cocomo's.** This outdoor pool bar presents reggae bands, calypso, and soft rock music on weekends during the warmer months. *200 Madonna Blvd., Tierra Verde, FL 33715; tel. 813-867-8710. Open Sat.-Sun. Apr.-Nov. At Tierra Verde Yacht & Tennis Resort.*

# SHOPPING

You will find only one shop located in Fort DeSoto Park, but there are many others in the surrounding area.

♦ **Fort DeSoto Gift Shop.** Mostly souvenirs and park T-shirts are sold here. *Next to the fort ruins on Anderson Blvd. Open daily.*

# BEST FOOD SHOPS

**SANDWICHES:** ♦ **7-Eleven.** *150 Pinellas Bayway, Tierra Verde, FL 33715; tel. 813-867-8698. Open daily.*

**SEAFOOD:** ♦ There's no store specializing in seafood in the immediate area, but Madeira Beach and Indian Rocks Beach, about a half-hour away, are known for their seafood marts. It's worth the drive. *Take Pinellas Bayway to Gulf Blvd. (Rte. 699) and follow it north.*

**FRESH PRODUCE:** ♦ **Tierra Verde Produce.** *Alongside the gas station at the corner of Pinellas Bayway and Madonna Blvd., Tierra Verde, FL 33715; tel. 813-866-6155. Open daily.*

**BEVERAGES:** ♦ **7-Eleven.** *150 Pinellas Bayway, Tierra Verde, FL 33715; tel. 813-867-8698. Open daily.*

**WINE:** ♦ **B&S Liquors.** *1120 Pinellas Bayway, Tierra Verde, FL 33715; tel. 813-867-0180. Open daily.*

# HISTORY

♦**Fort DeSoto.** Part of the fortifications—chiefly the gun emplacements and the ammunition rooms—are well-preserved. Four 12-inch mortar cannons, the only ones of their type remaining in North America, guard the walls. Even if you aren't a history buff, it's worth climbing to the top of the fort for a magnificent view of the Gulf, the Skyway Bridge, and Tampa Bay. The fort is listed in the National Register of Historic Places, but it should not be confused with the DeSoto National Memorial in Bradenton, Florida, site of the Spanish explorer's first landfall in North America. *Tel. 813-866-2484. Open daily sunrise-sunset. From Pinellas Bayway, turn right on Anderson Blvd. and drive west 1 mi.*

# SPORTS
## FISHING

With its two long fishing piers and a half dozen bridges, Fort DeSoto Park is a paradise for devoted anglers. You'll usually find a bait truck parked beyond the toll entrance to the park, alongside a popular fishing bridge over Bunces Pass. For deep-sea excursion boats and fishing charters, you must drive outside the park to the various marinas in St. Pete Beach and other communities to the north (see Chapter 10, Pass-A-Grille).

♦ **Bait Bucket.** Sells bait, tackle, and fishing licenses. *108 Pinellas Bayway, Tierra Verde, FL 33715; tel. 813-864-2108. Open daily.*

## BOATING

You can launch your boat at the park's ramp area on Madelaine Key, which has rest rooms, picnic areas, and ample parking.

♦ **Tierra Verde Boat Rentals.** Rents outboards and powerboats by the hour, half day, and full day. *100 Pinellas Bayway, Tierra Verde, FL 33715; tel. 813-867-0077. Open daily. At Tierra Verde Marina*

♦ **Destiny Yacht Charters.** The 41-foot *Destiny* sails to Shell Key on half-day cruises that include dolphin- watching and shell-collecting. Sunset-watching cruises are also popular. *100 Pinellas Bayway, Tierra Verde, FL 33715; tel. 813-430-7245. Open daily. At Tierra Verde Marina.*

## BICYCLING

Fort DeSoto park has about ten miles of wide, paved bike paths that are also used by Rollerbladers. There are no rentals here, so bring your own bicycles and skates.

## TENNIS

♦ **Tierra Verde Yacht & Tennis Resort.** Four lighted tennis courts are open to the public. *200 Madonna Blvd., Tierra Verde, FL 33715; tel. 813-867-8611, 800-934-0549. Tennis pro shop ext. 7103. Open daily.*

# NATURE

◆ **Fort DeSoto Park.** The best bird-watching is on North Beach, where blackwing skimmers, wood storks, and other shorebirds abound. Across the road, the Arrowhead Picnic Area nature trail, less than a mile long, introduces visitors to vegetation and other natural phenomena. Additional exhibits may be found at park headquarters on Anderson Boulevard. *Park open daily sunrise-sunset.*

# SAFETY TIPS

Obey warning signs at beaches and stay within designated swimming areas. When walking barefoot or in sandals, especially in grassy areas, beware of sand spurs: prickly seed pods that are painful.

# TOURIST INFORMATION

◆ **Fort DeSoto Park.** *Box 3, Tierra Verde, FL 33715; tel. 813-866-2484. Park headquarters open daily 8-5. At the junction of Pinellas Bayway and Anderson Blvd.*
◆ **St. Petersburg/Clearwater Area Visitors Bureau.** *St. Petersburg ThunderDome, One Stadium Dr., Suite A, St. Petersburg, FL 33705; tel. 813-892-7892. No visitors center.*

## CHAPTER 12

# Siesta Key

**M**aintaining a carefree character all its own, Siesta Key is a gem in the necklace of barrier islands fronting the city of Sarasota. Its greatest natural asset is its sand, which has been proclaimed the whitest in the world. The community is distinctive, too. Connected to the mainland by two short bridges, the island derives much of its character from the cadre of artists and writers who began settling here in the 1920s. Among them were mystery writer John D. MacDonald and author MacKinlay Kantor.

| | |
|---|---|
| Beauty | B+ |
| Swimming | B+ |
| Sand | A |
| Hotels/Inns/B&Bs | A |
| House rentals | B+ |
| Restaurants | A |
| Nightlife | A- |
| Attractions | C |
| Shopping | B+ |
| Sports | A- |
| Nature | C+ |

Today, the artsy folk share the famous sands with beachcombers and resident millionaires, along a dazzling seven-mile beach that, though developed, has many unspoiled enclaves. Recreational areas are well-maintained and accommodating to water-sports lovers; fishing and snorkeling are especially popular pursuits. In Siesta Key village, at the north end of the island, veggie cafes and swanky restaurants cater to a diverse clientele. Culture is but a short drive away in Sarasota, where John Ringling has left a legacy of fine art and theater appreciation since the 1920s, when the city was the winter headquarters of Ringling's circus.

Directly to the north of Siesta Key in the Sarasota island chain, Lido Key and companion St. Armands Key welcome visitors of diverse interests with a world-class shopping center and educational and recreational attractions.

# GULF BEACHES
## CRESCENT BEACH

| Beauty | B+ |
|---|---|
| Swimming | A |
| Sand | A+ |
| Amenities | A+ |

The experts at the Woods Hole Oceanographic Institution got it right when they declared Siesta's beaches the winner of the Great International White Sand Beach Challenge a few years ago. Powdered quartz contributes to the luminous, down-soft quality of these sands. Sarasota County, furthermore, puts lots of money into developing and maintaining facilities at its beaches. The beauty of the sand is compromised only by resort development all along this crescent-shaped strand at the northern end of the island. No pets are allowed on the beach.

*Swimming:* Clear, warm waters and a gently sloping sand shelf make for ideal swimming, though there is some murkiness in winter. Posted beach flags warn about any hazardous swimming conditions. Water temperatures average around 69 degrees from February through April, and climb as high as 86 in the summer.

*Sand:* The white beach stretches wide, soft, fluffy, and devoid of shells. The sand stays cool year-round. Where the waves wash it, the beach is as hard as cement.

## HOW TO GET THERE

◆ From I-75 (about 25 minutes from Siesta Key), there are two approaches to the island. To reach the north end, take Exit 38 and drive west on Bee Ridge Rd. Cross Hwy. 41 (Tamiami Trail), and turn right on Osprey Ave. Turn left on Siesta Dr., which leads to North Bridge and the island.

◆ To reach the south end, take Exit 37 and drive west on Clark Rd. (Rte. 72). After crossing Hwy. 41 (Tamiami Trail), the name of the road changes to Stickney Point Rd. Follow it for another mile and cross South Bridge onto the island.

*Amenities:* The six public accesses along Beach Road have no facilities. Siesta County Beach has rest rooms, a fitness trail, a playground, a soccer field, picnic tables and shelters, a pavilion, two food stands, and a souvenir shop. Lifeguards on duty.

*Sports:* A concession at the county beach rents catamarans, water bikes, and other water toys. There are also tennis courts, ball fields, volleyball courts, and volleyball nets strung along the beach.

*Parking:* Expect problems if you're a late-riser. Five of the six Beach Road accesses have small lots, and they fill up quickly. Though the county beach has one of the Gulf Coast's largest lots, its 800 spaces stay filled from early morning until after sunset.

## Beach Road Accesses

Preferred by those who want to avoid the crowds at the county beach, these six spots offer attractive beaching. Parking is limited, so get there early. *Off Beach Rd., between Columbus Blvd. and Calle Florida.*

## Siesta County Beach

Everything here, from the sand to the facilities, can be described in superlatives. This legendary, half-mile strand does draw crowds, but luckily it's wide enough to accommodate them. *On Midnight Pass Rd. at Beach Way Dr., about 2 1/2 mi. south of North Bridge.*

| Beauty | B+ |
|--------|----|
| Swimming | B |
| Sand | B+ |
| Amenities | B |

## SOUTH SIESTA KEY BEACHES

South of Stickney Point Road, the sand may be coarser, but the beaches are less populated and more natural. Families and shell collectors prefer it here.

*Swimming:* Calm, warm waters. The bottom of Turtle Beach drops off abruptly at one point. Some swimmers venture into the park's lagoon, which has a muddy bottom.

*Sand:* The sands at Point of Rocks are as fine and white as those to the north. At Turtle Beach, the sand is darker and coarser, and it contains shells.

*Amenities:* The public accesses at Point of Rocks have no facilities. At Turtle Beach, there are rest rooms. Picnic facilities are back from the beach, around the lagoon. Restaurants and bars are just across the street. No lifeguard.

*Sports:* Point of Rocks is near resort concessions that rent equipment for snorkeling, scuba diving, and fishing. Turtle Park offers such things as horseshoes, volleyball, a swing set, and boat ramps.

*Parking:* Of the two accesses at Point of Rocks, only the one just south of South Bridge has parking, and it's limited. Turtle Beach has ample, free parking. Drivers of RVs will find room to pull in here.

## Point of Rocks

Clear water and underwater rock formations make Point of Rocks popular with swimmers, snorkelers, and scuba divers. Although there's dense resort and commercial development nearby, it's still a great beach. *Just south of the intersection of Midnight Pass Rd. and Stickney Point Rd. For parking, look closely for the No. 12 access sign near the Siesta Breakers resort.*

## Turtle Beach

The tone here is much more relaxed than on Siesta County Beach, and commercial development is less intrusive. Exclusive resorts replace the clusters of shops and restaurants found at the north end of the island. True, there's a trailer park next door, but high dunes hide this and other evidence of development from people on the beach. *3 mi. south of South Bridge, at the junction of Blind Pass Rd. and Turtle Beach Rd.*

# HOTELS/INNS/B&Bs

You won't find any chain hotels on Siesta Key, but you will find something to suit every vacationing preference and budget. Accommodations range from hotel towers to homey motels and cottages. Each has its own personality.

♦ **Banana Bay Club** (expensive). Well away from the beach, this unusual property is on the brink of a quiet lagoon, which is a bird sanctuary. Its seven guest units, decorated with a tropical flair, range from a studio apartment to a two-bedroom house. All have kitchens. The club, which has a small, heated swimming pool, also provides bicycles, boats, and fishing equipment. *8254 Midnight Pass Rd., Sarasota, FL 34242; tel. 941-346-0113.*

◆ **The Wildflower Inn B&B** (moderate). Smack in the middle of the village shopping area, four apartments sit above Siesta's popular vegetarian restaurant of the same name. Rates include breakfast in the restaurant. Each of the recently refurbished units has a full kitchen, a bedroom, and a living area. The Dolphin room, with its porpoise motif, is a favorite. *5218 Ocean Blvd., Sarasota, FL 34242; tel. 941-346-1566.*

◆ **Crescent House B&B** (moderate). Situated across the road from the beach, this four-room B&B is as inviting as a friend's home. The fireplace and antique furnishings lend an air of gentility, but it's not stuffy. Guests share bathrooms and the hot tub. *459 Beach Rd., Sarasota, FL 34242; tel. 941-346-0857.*

# HOUSE RENTALS

Technically, there's a one-month minimum rental on houses, but it's not always clear which dwellings this covers. Most vacationers on Siesta rent an apartment, a condominium, or part of a house. Make it easy on yourself and work through the Siesta Key Chamber of Commerce, which has standardized the listings process. Rents start at $2,000 a month.

◆ **Siesta Key Chamber of Commerce.** *5100 Ocean Blvd., Unit B, Siesta Key, FL 34242; tel. 941-349-3800; fax 941-349-9699. Open Mon.-Fri. 10-5.*

# RESTAURANTS

The Sarasota area has a reputation for top-notch restaurants, and Siesta Key contributes its share, from casual beach eats to fine Continental cuisine.

◆ **Summerhouse** (expensive). Acclaimed for its bring-the-outdoors-in design, Summerhouse does an impeccable job of preparing traditional Continental cuisine. Lighter fare is available upstairs in the bar. *6101 Midnight Pass Rd., Sarasota, FL 34242; tel. 941-349-1100. Open daily for dinner.*

◆ **Coasters Seafood House** (moderate). There's lots of seating outside the New England-style building, so diners can watch boat traffic on the Intracoastal Waterway as they enjoy imaginatively prepared fish-house fare. The fish cakes with remoulade sauce are top-of-the-line. Reservations recommended. *1500 Stickney Point Rd., Sarasota, FL 34231; tel. 941-923-4848. Open daily for lunch and dinner. In the Boatyard Shopping Village, at the mainland end of South Bridge.*

◆ **Phillippi Creek Village Oyster Bar** (moderate). It's worth leaving the island to try this popular waterside fish house, known for its steamed seafood and casual atmosphere. Ask for a seat out on the floating dock. Seafood lovers shouldn't miss the combo pot for two, a Florida-style clam bake. *5353 S. Tamiami Trail, Sarasota, FL 34231; tel. 941-925-4444. Open daily for lunch and dinner. From Stickney Point Rd., go north on Hwy. 41 (Tamiami Trail) about 1/2 mi., to Phillippi Creek Village.*

◆ **The Old Salty Dog** (inexpensive). Casual seafood and sandwich favorites are served in a pub setting with outdoor seating. Best bets: fish-and-chips, filet of fresh Florida fish made the way you like it, or a custom-order burger. *5023 Ocean Blvd., Sarasota, FL 34242; tel. 941-349-0158. Open daily for lunch and dinner.*

# NIGHTLIFE

**S**iesta can be a partying place for people of all ages. Not far from Sarasota's theater and nightlife scene, it lets you be as involved as you wish.

◆ **Coasters.** Listen and dance to light rock and Top 40s stuff while overlooking the Intracoastal Waterway. *1500 Stickney Point Rd., Sarasota, FL 34231; tel. 941-923-4848. Open nightly. Live music Wed.-Sat. In the Boatyard Shopping Village, at the mainland end of South Bridge.*

◆ **Beach Club.** With the atmosphere of a rowdy college bar, it hosts local rock, jazz, and reggae groups. *5151 Ocean Blvd., Sarasota, FL 34242; tel. 941-349-6311. Open nightly. In Siesta Key village.*

◆ **Fandango's.** The spot for jazz, and it's right on the island. *5148 Ocean Blvd., Sarasota, FL 34242; tel. 941-346-1711. Live jazz Thu.-Sat. In Siesta Key village.*

♦ **Crescent Club.** Appealing to the mature crowd, its dance floor and live entertainment recall the big-band era. *6519 Midnight Pass Rd., Sarasota, FL 34242; tel. 941-349-1311. Open nightly. 3 mi. south of South Bridge, at Turtle Beach.*

♦ **Summerhouse.** Upscale entertainment includes live jazz. *6101 Midnight Pass Rd., Sarasota, FL 34242; tel. 941-349-1100. Open nightly. Live music Tue.-Sat.*

♦ **Sarasota Quay.** After dark, you'll find everything from live jazz to sound-and-light shows at this collection of clubs, restaurants, and stores. *105 Sarasota Quay, Sarasota, Fl 34236; tel. 941-957-0120. Open nightly. From Stickney Point Rd., go north on Hwy. 41 about 6 mi. to the intersection with Fruitville Rd.*

♦ **Sarasota Opera at A.B. Edwards Theatre.** In this historic centerpiece of downtown Sarasota's theater-and-arts district, a professional troupe has performed classical works for more than 30 years. *61 N. Pineapple Ave., Sarasota, FL 34231; tel. 941-953-7030. Open nightly Mon.-Sat.; matinee Sun. Box office open Mon., Wed., Fri. 10-2. Take Hwy. 41 north, turn left on Main St. and go west to Pineapple Ave.*

♦ **Florida Studio Theatre.** A professional company stages experimental theater in winter and hosts the New Plays Festival in summer. *1241 N. Palm Ave., Sarasota, FL 34236; tel. 941-366-9796. Box office open daily; performances Tue.-Sun. from Dec. through the first week in Aug. Take Hwy. 41 north, turn left on Main St., and go west to Palm Ave.*

# SHOPPING

Siesta Key village shops run the gamut from tacky to tasteful. Come barefoot. Die-to-buy types should, however, put on their shoes and hop up to the next island to canvass St. Armands Circle for serious spending. For unequaled art shopping, head for South Palm Avenue in downtown Sarasota.

♦ **Sea Chantey.** Specializing in unusual objets d'art, jewelry, and women's clothes, this shop rises above the pink flamingos and T-shirts for sale on the island. *5150 Ocean Blvd., Siesta Key, FL 34242; tel. 941-349-6171. Open daily. In Siesta Key village.*

♦ **Uniquely Florida.** Jewelry, coins, and other collectibles. *1512 Stickney*

*Point Rd., Sarasota, FL 34231; tel. 941-921-7028. Open Mon.-Sat. In the Boatyard Shopping Village, at the mainland end of South Bridge.*

# BEST FOOD SHOPS

**SANDWICHES:** ♦ **Phil Pickle's Diner.** *5239D Ocean Blvd., Sarasota, FL 34242; tel. 941-346-2005. Open daily.*

**SEAFOOD:** ♦ **Siesta Fish Market.** *221 Garden Ln., Sarasota, FL 34242; tel. 941-349-2602. Open daily.*

**FRESH PRODUCE:** ♦ **Siesta Market.** *205 Canal Rd., Sarasota, FL 34242; tel. 941-349-1474. Open daily.*

**BAKERY:** ♦ **Strudels 'N Cream.** *5104 Ocean Blvd., Siesta Key, FL 34234; tel. 941-349-8930. Open daily.*

**ICE CREAM:** ♦ **Big Olaf Creamery.** *5208 Ocean Blvd., Sarasota, FL 34242; tel. 941-349-9392. Open daily.*

**WINE:** ♦ **Siesta Spirits.** *5253 Ocean Blvd., Sarasota, FL 34242; tel. 941-349-4759. Open daily.*

# SPORTS

## FISHING

Fishermen find plenty of opportunity on Siesta Key to cast from land. Favorite spots at the north end of the island include Siesta Bridge, and Sarasota Big Pass at Shell Road. At the south end, there's Stickney Point Bridge or seawall, the beach at Point of Rocks, the Turtle Beach lagoon, and Midnight Pass (at the south end of Turtle Beach).

♦ **Midnight Pass Marina.** Look here for fishing guides to take you to local waters or far out in the Gulf. *8865 Midnight Pass Rd., Sarasota, FL 34242; tel. 941-349-8884. Open daily.*

♦ **Mr. CB's.** This is water-sports headquarters, with fishing charters, bait, tackle, and fishing licenses. *1249 Stickney Point Rd., Sarasota, FL 34242; tel. 941-349-4400. Open daily. At the island end of South Bridge.*

## BOATING

Cruising the Intracoastal Waterway between Sarasota and its off-shore islands is a favorite pastime for vacationers.

♦ **Mr. CB's.** Rents runabouts and pontoon boats. *1249 Stickney Point Rd., Sarasota, FL 34242; tel. 941-349-4400. Open daily. At* *the island end of South Bridge.*

♦ **Siesta Key Boat Rental.** *1265 Old Stickney Point Rd., Sarasota, FL 34242; tel. 941-349-8880. Open daily. At Siesta Key Marina, near the island end of South Bridge.*

♦ **Sweetwater Kayaks.** Rents kayaks and leads tours with instruction. Most popular: the morning dolphin paddle and the sunset tour. *5263 Ocean Blvd., No. 7, Sarasota, FL 34242; tel. 941-346-1179. Open daily.*

## BICYCLING

Cyclists and joggers take to the path that runs from Siesta Bridge on the north to Turtle Beach on the south.

♦ **Mr. CB's.** Bicycle rentals. *1249 Stickney Point Rd., Sarasota, FL 34242; tel. 941-349-4400. Open daily. At the island end of South Bridge.*

## GOLF

Though Siesta Key has no golf courses, the mainland is rife with them.

♦ **Gulf Gate Country Club.** Closest to the island, it has a nine-hole and an 18-hole course. *2550 Bispham Rd., Sarasota, FL 34231; tel. 941-921-5515. Open daily.*

## TENNIS

♦ **Siesta County Beach.** Four courts for public use. *Open daily. On Midnight Pass Rd., at Beach Way Dr.*

# HISTORY

♦ **Historic Spanish Point.** Several eras of local history can be explored at this 30-acre site, which has prehistoric burial mounds, a pioneer homestead, an old cemetery, a rebuilt citrus packing house, and an archaeological exhibit. Every Sunday from mid-December to mid-April, actors portray life at the turn of the century. *500 N. Tamiami Trail, Osprey, FL 34229; tel. 941-966-5214. Admission. Open Mon.-Sat. 9-5; Sun. noon-5. From Stickney Point Rd., drive south on Hwy. 41 (Tamiami Trail) about 5 mi., to Osprey.*

# NATURE

♦ **Sarasota Bay Walk.** This nature walk, less than a mile long, takes you along lagoons, estuaries, and upland, with interpretation along the way. *1550 Ken Thompson Pkwy., Sarasota, FL 34236; tel. 941-361-6133. Open daily. Take Hwy. 41 north, turn left on Main St., and go west to St. Armands Key. The starting point is to the north, on City Island.*

♦ **Mote Marine Laboratory and Aquarium.** Known for the 135,000-gallon tank that's home to sharks and other marine life, this research center displays local and exotic creatures in 22 aquariums and touch tanks. Exhibits deal with the coastal environment and marine mammal rehabilitation. *1600 Ken Thompson Pkwy., Sarasota, FL 34236; tel. 941-388-2451, 800-691-6683. Open daily. Admission. Take Hwy. 41 north, turn left on Main St. and go west to St. Armands Key. The laboratory and aquarium are north, on City Island.*

♦ **Pelican Man's Bird Sanctuary.** Indigenous birds of all sorts are treated here for broken wings and other injuries. *1708 Ken Thompson Pkwy., Sarasota, FL 34236; tel. 941-388-4444. Open daily. Take Hwy. 41 north, turn left on Main St. and go west to St. Armands Key. The sanctuary is north, on City Island.*

♦ **Oscar Scherer State Recreation Area.** Rare Florida scrub jays, bald eagles, bobcats, alligators, and river otters make their home in this 462-acre park. Explore by canoe or on foot. Swimming and camping facilities available. *1843 S. Tamiami Trail, Osprey, FL 34229; tel. 941-483-5956. Open daily. From Stickney Point Rd., drive south on Hwy. 41 (Tamiami Trail) about 5 mi., to Osprey.*

# SAFETY TIPS

Siesta Key's quartz-white sand reflects the sun powerfully and causes you to burn quickly. It's also hard on the eyes, so bring sunscreen, a hat, and sunglasses.

# TOURIST INFORMATION

♦ **Siesta Key Chamber of Commerce.** *5100 Ocean Blvd., Unit B, Siesta Key, FL 34242; tel. 941-349-3800; fax 941-349-9699. Open Mon.-Fri. 10-5.*

♦ **Sarasota Convention & Visitors Bureau.** *655 N. Tamiami Trail, Sarasota, FL 34236; tel. 941-957-1877, 800-522-9799. Open Mon.-Fri. 9-5.*

## CHAPTER 13

# Manasota Key

M anasota Key has a split personality. At its northern extreme, which lies in Sarasota County, it is ultra-exclusive and sparsely developed. This is what most people regard as Manasota Key. But the southern portion, which is in Charlotte County, is very much a part of the island, although the culture couldn't be more different. This four-mile stretch, known as Englewood Beach, is an extension of the mainland town of Englewood. With some of the least expensive lodging, restaurants, water sports,

| Beauty | B+ |
|---|---|
| Swimming | B |
| Sand | B |
| Hotels/Inns/B&Bs | B |
| House rentals | A |
| Restaurants | B |
| Nightlife | B |
| Attractions | C+ |
| Shopping | B- |
| Sports | A |
| Nature | A |

and stores to be found anywhere on Florida's coast, it's the antithesis of the north-end community.

Manasota Key's north end is a designated wildlife sanctuary. The road running along the narrow spine between Gulf and bay is quiet and wooded. Palatial mansions and older, humbler beach houses are evidence of the wealth that controls development. There are a couple of intimate resorts but no restaurants or shops. You see people only at the two beach parks.

Despite the impression you get from the southern end, Manasota Key is one of Florida's most out-of-the-way beach destinations. Far from the state's booming metropolises, it draws primarily from nearby mainland communities. The key attracts what one resident describes as "regular people," making it a friendly place for families and retirees.

It combines the benefits of commercialization with a beautiful beach and a persistence of the natural. Besides the facilities in Englewood Beach, visitors have their pick of hotels, restaurants, marinas, and shops in nearby Englewood. Lemon Bay, which separates the key from the mainland, is part of the Cape Haze Aquatic Preserve.

The vast, lightly settled land between Englewood Beach and the commercial strip to the east along Highway 41 is riddled with mangrove-shaded rivers, creeks, and bayous that lend the area an uncommon natural beauty.

Manasota Key beachers find warm waters (average temperature, 86 degrees) and coarse, black-specked, gray sand. The salt-and-pepper effect comes from fossilized prehistoric bones and shark's teeth, pulverized over the aeons and spit ashore.

# GULF BEACHES
## NORTH MANASOTA KEY

The beauty of these beaches lies mainly in their unblemished backdrop: There's not a high-rise in sight. The north beach is having erosion problems, however, which is why this otherwise perfect beach gets a B+ for beauty. Both beaches are kept nat-

| Beauty | B+ |
|---|---|
| Swimming | B |
| Sand | B |
| Amenities | C+ |

## HOW TO GET THERE

◆ From Fort Myers's Southwest International Airport (1 1/2 hours from Manasota Key), follow Daniels Pkwy. to I-75. Drive north on I-75 for 30 mi. and get off at exit 31. Turn left on Peachland Blvd. and drive for 4 mi., following signs for Hwy. 41. Turn right on Hwy. 41, then left on Rte. 776. Follow Rte. 776 for 16 1/2 mi., until it veers left and becomes Beach Rd., which crosses the south bridge to Manasota Key and the community of Englewood Beach.

ural, and they are well-maintained. Dune daisies, scaevola, sea grapes, cabbage palms, and grasses grow in profusion at Manasota Beach and its adjacent park.

*Swimming:* The bottom has a slightly steep slope and is shelly. Normally the water is fairly calm, and the swimming is good.

*Sand:* It's a beach of varied textures, with black-specked sand plus shells and shark teeth that wash up.

*Amenities:* Rest rooms and outdoor showers at both beaches. Manasota Beach has picnic pavilions, and barbecue grills. Lifeguard on duty.

*Sports:* Manasota Beach has volleyball and a boat launch. Beach hikers find plenty of uninterrupted miles to cover.

*Parking:* Park free in unpaved lots with plenty of spaces. The later you get there, the farther you'll have to walk to the beach.

## Manasota Beach

The more popular of the two, the 14-acre park's beach draws crowds around its parking area, where the beach is narrow. From here, you can walk north and south to secluded sands. About 1 1/2 miles north you'll reach Venice's Casperson Beach, also known for its remoteness. *At the west end of the north bridge, at 8570 Manasota Beach Rd..*

## Middle (Blind Pass) Beach

Locals refer to it as Blind Pass Beach (there's no actual pass here), even though in recent years it's been renamed. The 63-acre beach widens at the access and feels less cramped than its northern counterpart. *Open 8-8. About 3 1/2 mi. south of the north bridge, at 6725 Manasota Beach Rd.*

## ENGLEWOOD BEACHES

Of the two beaches at Manasota Key's south end, the one at Port Charlotte State Recreation Area is by far the lovelier and less developed. There are no facilities there, however. Chadwick Park is tops on the island for providing amenities or hav-

| | |
|---|---|
| Beauty | A- |
| Swimming | B+ |
| Sand | B |
| Amenities | A- |

ing them nearby. Fortunately, development in the area is low-rise, so you don't feel as if you're surrounded by a city.

*Swimming:* For safe, shallow water, Chadwick Park is the spot. Swift currents run through Stump Pass at the south end of Port Charlotte Park.

*Sand:* The shell-strewn, black-specked sand is of the same quality as that to the north. The beach is narrowest around Chadwick Park's south parking lot, but widens in both directions from there.

*Amenities:* Port Charlotte State Recreation Area has no facilities. At Chadwick Park, you'll find rest rooms, showers, beach-chair rentals, a food concession, and a picnic ground with play areas and grills. To use the picnic pavilions, you must reserve ahead at the concession shop. Nearby are all sorts of restaurants, shops, and rentals. No lifeguard.

*Sports:* Sports enthusiasts favor Chadwick Park, where there are volleyball and basketball courts and water-sports rentals can be found within easy walking distance. Stump Pass, at the end of the Port Charlotte beach, offers prime fishing.

*Parking:* Chadwick Park has two gated lots where you pay $1 a day. These both fill up by midday in season (December through March). The Port Charlotte park has three free spaces (good luck getting one) and no legal street parking (this area is patrolled). Hard-core seclusionists drop off the gang and gear at the beach entrance, park at Chadwick, and walk back almost two miles.

## Chadwick Park Beach

When people talk about Englewood Beach, this is usually what they mean. The beach gets crowded around the two parking lots but stretches for a long way in either direction. An elevated boardwalk edges the beach. *Open 6-11. At the end of the road that crosses the south bridge.*

## Port Charlotte State Recreation Area

Not many people find their way to this beach. Because of its parking problem, it's used primarily by guests of local resorts. Your best bet is to bicycle there. There's a bike path leading to it, and the park has bike racks. The beach is unspoiled, with little visual offense from development. It extends about one mile from the end of Beach Road to Stump Pass with nothing but vegetation along the way. A sandy trail runs the length of the beach. *At the south end of Gulf Blvd., 2 mi. from the south bridge.*

# HOTELS/INNS/B&Bs

**M**ost of the island's accommodations are near Englewood Beach. They range from luxury condo beach clubs to fishing cottages.

◆ **Manasota Beach Club** (very expensive). Demure, not fancy. Rustic cabins, without TV or phones, have the feel of a kid's camp. Its "very expensive" price tag includes all meals in season. (In November, December, and late April, guests can rent cottages with kitchens.) Besides bird-watching and secluded beaching, the wooded Gulf-to-bay property has a swimming pool, tennis courts, croquet, bocci, and other sports. *7660 Manasota Key Rd., Englewood, FL 34223; tel. 941-474-2614. Closed mid-May to mid-Dec. On the north end of Manasota Key.*

◆ **Weston's Resort** (inexpensive). Its pale yellow stucco buildings occupy two sides of the street. The east side is devoted to fishermen, with a fishing dock, boat ramp, and rentals. The west side faces the beach. Its 82 units range from efficiencies to three-bedroom apartments, which get into higher price ranges. They accommodate three to eight people. Each unit has a kitchen and use of two pools, tennis courts, and fishing facilities. *985 Gulf Blvd., Englewood Beach, FL 34223; tel. 941-474-3431. South of Beach Rd. on Manasota Key.*

# HOUSE RENTALS

◆ **Manasota Key Realty.** There are many different types of vacation rentals to choose from on Manasota Key: grandiose north-end mansions, beachside cottages, and bayside homes. Sarasota County (the island's north end) requires a one-month minimum stay. Rates range from $1,200 to $4,000 a month. *1385 Gulf Blvd., Englewood, FL 34223; tel. 941-474-9534, 800-881-9534. Open Mon.-Sat.*

# RESTAURANTS

◆ **New Captain's Club** (moderate). Occupying a historic building, it gives diners a chance to enjoy their meal while taking in a view of the bay. There's a wide choice of fish dishes, ribs, salads, sandwiches, and meat. *1855 Gulf Blvd., Englewood Beach, FL 34223; tel. 941-475-8611. Open daily for lunch and dinner. Across the street from Chadwick Park's south end. Boat docking available.*

◆ **Rum Bay** (moderate). For an unusual dining beach experience, it's worth driving 20 minutes and taking a ferry to Palm Island resort. Its casual restaurant specializes in baby back ribs for dinner. Go for lunch and enjoy some beach time while you're on the island. The specialty ham sandwich is terrific. Reservations advised. *Palm Island Resort, Cape Haze, FL 33946; tel. 941-697-0566. Open daily for lunch and dinner. Take Rte. 775 south to the ferry dock (call ahead for reservations and directions). The ferry makes hourly trips to the island. Fare: $1 per person.*

◆ **Barnacle Bill's** (inexpensive). A longtime favorite, it stakes its reputation on Dagwoodesque sandwiches and homemade soups and pies favored by the beach crowd. Its dinners star local seafood. *1975 Beach Rd., Englewood Beach, FL 34223; tel. 941-474-9703. Open Mon.-Sat. for lunch and dinner. Across the street from Chadwick Park. Boat docking available.*

◆ **Flying Bridge II** (inexpensive). A local favorite on the mainland. Specialties include baby back ribs, char-grilled grouper, and blackened catfish. View of back-bay waters. *2080 McCall Rd. S., Englewood, FL 34223; tel. 941-474-2206. Open daily for lunch and dinner. About 15 minutes east of Beach Rd. on Rte. 776.*

# NIGHTLIFE

◆ **Beaches.** A good place to watch the sunset and enjoy live contemporary music. *2095 N. Beach Rd., Englewood Beach, FL 34223; tel. 941-473-9229. Open daily. Across from Chadwick Park's north end.*

◆ **Lemon Bay Playhouse.** The local community theater group performs comedies and mysteries in an intimate 71-seat house. *Box 124, Englewood, FL 34295; tel. 941-475-6756. Box office open Mon., Wed., Sat. Admission. In downtown Englewood, off Rte. 776 on Dearborn Ave.*

◆ **New Captain's Club.** It features an outdoor tiki bar and live music. *1855 Gulf Blvd., Englewood Beach, FL 34223; tel. 941-475-8611. Open daily. Across the street from Chadwick Park's south lot.*

# ATTRACTIONS

◆ **Pelican Pete's Playland.** Miniature golf, go carts, batting cages, a game room, and rides give kids a fun time off the beach. *3101 McCall Rd. S., Englewood, FL 34224; tel. 941-475-2008. Open daily. Hours change according to season—call ahead. Admission. About 15 minutes east of Beach Rd. on Rte. 776.*

# SHOPPING

A few beach and souvenir shops cluster around Chadwick Park on the island. Across the bridge in Englewood, strip malls and an assortment of major discount stores and groceries line Route 776.

◆ **Necessary Nonsense.** This store advertises "tropical shopping": Jewelry, art, and musical instruments follow a primitive theme. *1450 Beach Rd., Englewood, FL 34223; tel. 941-474-3180. Hours vary. Just east of the Beach Rd. drawbridge.*

# BEST FOOD SHOPS

Because of the limited selection of stores on Manasota Key, some of the shops listed below are on the mainland.

**SANDWICHES:** ◆ **Hungry Howie's Pizzas & Subs.** *1720 McCall Rd. S., Englewood, FL 34223; tel. 941-475-8384. Open daily. East of the Beach Rd. bridge, on Rte. 776.*

**SEAFOOD:** ◆ **Island Court.** *1939 Beach Rd., Englewood, FL 34223; tel. 941-474-8236. Open daily.*

**FRESH PRODUCE:** ◆ **Roadside produce stand.** *Rte. 776 & Oriole Blvd., Englewood, FL 34223. Hours vary. In an old boat-yard building.*

**BAKERY:** ◆ **Englewood Bakery.** *67 McCall Rd. S., Englewood, FL 34223; tel. 941-474-1603. Open Mon.-Sat. South of Beach Rd. on Rte. 776.*

**ICE CREAM:** ◆ **Twistee Treat.** *1675 McCall Rd. S., Englewood, FL 34223; tel. 941-475-6056. Open daily. Drive a short distance south* *of the Beach Rd. bridge on Rte. 776.*

**BEVERAGES:** ◆ **Starvin' Marvin.** *1680 McCall Rd. S., Englewood, FL 34223; tel. 941-475-2809. Open daily. South of Beach Rd. on Rte. 776.*

# SPORTS
## FISHING

Nearby Boca Grande Pass and Charlotte Harbor are famous for summer tarpon. In season, Lemon Bay teems with back-bay fish. Grouper and shark are favored deep-water catches. Deep-sea charters cost about $45 per person for half a day. Fishing piers are along Beach Road on the east side of the drawbridge.

◆ **Island Court.** Sells fishing tackle and live and frozen bait. *1939 Beach Rd., Englewood, FL 34223; tel. 941-474-8236. Open daily.*

◆ **Silver Dollar Charters.** Go deep-sea fishing aboard the 32-foot *Ramblin' Rose. 1961 Beach Rd., Englewood, FL 34223; tel. 941-475-0512. Open daily.*

## BOATING

Boaters can launch at Manasota Beach ramp, in Indian Mound Park, off the south bridge, or for a fee, at most local marinas.

◆ **Bay Breeze Boat Rentals.** Rents pontoon, fishing, and bow-rider boats. *1450 Beach Rd., Englewood, FL 34223; tel. 941-475-0733. Open daily. Just east of the drawbridge on Beach Rd.*

◆ **Bikes & Boards.** Rents kayaks, sailboards, and other water-sports equipment. *1249 Beach Rd., Englewood, FL 34223; tel. 941-474-2019. Open daily. East of the Beach Rd. drawbridge.*

◆ **Lantern Queen Cruise & Dine.** Take a lunch or dinner excursion aboard an elegant paddlewheel boat. Reservations required. *8251 Esther St., Englewood, FL 34223; tel. 941-697-2244. Open Tue.-Sun. On Rte. 775, 5 mi. south of the Rte. 776 intersection.*

◆ **Rocky's Recreational Rentals.** Rents 16- to 21-foot skiffs and other water-sports equipment. *1863 Gulf Blvd., Englewood Beach, FL 34223; tel. 941-474-1022, 800-314-4838. Open daily. At The Beach Place, across the street from Chadwick Park's south lot.*

## BICYCLING

Englewood Beach designates widened shoulders on both sides

of Beach Road and Gulf Boulevard as bike paths. You can rent at the places listed below.

◆ **Bikes & Boards.** *1249 Beach Rd., Englewood, FL 34223; tel. 941-474-2019. Open daily. East of the Beach Rd. drawbridge.*

◆ **The Beach Place.** *1863 Gulf Blvd., Englewood Beach, FL 34223; tel. 941-474-1022, 800-314-4838. Open daily. Across the street from Chadwick Park's south lot.*

## GOLF

◆ **Oyster Creek Golf & Country Club.** A semiprivate club with 18 holes. *6500 Oriole Blvd., Englewood, FL 34224; tel. 941-475-0334. Open daily. Admission. Off Rte. 776, about 1 1/2 mi. east of the Rte. 775 intersection.*

## TENNIS

◆ **Englewood Recreation Center.** Four courts are open to the public. *101 N. Orange St., Englewood, FL 34223; tel. 941-474-3570. Open daily. In downtown Englewood. Take Rte. 776 north of Beach Rd. on the mainland. Turn left on Dearborn Ave., right on Orange.*

◆ **Englewood Tennis Club.** A semiprivate club with six clay courts. *2280 Englewood Rd., Englewood, FL 34223; tel. 941-475-3386. Open daily. Admission. South of Manatee Beach Rd. on Rte. 776.*

# HISTORY

◆ **Indian Mound Park.** Hike atop an ancient midden, where Native Americans tossed the shellfish remains of their dinners more than 2,000 years ago. Magnificent view of Lemon Bay and Manasota Key. Nature trail. *Tel. 941-474-3570. Open daily. From the mainland side of the Beach Rd. bridge, go north on Rte. 776 to Dearborn Ave. Take a left into downtown Englewood and follow the signs. At the end of Winson Ave.*

# NATURE

Lemon Bay and Stump Pass belong to the 7,667-acre Cape Haze Aquatic Preserve, which ensures that public recreational activities do not conflict with wildlife preservation.

Manatees, Florida's lovable but endangered 1,300-pound sea mammals, favor the protected waters of Lemon Bay and its tributaries.

# TOURIST INFORMATION

◆ **Englewood Area Chamber of Commerce.** *601 S. Indiana Ave., Englewood, FL 34223; tel. 941-474-5511; fax 941-475-9257. Open Mon.-Fri. 9-5.*

## CHAPTER 14

# Sanibel/Captiva

**S**anibel and Captiva are two of Florida's most natural and, at the same time, accommodating beach destinations. They are remote enough to stand pristine but sufficiently developed to offer the amenities of resort life for those who desire them. Although the two islands are hooked together by a bridge, each has a distinct personality. Sanibel, linked to the mainland by a causeway, is more touristy than Captiva, which moves at the unhurried pace of a seaside community. Vacationers seeking an even more remote setting can take a boat

| | |
|---|---|
| Beauty | A- |
| Swimming | B+ |
| Sand | B |
| Hotels/Inns/B&Bs | A |
| House rentals | A |
| Restaurants | A- |
| Nightlife | C+ |
| Attractions | B |
| Shopping | B |
| Sports | A |
| Nature | A+ |

to North Captiva Island (also called Upper Captiva) or Cayo Costa, two outlying islands that provide ideal getaways for the devoted beach escapist.

Sanibel, once a stronghold of the wealthy winter vacationer, has become more popular with families over the past decade, and tourism figures have soared. Still, half of the island remains a national wildlife refuge, and islanders are stridently protective of Sanibel's natural gifts. Captiva offers both exquisite scenery and a reputation for glamour. Celebrities from Charles Lindbergh to Jimmy Buffett have found refuge here, and South Seas Plantation, a resort that takes up a third of the skinny island, often hosts the rich and powerful.

In 1921, a hurricane separated Captiva's northernmost portion, forming the island known as North Captiva. Still largely left to nature, it is a favorite destination for recreational boaters who relish a beach of their own or an adventurous picnicking experience. Most of North Captiva is state park, but there is also the Safety Harbor Club, a community of modern homes and condos that bills itself as the ultimate getaway.

Island-hoppers can continue north to Cayo Costa for more secluded beaches in primordial Florida wilderness. Here, another state park offers picnic grounds, rustic cabins, shady tent sites, and showers. But there is no electricity and no drinking water.

Sanibel and Captiva were much like Cayo Costa when they were settled, first by Calusa Indians, then by Cuban fishermen, intrepid farmers, and other pioneers. Only after the islands were discovered by the rich did resorts begin to flourish. Teddy Roosevelt came to yank large, silvery tarpon from the Gulf waters. Later, such stars as Shirley Temple and Hedy Lamarr sought seclusion on the islands.

Among the celebrities was J.N. (Ding) Darling, an avid con-

## HOW TO GET THERE

◆ From exit 21 on I-75 in Fort Myers (a 45-minute drive from Sanibel), head west on Daniels Pkwy., following signs for the beaches. Turn left onto Six Mile Cypress Pkwy. and follow it across Hwy. 41 (Tamiami Tr.) where it becomes Gladiolus Dr. Continue to Summerlin Rd. (Rte. 869) and turn left. Follow Summerlin about 8 mi. to the Sanibel Causeway. Cross the causeway ($3 toll) to Sanibel Island.

To continue to Captiva Island (about 12 mi. from the Sanibel Causeway), take a right at the four-way stop sign onto Periwinkle Way, Sanibel's main road. When Periwinkle ends, go right on Tarpon Bay Rd., then left on Sanibel-Captiva Rd. Cross the bridge over Blind Pass, which separates the two islands.

servationist and Pulitzer Prize-winning political cartoonist from Iowa Thanks to Darling, who later ran what is now the U.S. Fish and Wildlife Service, much of the bird life and mangrove wilderness of Sanibel has been preserved. The conservation attitude remains, and visitors find less cement and more green than on Florida's developed coastlines.

Sanibel and Captiva are known for their arts scene, restaurants, and top-rated resorts. Vacationers looking for wild nightlife, however, should head elsewhere.

Sanibel has also gained a worldwide reputation for its seashells. Because the island faces south, it nets exotic shells that wash up in more abundance than on other beaches. Although live shelling was recently banned, collectors come to cull the long beachfront for empty shells, browse in the many shell shops, and attend the annual Shell Fair, which has been held for more than 50 years old.

Other recreational opportunities abound: fishing, windsurfing, sailing, boating, scuba diving, and parasailing. In addition, a scenic, 30-mile bicycle path loops around Sanibel.

# GULF BEACHES
## SANIBEL ISLAND

A wide apron of sand skirts the entire 15-mile Gulf shore of Sanibel Island. Every beach is public, and local ordinances prevent buildings from encroaching. Resorts border much of the southern waterfront, while private homes and woods line the northern shoreline.

| Beauty | A- |
|--------|----|
| Swimming | B |
| Sand | B |
| Amenities | C |

*Swimming:* Gulf waters tend to be murky because of runoff from nearby rivers. The Gulf bottom is sandy and gently sloping, with sandbars offshore. On the south and north ends of the island, the undertow in the passes between Gulf and bay precludes safe swimming. Wave action is normally low elsewhere. Water temperatures range from a winter low of 66 degrees to a summer high of 87.

*Sand:* Beaches are wide and mostly flat. The fine, white sand is strewn with shells and other beachcombing treasures.

*Amenities:* To preserve the environment, Sanibel sticks to the basics. The parking lots are unpaved, and there are no permanent food stands at the public beaches. All beaches have rest rooms. Gulf Park and Bowman's have picnic tables. No lifeguard.

*Sports:* Concessionaires are not allowed near public beaches. Some resorts have their own sailboat, cabana, and beach-toy rentals, many of which serve the public.

*Parking:* Three major public beaches have metered parking (75 cents per hour), and a fourth, Bowman's, has day parking ($3). Oversize vehicles are accommodated at Tarpon Beach. Restricted accesses, marked A or B, are primarily for resident parking, but pedestrians and bicycle riders can use them. Nonresident drivers may buy a B sticker for $30 at the city police department office.

## Lighthouse Beach

Site of the historic Sanibel Lighthouse, this most-developed of Sanibel beaches rounds the island's southern tip, Gulf to bay, and includes a fishing pier and a nature trail. Popular with teens and spring-breakers, it gets heavily populated in March and April. Tall casuarina (Australian pine) trees and sea oats edge the shelly sands. Swimming at the southern tip can be dangerous because of currents. A mobile food concession often sells snacks. *At the south end of Periwinkle Way.*

## Gulfside Park

An abundance of casuarinas attracts sand flies (no-see-ums), so avoid this spot on calm days. The beach is wide but somewhat sloped. Not easy to find, it's less crowded than others. *From Periwinkle Way, take Casa Ybel Rd. across from Jerry's Shopping Center. Go left on Algiers Ln.*

## Tarpon Bay Beach

The parking lot across the road is often full at this popular beach, so arrive early. A food wagon can be found here most days between December and January. *Take Periwinkle Way to the end, and go left on Tarpon Bay Rd. The parking lot is on the left before you get to the beach.*

## Bowman's Beach

This long, remote stretch of sand is the most natural of Sanibel's beaches and the only one with a good sunset view. It once was frequented by nudists, but town law now prohibits nude sunbathing. The parking lot ($3 per day) is about one-quarter mile from the sea, but the walk to the beach crosses a lovely estuary where wildlife can be seen. Cactus and other dune growth border the wide sands, framed by tall casuarinas. Points of land at each end turn the beach into a long cove. Owned by the county, this is the only beach where alcoholic beverages and pets are not allowed. *On Bowman's Beach Rd., off Sanibel-Captiva Rd., around mile marker 5.*

## CAPTIVA ISLAND BEACHES

As with many barrier beaches, conditions on Captiva vary because of erosion from storms and tides. You may find wide or narrow beaches, depending on nature's whims and the success of human efforts to counter them. Yet

| | |
|---|---|
| **Beauty** | **B** |
| **Swimming** | **B+** |
| **Sand** | **C+** |
| **Amenities** | **C** |

this is a great spot for beachgoers, especially those who want to be somewhat removed from the madding crowd. The shell collecting is not as impressive as Sanibel's, but Captiva is ideal for enjoying sunsets. Captiva is not incorporated, so county restrictions against alcohol and pets apply at all beaches.

*Swimming:* Conditions are much the same as on Sanibel, though the waters are somewhat clearer. In stormy weather, however, surfers prefer the whipped-up waters of Captiva.

*Sand:* Because of erosion, Captiva beaches have to be rebuilt periodically. Sand dredged up in the process tends to be grayish, but it is clean. Shell collecting is best around Mucky Duck Restaurant—and better anywhere after dredging.

*Amenities:* Turner's Beach is in the heart of the Blind Pass community known as Santiva, which has restrooms, food stores, and restaurants. There are no facilities at Captiva Beach, but restrooms, upscale restaurants, and stores are located at a shopping center a quarter mile from the parking lot entrance.

*Sports:* No concessions on the beach. Equipment may be rented

at Castaways Resort in Santiva or in the village of Captiva.
*Parking:* The island has only two beach accesses. Parking is a problem at both, but free. Go early in the morning. Many people have lunch at the Mucky Duck and park there while at the beach.

## Turner's Beach

This beach is on both sides of Blind Pass, but nonresident parking is available only on the Captiva side. Swimming is dangerous, but the fishing is great. Blind Pass bridge is a popular spot with anglers. Pedestrians can easily cross the bridge from one side to the other. There are portable rest rooms on the Captiva side; restaurants and groceries on the Sanibel side. Captiva's beach is wide, but it drops off quickly once you're in the water. Boulders rim the sands on one side. On the Sanibel side of Turner's Beach, there is a good place east of the bridge to take toddlers to splash around in the shallow waters. *On Sanibel-Captiva Rd. at Blind Pass, about 7 mi. north of Tarpon Bay Rd.*

## Captiva Beach

Especially popular for sunsets, this beach fills up from December through April. It is at the southern edge of South Seas Plantation, so you can walk the resort's beach front. If you want to avoid crowds, head in the opposite direction where the vegetation is bountiful and there are no condos. The sand slopes steeply and is flecked with chips of shells. *Follow Sanibel-Captiva Rd. until it turns into Captiva Dr. and continue until it dead-ends at the beach parking lot.*

## OUTLYING ISLANDS

For the adventurous, the islands to the north of Captiva offer solitude and a variety of flora and fauna. There are no bridges, so you must go by boat. Amenities are few, and, aside from the Safety Harbor Club, there's no hint of

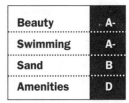

| Beauty | A- |
| --- | --- |
| Swimming | A- |
| Sand | B |
| Amenities | D |

resort life. If you're leery of roughing it, you can boat into the harbor on the bay side of North Captiva and follow the buoys and signs to Grady's Restaurant, on a side canal to the left. Grady's rents golf carts, the only means of motorized transportation on the island. There's a campground on Cayo Costa. A few wild pigs still roam the island, but they won't bother you when you're working on your perfect suntan at the beach. Look for a pioneer cemetery and remnants of a military quarantine station.

*Swimming:* The water is usually warm and calm, and the sea bottom varies in slope.

*Sand:* The fine, white beach is rich in shellfish egg cases, seaweed, and other natural debris. North Captiva's beach varies in width due to erosion.

*Amenities:* On North Captiva, rest rooms are a half-mile walk from the north end of the beach. Cayo Costa has a picnic ground with rest rooms, showers, and camping facilities.

## North Captiva Beach

Boaters anchor offshore on the Gulf side to picnic, sunbathe, swim, and beachcomb au naturel. At the north end, there are sandy paths to restaurants and numerous bayside accommodations. *Must go by boat. Water taxis run from Jensen's Marina on Captiva.*

## Cayo Costa Beach

Cayo Costa provides much the same beach experience as North Captiva: natural, unpopulated strands with lots of driftwood and other interesting bits to investigate. At the south end, beachgoers are few. At the north, there is a dock and trails that cross from the picnic ground to the bay. *Must go by boat. Water taxis, which can cost up to $100, run from Jensen's Marina on Captiva.*

## Johnson Shoals

At the northern tip of Cayo Costa (tides permitting), an exposed sandbar juts into the Gulf of Mexico. This is an excellent place to find a variety of sand dollars and seashells. *Must go by boat. Many Sanibel-Captiva shelling charters can be hired to take you there.*

# HOTELS/INNS/B&Bs

anibel and Captiva have accommodations aplenty, from basic beach cottages to grand resorts. If you plan to vacation anytime from December through April, book well in advance. North Captiva offers condo and home rentals. On Cayo Costa, you'll find only primitive camping.

♦ **Sundial Beach Resort** (very expensive). A complete destination resort, Sundial specializes in families, with suite accommodations and a first-class children's program. The beach-view units are best. Sundial has it all: beachfront, restaurants, 13 tennis courts, five heated swimming pools, and ten Jacuzzis. *863 E. Gulf Dr., Sanibel, FL 33957; tel. 941-472-4151, 800-237-4184.*

♦ **South Seas Plantation** (very expensive). Hidden behind security gates, South Seas is one of Florida's top destination resorts. You can select your digs from among tennis villas, beach cottages, harborside hotel rooms, and other types of accommodations. The most fashionable and the best for views are the condos of Land's End where visiting celebrities often stay. The resort boasts 2 1/2 miles of well-maintained beach, 600 guest units, three restaurants, shops, a nine-hole golf course, a physical fitness center, a yacht harbor, 18 swimming pools, 21 tennis courts, water-sport rentals and lessons, excursion cruises, and organized activities for children and teenagers. *Box 194, Captiva, FL 33924; tel. 941-472-5111, 800-237-3102.*

♦ **'Tween Waters Inn** (expensive). A sprawling resort that spans from Gulf to bay, 'Tween Waters is terrific for those who love the beach and water sports. The beautiful beach just across the road from the inn is used mostly by resort guests. Accommodations range from rooms and cottages to efficiencies and apartments. The older cottages have historic charm. 'Tween Waters also provides the only nightlife on the islands. This may bother some cottage-dwellers, because the parking lot is at their doorstep. Cottages around the resort entrance and tennis courts are quieter. The cottage efficiencies are the best buy. *Box 249, Captiva, FL 33924; tel. 941-472-5161, 800-223-5865.*

♦ **The Castaways** (expensive). With its marina and cottages, The Castaways embodies the perfect barefoot beach destination. Beach-lovers should ask for cottages on the Gulf side, though things get a bit hectic on the road that separates them from the front office, the marina, and the pool. Cottages are old but well-kept, with one to three bedrooms. *6460 Sanibel-Captiva Rd., Sanibel, FL 33957; tel. 941-472-1252.*

♦ **Island Inn** (expensive).The closest thing to historic lodging on Sanibel, this beach resort effects Old Florida style with white wicker, lattice, and a congenial, clubby atmosphere. Both cottage and lodge rooms have Gulf views, but the cottages have more character. Some date back to the early 1900s. Spoonbill, a duplex, is closest to the beach. In season (December through April), the resort operates on the Modified American Plan, which includes breakfast and dinner in the room rate. Off season, it's a B&B. *Box 659, Sanibel, FL 33957; tel. 941-472-1561.*

♦ **Kona Kai Motel** (moderate). One of Sanibel's few lower-cost lodging options, it has a pool and barbecue grills and sits conveniently in a garden setting along the main drag of shops and restaurants. The rooms and efficiencies have peaked roofs in a South Seas motif. Some include telephones ; all have TVs.

# HOUSE RENTALS

Furnished homes, usually on a beach or a golf course, are available throughout Sanibel (one-month minimum), Captiva (one-week minimum), and North Captiva (three-day minimum) from local real estate agencies. Range of rates: Sanibel, $2,000 to $5,000 monthly; Captiva, $1,500 to $8,000 weekly; North Captiva, $795 to $3,500 weekly (includes use of club facilities). The agencies have condominiums available at lower prices and with only a one-week minimum required on Sanibel.

♦ **Vacations in Paradise.** *8250 College Pkwy. #102, Fort Myers, FL 33919; tel. 941-481-3636, 800-237-8906. Open daily.*

♦ **Sanibel Realty.** *1630 Periwinkle Way, Sanibel, FL 33957; tel. 941-472-6565, 800-572-6423. Open daily.*

♦ **North Captiva Island Club.** Handles house rentals around Safety Harbor on North Captiva. *Box 1000, Pineland, FL 33945; tel. 941-395-1001, 800-576-7343. Open daily.*

# RESTAURANTS

Island restaurants are known for their seafood, particularly local shrimp, which is sometimes called Sanibel shrimp. There is also a burgeoning new-Florida style of cooking. Most restaurants do not accept reservations.

♦ **Mad Hatter** (expensive). Great for sunset if you reserve early, this place excels in eclectic cuisine with an accent on fresh seafood and produce. Menu changes nightly. Sesame soy marinated mahi-mahi and grilled yellowfin tuna with miso vinaigrette are very popular items. Reservations required. *6460 Sanibel-Captiva Rd., Sanibel, FL 33957; tel. 941-472-0033. Open daily for dinner. Closed for two weeks after Labor Day.*

♦ **McT's Shrimp House & Tavern** (moderate). This longtime island tradition serves shrimp in every guise imaginable, including all-you-can-eat steamed in the shell. The atmosphere is casual and friendly. *1523 Periwinkle Way, Sanibel, FL 33957; tel. 941-472-3161. Open daily for dinner.*

♦ **Mucky Duck** (moderate). As much a tourist attraction as a restaurant, this beachside pub adds fish and chips and shepherd's pie to the usual island fare, poking fun at British pub ambience in the process. Try the barbecue shrimp and bacon. Sunset at "The Duck" is an island ritual. You can also lunch at Mucky Duck on your way to or from the beach. Parking can be a problem, though, so arrive early. *Andy Rosse Ln., Captiva, FL 33924; tel. 941-472-3434. Open Mon.-Sat. for lunch and dinner.*

♦ **Tarwinkles Seafood Emporium** (moderate). Fresh fish and shellfish get treated to innovative tropic preparations, with selections changing nightly. The triple saute pasta-seafood dish, consisting of shrimp, lobster, and scallops on linguine, is a favorite. Reservations recommended. *Periwinkle Way and Tarpon Bay Rd., Sanibel, FL 33957; tel. 941-472-1366. Open daily for lunch and dinner.*

♦ **Barnacle Phil's** (inexpensive). Although this place on North Captiva is unpretentious and laid-back, notables continue to contribute to its notoriety. Henry Winkler once had six quarts of its famous black beans and rice flown to Hollywood. Casual fare is served in a squat shack or outside on picnic tables. *4401*

*Point House Tr., North Captiva, FL; tel. 941-472-6394. Open Fri.-Wed. for lunch and dinner; Thu. for lunch only. At Safety Harbor on North Captiva Island.*

♦ **Lazy Flamingo** (inexpensive). A favorite of locals, the original Lazy Flamingo has a Key West temperament and casual attitude. The menu concentrates on seafood and finger foods. The grilled grouper sandwich is a sure bet, but beware the Dead Parrot Buffalo Wings. (Note: There is another Lazy Flamingo on the island that does not measure up to the original.) *6520 Pine Ave. at Santiva, Sanibel, FL 33957; tel. 941-472-5353. Open daily for lunch and dinner.*

# NIGHTLIFE

With an older population and many family-oriented resorts, Sanibel and Captiva shy away from nightlife. Street lights are taboo, and bars on Sanibel close their doors at 1 a.m. With a few exceptions, the arts scene rules over the bar scene.

♦ **Jacaranda Patio Lounge.** Live music played by local bands in a variety of contemporary genres. *1223 Periwinkle Way, Sanibel, FL 33957; tel. 941-472-1771. Open nightly.*

♦ **Old Schoolhouse Theatre.** In the setting of an historic schoolhouse, this cozy theater has served for years as the island's cultural mainstay. Recently renovated, it hosts musical productions by a professional troupe December through May and community theater in the summer. *1905 Periwinkle Way, Sanibel, FL 33957; tel. 941-472-6862. Open Mon.-Sat.*

♦ **Pirate Playhouse.** Professional actors present comedies, musicals, and drama in this modern theater-in-the-round. *2200 Periwinkle Way, Sanibel, FL 33957; tel. 941-472-0006. Open Mon.-Sat.*

♦ **Island Cinema.** First-run movies show in this small, old house. *Periwinkle Way and Tarpon Bay Rd., Sanibel, FL 33957; tel. 941-472-1701. Open nightly. At Bailey's Shopping Center.*

♦ **Comedy Club.** Nationally known comics do stand-up routines. *975 Rabbit Rd., Sanibel, FL 33957; tel. 941-472-8833. Open Wed.-Sun. Next to Loco's Restaurant.*

♦ **Crow's Nest Lounge.** The only hot spot on the islands, this resort bar features live dance bands. On Mondays, crab races begin at 6. *Captiva Dr., Captiva, FL 33924; tel. 941-472-5161. Open daily. At 'Tween Waters Inn.*

# SHOPPING

For shells, shell art, resort fashions, wildlife art, and sea-related gifts, Sanibel and Captiva shops are tops. Prices are higher than on the mainland, but the lush, unhurried atmosphere is much nicer than the stress of crowded malls.

◆ **Showcase Shells.** Among Sanibel's many shell shops, this one is most elegant, even gallery-like. *1614 Periwinkle Way, Sanibel, FL 33957; tel. 941-472-1971. Open daily. In Heart of the Islands Center.*

◆ **Chico's.** A nationwide chain of stores (and the trend toward its distinctive tropic wear) began here. There are now three outlets on Sanibel and Captiva. *The original store is at 2075 Periwinkle Way, Sanibel, FL 33957; tel. 941-472-0202. Open daily. At Periwinkle Place Shopping Center.*

◆ **MacIntosh Books.** This tiny shop is packed with books about Florida and many other topics. There is a music shop and special rooms for children's and travel books. *2365 Periwinkle Way, Sanibel, FL 33957; tel. 941-472-1447. Open daily.*

◆ **Jungle Drums.** Local and national artists depict wildlife themes in various media in this creatively decorated gallery. *11532 Andy Rosse Ln., Captiva, FL 33924; tel. 941-395-2266. Open Mon.-Sat.*

# BEST FOOD SHOPS

**SANDWICHES:** ◆ **Huxters Deli.** *1203 Periwinkle Way, Sanibel, FL 33957; tel. 941-472-2151. Open daily.*

**SEAFOOD:** ◆ **The Timbers Fish Market.** *703 Tarpon Bay Rd., Sanibel , FL 33957; tel. 941-395-2722. Open daily. In the Timbers Restaurant.*

**FRESH PRODUCE:** ◆ **Bailey's.** *Periwinkle Way and Tarpon Bay Rd., Sanibel, FL 33957; tel. 941-472-1516. Open daily. At Seahorse Shoppes center near Sanibel Lighthouse beach.*

**BAKERY:** ◆ **Pinocchio.** *362 Periwinkle Way, Sanibel, FL 33957;*

*tel. 941-472-6566. Open daily.*

**ICE CREAM:** ◆ **Pinocchio.** 362 *Periwinkle Way, Sanibel, FL 33957; tel. 941-472-6566. Open daily.*

**BEVERAGES:** ◆ **Huxters Deli.** 1203 *Periwinkle Way, Sanibel, FL 33957; tel. 941-472-2151. Open daily.*

**WINE:** ◆ **Grog Shop.** *Periwinkle Way and Tarpon Bay Rd., Sanibel, FL 33957; tel. 941-472-1682. Open daily. In Bailey's Shopping Center.*

# SPORTS
## FISHING

Two major fishing tournaments take place on Captiva every May: the Tarpon Tide Tournament and the Caloosa Catch & Release Fishing Tournament. Of course, there is plenty of fishing during the rest of the year, too.

◆ **Bait Box.** Buy bait, tackle, and fishing licenses here. *1041 Periwinkle Way, Sanibel, FL 33957; tel. 941-472-1618. Open daily.*

◆ **Sanibel Marina.** Longtime guides include Jim Burnsed and Dave Case. *634 N. Yachtsman Dr., Sanibel, FL 33957; tel. 941-472-2723. Open daily.*

◆ **'Tween Waters Marina.** Captain Mike Fuery is the most knowledgeable. He's taken former president Jimmy Carter fly-fishing. *Captiva Dr., Captiva, FL 33924; tel. 941-472-5161. Open daily.*

◆ **South Seas Plantation Marina.** Although part of a private resort, it offers a variety of charters to the public, with advance reservation. *Captiva, FL 33924; tel. 941-472-5111. Open daily.*

## BOATING

Marinas rent powerboats for half and full days, to use in intracoastal waters only. Many resorts rent small sailboats, paddleboats, kayaks, and other craft. Charters and tours out of Sanibel Marina, and from Jensen's Marina and 'Tween Waters Marina on Captiva, go to North Captiva, Cayo Costa, and other outlying islands for day trips.

◆ **The Boat House.** *634 North Yachtsman Dr., Sanibel, FL 33957; tel. 941-472-2531. Open daily. At Sanibel Marina.*

◆ **Tarpon Bay Recreation.** The concessionaire at this marina rents canoes and kayaks for use in the bay and in the Ding

Darling Refuge. *900 Tarpon Bay Rd., Sanibel, FL 33957; tel. 941-472-8900. Open daily.*

◆ **Castaways Marina.** Rents pontoon boats and canoes. *6460 Sanibel-Captiva Rd., Sanibel, FL 33957; tel. 941-472-1112. Open daily.*

◆ **Captiva Cruises.** A complete menu of sightseeing and luncheon trips is available aboard the 150- passenger *Jean Nicolet. South Seas Plantation, Captiva, Fl 33924; tel. 941-472-7549. Open daily.*

◆ **New Moon.** This 35-foot sailboat can carry six passengers on each trip. *'Tween Waters Marina, Captiva Dr., Captiva Island, FL 33924; tel. 941-395-1782. Open daily.*

◆ **'Tween Waters Marina.** This marina rents motorboats, sailboats, canoes, kayaks, and aquabikes. *Captiva Dr., Captiva Island, FL 33924; tel. 941-472-5161. Open daily.*

◆ **Jensen's Twin Palm Marina.** Pontoon boats and other motor boats are available for rent. *15107 Captiva Dr., Captiva Island, FL 33924; tel. 941-472-5800. Open daily.*

## BICYCLING

Sanibel's 30 miles of paved bicycle paths cover the island tip to tip and encourage unhurried sightseeing. The newer trails take you away from road traffic. Bikers on Captiva vie with motor traffic on the serpentine road. In high season, this can be tricky, if not dangerous. Some resorts provide or rent bikes. Otherwise, try the following rental places.

◆ **Bike Route.** *2330 Palm Ridge Rd., Sanibel, FL 33957; tel. 914-472-1955. Open Mon.-Sat.*

◆ **Finnimore's Cycle Shop.** *2353 Periwinkle Way, Sanibel, FL 33957; tel. 941-472-5577. Open daily.*

◆ **Jim's Bike Rental.** *11534 Andy Rosse Ln., Captiva, FL 33924; tel. 941-472-1296. Open daily, weather permitting.*

## GOLF

Two semiprivate, 18-hole golf courses grace Sanibel's sands. (South Seas Plantation Resort's nine-hole course is open to guests only.)

◆ **Dunes Golf & Tennis Club.** *949 Sandcastle Rd., Sanibel, FL 33957; tel. 941-472-3355. Open daily.*

◆ **Beachview Golf Course.** *110 Par View Dr., Sanibel, FL 33957; tel. 941-472-2626. Open daily.*

## TENNIS

◆ **City Recreation Complex.** Five lighted courts are open to the public. *3840 Sanibel-Captiva Rd., Sanibel, FL 33957; tel. 941-472-0345. Open daily. At Sanibel Elementary School.*

# HISTORY

◆ **Sanibel Historic Village.** Relics of the past, including entire buildings, have been assembled to evoke the era before a causeway joined the island to the mainland. A pioneer abode houses a museum. The original island post office dates from the mid-1920s. The relocated Old Bailey Store has an authentic cracker-barrel atmosphere, and Miss Charlotta's Tea Room serves sweets as it did when it stood at the ferry landing. *850 Dunlop Rd., Sanibel, FL 33957; tel. 941-472-4648. Open Wed.-Sat. 10-4. Off Periwinkle Way near City Hall.*

◆ **Sanibel Lighthouse.** One of the island's first permanent structures, it was built in 1884 at the southeast end and still functions as a beacon of warning and welcome. The lighthouse and Old Florida-style lightkeeper's cottage were renovated in 1991. The public is not admitted, but you can enjoy them from the outside. *At the south end of Periwinkle Way.*

◆ **Captiva History House.** Through photographs, memorabilia, and story boards, this tiny museum in a plantation worker's home relates Captiva Island's progress from prehistoric inhabitants through the farming and fishing eras of the early 1900s. South Seas Plantation, Captiva, FL 33924; tel. 941-472-5111. *Open Sun. and Tue.-Fri. 10-4. At the entrance to South Seas Plantation resort.*

◆ **Chapel-By-The-Sea.** This 1904 clapboard church on Captiva is popular for weddings, Sunday services, and seaside meditation. Many Captiva pioneers are buried in a cemetery beside the chapel. *Interdenominational services Sun. at 11. Open daily 9-5. From Captiva Dr., turn on Wiles Dr. and go to Chapin St. Parking is in the library lot.*

# NATURE

◆ **Aqua Trek and Sealife Learning Center.** Kids enjoy the touch tank, 15 aquariums, and other displays about marine life in the Gulf. The center serves as a marine laboratory and departure point for informative beach walks by a marine biologist. *2353 Periwinkle Way, Sanibel, FL 33957; tel. 941-472-8680. Open Mon.-Sat. 9-5.*

◆ **The Bailey-Matthews Shell Museum.** This facility builds on Sanibel's shell-collecting reputation with educational exhibits that reveal the role of shells in natural and human history. A special attraction is the collection of the late Raymond Burr, the actor, who frequented Sanibel and helped to fund the new museum. *Sanibel-Captiva Rd., Sanibel, FL 33957; tel. 941-395-2233. Open Tue.-Sun. 10-4.*

◆ **Sanibel-Captiva Conservation Center.** Guided and self-guided tours introduce you to indigenous wetland flora and natural bird habitats along four miles of walking trails crowned by an observatory tower. *3333 Sanibel-Captiva Rd., Sanibel, FL 33957; tel. 941-472-2329. Open Mon.-Fri. 8:30-3. Admission.*

◆ **J. N. Ding Darling National Wildlife Refuge.** Within its 5,030 acres, manatees, alligators, waterfowl, and snakes may be found. Native plants flourish in its Everglades-like atmosphere. See it by canoe (at high tide, to avoid portaging through the alligators' turf), tram, bicycle, or car. Best wildlife spotting times are early morning and sunset. *1 Wildlife Dr., Sanibel, FL 33957; tel. 941-472-1100. For tram or canoe tours, call 941-472-8900. Wildlife Dr. open daily sunrise-sunset. Visitor center open  Sat.-Thu. 9-4. Admission. Off Sanibel-Captiva Rd.*

# SAFETY TIPS

**S**anibel and Captiva are relatively crime-free because they are accessible by a single causeway. However, lock your car at the beaches and fishing pier and keep valuables out of sight.

# TOURIST INFORMATION

◆ **Sanibel-Captiva Islands Chamber of Commerce.** *Box 166, Sanibel, FL 33957; tel. 941-472-1080. Open Mon.-Sat. 9-7; Sun. 10-5. On the right, just after you get off the causeway entering Sanibel.*

◆ **Lee County Visitor and Convention Bureau.** *Box 2445, Fort Myers, FL 33902; tel. 941-335-2631, 800-237-6444. No visitors center.*

## CHAPTER 15

# Bonita

**B**onita Springs promotes itself as the Gateway to the Gulf because its beaches are closest of any to Interstate 75, but this stretch of coast has a lot more going for it than proximity. It contains some of Florida's best-preserved coastlands and estuaries. Fortunately, state and county governments have stepped in to ensure that these precious habitats survive.

Commercial development came late to this area, compared to other parts of Florida. For centuries, it remained in the hands of first Calusa Native Americans, then adventuresome explorers and pioneers. Rich are the legends surrounding the islands and bayous of Estero Bay, replete with Native American kingdoms, fiery Spanish missionaries, gold-hoarding pirates, and outlaws of the James gang.

| | |
|---|---|
| **Beauty** | A |
| **Swimming** | A- |
| **Sand** | B |
| **Hotels/Inns/B&Bs** | B- |
| **House rentals** | B+ |
| **Restaurants** | B- |
| **Nightlife** | C |
| **Attractions** | B |
| **Shopping** | B- |
| **Sports** | A |
| **Nature** | A |

For many years, Little Hickory Island, known as Bonita Beach, was the stronghold of commercial fishermen, and much of that heritage remains today. Then, development began in earnest during the 1940s, and acres of wetlands were dredged and filled to extend the real estate.

On the nearby mainland, Bonita Springs remained a small agricultural town known for its tomato farming, while its neighbors grew fat on tourism. A greyhound race track began to draw tourists in the 1960s, and the rural community took off with it. Grandiose golf resorts gradually gobbled up most of the farmland.

The cluster of islands that make up the area known as Lover's Key remained aloof from development, however. Sandwiched between the booming resort of Fort Myers Beach on the north and Little Hickory Island to the south, they were not discovered until two parks opened on Long Key and Black Island, once the home of pirate Black Augustus. Carl E. Johnson Park was built by the county, and Lover's Key State Recreation Area by Florida. Both connect to the beach via footbridges.

# GULF BEACHES
## BONITA SPRINGS AREA

| | |
|---|---|
| Beauty | A- |
| Swimming | A- |
| Sand | B |
| Amenities | B+ |

Bonita Beach turned from fishing to tourism as bridges were built in the mid-1950s to connect it with the mainland and the islands to the north. Today, the community has the most developed beaches in the Bonita Springs area. Although its sands are still beautiful at any time of year, traffic snarls its two-lane road from February through April.

*Swimming:* Sandbars offshore keep the waves small. The shoreline steps off a bit along the water, and shells are hard on bare feet, but otherwise, swimming conditions are favorable. Waters are generally warm enough for swimming year-round.

*Sand:* Shells amass at water's edge along this wide stretch of blond sand. Shell fragments hinder barefoot walking.

*Amenities:* Barefoot Beach has food concessions, rest rooms,

## HOW TO GET THERE

◆ From the Bonita Springs exit (18) on I-75 (about 10 minutes from Bonita Beach), drive west on Bonita Beach Rd. Follow it alongside the mainland town of Bonita Springs and across the Tamiami Trail (Hwy. 41) until you reach the southernmost beaches of the area. The beaches of Lover's Key can be reached by continuing north from Bonita Beach on Rte. 865 for 13 mi. or by driving south from Fort Myers Beach.

changing rooms, and showers. At Bonita Beach, you'll find rest rooms, a restaurant, a bar, food stands, and picnic tables. Lifeguards are on duty at Bonita Beach but not at Barefoot.

*Sports:* Sailboats and other water-sports equipment are available at the main public access and at outlets on Bonita Beach Road. *Parking:* Barefoot Beach has three free lots, but these fill early in the height of season (February through April). You can park along the road inside the park too. Bonita Beach charges 75 cents an hour for parking. It fills before Barefoot Beach.

## Barefoot Beach Preserve

This county facility encompasses 342 acres with 1 1/2 miles of beach. Sea grapes, cabbage palms, and sea oats adorn the beaches and the squat sand dunes. Good views with little interference from man-made structures. Boardwalks cross the dunes. *Open 8-sunset. At Hickory Blvd. and Bonita Beach Rd., you'll see signs for Barefoot Beach. Turn south at a security gate and drive through. Follow the road 2 mi. over speed bumps.*

## Bonita Public Beach

The area's most easily reached beach, this popular spot is favored by young volleyball players and water-sportsters. The sand widens here and has fewer shells. Vegetation gives way to tall buildings along the skyline. *On Hickory Blvd. at Bonita Beach Rd.*

## Bonita Beach Accesses

About ten public accesses lie north of the public beach, cropping up every few blocks along the length of the island. Limited parking keeps the crowd down, but spaces fill early.

## LOVER'S KEY BEACHES

Plans are in the works for improving the facilities by combining two quiet getaways into one state park. Carl E. Johnson, at 130 acres, and Lover's Key, at 434, unfold a rich tapestry of estuary and beach environments removed from development. The entrance to each is located on a separate island in Estero Bay, but

| Beauty | A+ |
| --- | --- |
| Swimming | A- |
| Sand | B |
| Amenities | B |

**146**

they already share a common island as their Gulf beach front.

Visitors park on one of the main islands and then cross a bridge to the beach. At Lover's Key, this means walking along a boardwalk over a mangrove estuary. At Carl Johnson, you can take a tram.

*Swimming:* The water is calmer here than at Bonita Beach and fairly shallow. Currents are too strong for swimming at the north end of Lover's Key.

*Sand:* The beaches are entirely natural. Shells, small sponges, and tree droppings accumulate at the high-tide line. Washed-out trees form driftwood sculptures at the state park. Beach width is ten feet or more.

*Amenities:* Lots of Australian pines offer shade for picnic tables. Johnson Park has pavilions, barbecue grills, and a soda machine. Both have rest rooms and outdoor showers and offer up-close-and-personal wildlife encounters. No lifeguard, but 911 call boxes are located on the beach.

*Sports:* Volleyball nets, playground equipment, and boat ramps are located across the street from the entrance to Carl Johnson. During the winter, the park offers programs on fishing, birding, and beach walking. Lover's Key park has a canoe launch for estuary explorers. Fishing is good from its bridges and on Big Carlos Pass.

*Parking:* Because these parks don't attract crowds, finding a space is less of a problem than at those to the south and north. It costs $3 on the honor system to park at Johnson Park and $2 at Lover's Key. The tram to the beach at Johnson Park is free.

## Carl E. Johnson Park

Families, retirees, and Europeans favor this beach. They bring their own lawn chairs and picnics to spend the day. The tram ride to the beach takes you through three-quarters of a mile of wildlife habitat. A visitor's guide tells you about what you're seeing: mangroves, ospreys, fiddler crabs, sea grapes. *Tel. 941-338-3300. Open 8-sunset. On Rte. 865 about 2 mi. north of Bonita Beach.*

## Lover's Key State Recreation Area

This access places you at the north end of the skinny key. Manatees and dolphins frequent the bay, Big Carlos Pass, and Gulf waters. Coconut palms nod along the vegetation line. *Tel.*

*941-597-6196. Open 9-5. About 2 1/2 mi. north of Bonita Beach.*

# HOTELS/INNS/B&Bs

**M**ost accommodations for this region are found in Bonita Beach, principally at either end of the island. These cater to everyone from fishermen to families. For a wider variety of hotels and resorts, look to Fort Myers Beach to the north or Bonita Springs to the east.

◆ **Days Inn at Lover's Key** (expensive). All the rooms in this 14-story hotel include kitchens, continental breakfast, daily sunset cocktails, and balconies overlooking either the Gulf across the road or the bay at the hotel's back door. It has a small beach with water-sports rentals, but better beaches are found on the Gulf nearby. *8701 Estero Blvd., Fort Myers Beach, FL 33931; tel. 941-765-4422, 800-325-2525. Above Bonita Beach, near Lover's Key, just south of the Rte. 865 bridge to Fort Myers Beach.*

◆ **Bonita Beach Resort Motel** (moderate). Wedged among the modern high-rises on Bonita Beach's north end, this small 20-unit property caters to fishermen. Right on the bay, it has docking, a boat ramp, and boat rentals. It also has Gulf access across the street. Clean, plain air-conditioned rooms. Some have kitchens, some views of the bay. *26395 Hickory Blvd., Bonita Springs, FL 33923; tel. 941-992-2137. Open year-round.*

◆ **The Beach & Tennis Club** (moderate). This condominium resort focuses on tennis, with ten Har-Tru courts and a pro shop. Two heated pools, a children's pool, beauty salon, restaurant, shuffleboard, and laundry. One-bedroom apartments stack up in five buildings. *5700 Bonita Beach Rd. S.W., Suite 3103, Bonita Springs, FL 33923; tel. 941-992-1121, 800-237-4934; fax 941-992-8035. Open year-round. At the south end of Bonita Beach, across from the public beach.*

# HOUSE RENTALS

**J**anuary through April, houses usually rent for three months, although technically only one week is required. Home rentals are abundant and of high quality, with weekly rates starting at $1,000. Better rates are available for longer stays.

◆ **Bluebill Properties.** *26201 Hickory Blvd., Bonita Springs, FL 33923; tel. 941-597-1102, 800-237-2010. Open daily.*

# RESTAURANTS

No world-class restaurants here, mostly small-but-good types. For more sophistication, go to Naples (*see* Chapter 16, North Naples). Seafood is the focus. With nearby Bonita Springs' reputation for vegetable farming, you can also expect fresh produce. Water views are plentiful.

◆ **McCully's Rooftop Restaurant** (expensive). The Rooftop boasts sweeping waterfront views. Depending upon where you sit in the 250-seat restaurant, you can watch the sun set, the boat traffic entering Hickory Pass, or manatees surfacing in Estero Bay. Specialty dishes include grouper *à la maison*, seafood strudel, and Derby pie (chocolate chip spiked with brandy). The family-run restaurant is known for its sumptuous Sunday brunch. *25999 Hickory Blvd., Bonita Springs, FL 33923; tel. 941-992-0033. Open Tue.-Fri. for lunch; Tue.-Sun. for dinner, and Sun. for brunch. At the north end of Bonita Beach.*

◆ **Big Hickory Fishing Nook Restaurant** (moderate). This old fish-shack restaurant sits at a marina with views of fishing boats and back bays. It adds healthy and vegetarian options to its traditional fish fare. The conch chowder is great. They give you a fifth of sherry on the side to do your own doctoring. Try the chocolate volcano, too. Ask for a back-porch seat if weather permits. *26107 Hickory Blvd. S.W., Hickory Island Center, Bonita Springs, FL 33923; tel. 941-992-0991. Open daily for breakfast, lunch, and dinner. Closed Tue. in off-season. At the north end of Bonita Beach, on the east side of the road.*

◆ **Doc's Beach House** (inexpensive). A casual beach restaurant, it specializes in burgers, grilled seafood, and snacks. You can get hotdogs, beverages, and take-out food downstairs or take an air-conditioned break with a second-story view of the beach action. *27908 Hickory Blvd., Bonita Beach, FL 33923; tel. 941-992-6444. Open daily for breakfast, lunch, and dinner in season and for lunch and dinner off season. At the south end of Bonita Beach, where Hickory Blvd. heads to the mainland.*

# NIGHTLIFE

**B**onita Beach is quieter than the beach towns to the north and south. Youthful dance and beach parties happen regularly at the north end of Fort Myers Beach, less than a half hour away.

◆ **Doc's Beach House.** Local bands entertain the crowd with contemporary music on the beach in season. *27908 Hickory Blvd., Bonita Springs, FL 33923; tel. 941-992-6444. Open nightly in season. At the south end of Bonita Beach, where Hickory Blvd. heads to the mainland.*

# ATTRACTIONS

◆ **Naples-Fort Myers Greyhound Track.** Pari-mutuel betting, with grandstand and clubhouse seating. *10601 Bonita Beach Rd. S.E., Bonita Springs, FL 33923; tel. 941-992-2411. Open Mon., Wed., and Fri.-Sun. at 11:30 for matinees and Mon.- Sat. at 6:30 for night races. Admission. 2 mi. west of I-75.*

# SHOPPING

**B**onita Springs is building shopping centers, especially along the Tamiami Trail. Nearer to the beach, you'll find small clusters of tourist- and marine-oriented shops. Neighboring Fort Myers Beach, at the north end, is a mecca of surf and souvenir shops. Hard-core shoppers will want to drive the 15 minutes to Naples (*see* Chapter 16, North Naples).

◆ **Island Hut/Tropical Treasures.** These two shops meld together, selling Florida-style gifts, straw hats, T-shirts, and cotton apparel. *26105 Hickory Blvd., Hickory Island Center, Bonita Springs, FL 33923; tel. 941-992-1851. Open daily. At the north end of Little Hickory Island.*

# BEST FOOD SHOPS

**SANDWICHES:** ◆ **Island Deli.** *26105 Hickory Blvd., Hickory Island Center, Bonita Springs, FL 33923; tel. 941-992-1112. Open daily.*
**SEAFOOD:** ◆ **Rodes Fresh & Fancy.** *3998 Bonita Beach Rd. S.W., Bonita Springs, FL 33923; tel. 941-992-4040. Open daily.*

**FRESH PRODUCE:** ◆ **Hickory Bay Farm Market.** *4906 Bonita Beach Rd. S.W., Bonita Springs, FL 33923. Open daily.*
**BAKERY:** ◆ **Goldie's Restaurant & Bakery.** *4951 Bonita Beach Rd., Bonita Springs, FL 33923; tel. 941-947-6605. Open daily.*
**ICE CREAM:** ◆ **Royal Scoop Homemade Ice Cream & Yogurt.** *15 Eighth St., Bonita Springs, FL 33923; tel. 941-992-2000. Open daily. Eighth St. at Bonita Beach Rd. near the beaches.*
**BEVERAGES:** ◆ **Publix.** *3306 Bonita Beach Rd. S.W., Bonita Springs, FL 33923; tel. 941-495-1600. Open daily.*
**WINE:** ◆ **White Lite Liquor.** *25999 Hickory Blvd., Bonita Springs, FL 33923; tel. 941-992-3839. Open daily.*

# SPORTS
## FISHING
Bonita Springs has adopted the slogan Snook Capital of the World. Snook, a.k.a. robalo, is a large silver fish with sweet, mild meat prized by seafood connoisseurs. It's against the law to sell it, so you must catch your own to experience it. There are season restrictions to protect it during spawning. Sheepshead, ladyfish, jack crevalle, mangrove snapper, and sea trout are more common finds in local estuary waters. You can buy fishing licenses at the K-mart on Highway 41 in Bonita Springs.

◆ **Big Hickory Fishing Nook.** Take care of all your fishing needs here: bait, tackle, fuel, rental boats, charters, rod and reel repair, gifts. *26107 Hickory Blvd., Hickory Island Center, Bonita Springs, FL 33923; tel. 941-992-3945. Open daily. At the north end of Bonita Beach.*

◆ **Estero Boat Tours.** The area's experts on local fishing and sights. Ask for Captain Charlie Weeks or Carl Johnson. *Weeks Fish Camp, Coconut Rd., Bonita Springs, FL 33923; tel. 941-992-2200. Open daily. Take the Tamiami Trail 5 mi. north of Bonita Beach Rd. and turn west on Coconut Rd.*

## BOATING
With its wildlife-rich bay waters and 150-plus small islands to explore, Bonita Springs affords endless opportunities for on-the-water adventure. Favorite destinations include archaeologically interesting Mound Key, sandy Big Hickory Island, and

waterside restaurants. There are boat-launching ramps on the bay side of Carl E. Johnson Park.

◆ **Back Bay Marina.** Rents pontoon boats and canoes. *4751 Bonita Beach Rd., Bonita Springs, FL 33923; tel. 941-992-2601. Open daily.*

◆ **Big Hickory Fishing Nook.** The focus is on fishing, but it rents pontoon boats and other craft for general use. *26107 Hickory Blvd., Hickory Island Center, Bonita Springs, FL 33923; tel. 941-992-3945. Open daily 7-8. At the north end of Bonita Beach.*

◆ **Bonita Beach Resort Motel.** Rents fishing boats. *26395 Hickory Blvd., Bonita Springs, FL 33923; tel. 941-992-2137. Open daily.*

◆ **G.R. Sailboats.** You can rent sailboats, Hobie Cats, sailboards, and pontoon boats. Sailing and windsurfing lessons. *4892 Bonita Beach Rd., Bonita Springs, FL 33923; tel. 941-947-4889. Open daily. Near the Bonita Beach Public Beach and the turn-off to Barefoot Beach Preserve.*

## BICYCLING

Bonita Beach recently undertook a gigantic project to widen its bike path, which runs the length of the nearly three-mile-long island. Heading south, the path connects with one in Vanderbilt Beach.

◆ **Bonita Beach Bike.** A full-service bike shop, it rents beach cruisers and single- and multispeed bikes. *4892 Bonita Beach Rd., Bonita Harbor Plaza, Bonita Springs, FL 33923; tel. 941-947-6377. Open Mon.-Sat.*

## GOLF

◆ **Pelican's Nest Golf Club.** One of the area's premier clubs, it has an 18-hole and a 9-hole course. *4450 Pelicans Nest Dr., Bonita Springs, FL 33923; tel. 941-947-4600, 800-952-6378. Open daily. Admission. About 3 mi. north of Bonita Beach Rd., off the Tamiami Trail.*

## TENNIS

◆ **Beach & Tennis Health Club.** The club is open to the public. It has ten Har-Tru courts (five lighted), plus a health club and lessons. *5800 Bonita Beach Rd., Bonita Springs, FL 33923; tel.*

*941-947-2330. Open daily. Admission.*

◆ **Bonita Springs Recreation Complex.** Its tennis courts are lighted. *26740 Pine Ave., Bonita Springs, FL 33923; tel. 941-992-2556. Open daily. Drive about 1 mi. north of Bonita Beach Rd. on the Tamiami Trail and turn east on Terry St. The park lies to the north on Pine Ave.*

# HISTORY

◆ **Koreshan State Historic Site.** A recreation area and historic site combined, it relates the fascinating story of a turn-of-the-century religious cult that founded a cultural and agricultural society on the banks of the Estero River. Members believed the world clung to the inside of a hollow globe that looked inward upon the solar system. Their buildings and experimental gardens are reconstructed here. *Tamiami Trail at Corkscrew Rd., Estero, FL 33928; tel. 941-992-0311. Open daily 8-sunset. Admission. On the Tamiami Trail (Hwy. 41), about 7 mi. north of Bonita Beach Rd.*

◆ **Mound Key.** Archaeologists and history buffs find their way to this bay island, named for the shell mounds that ancient Calusa Amerindians left behind. The island is supposed to have been headquarters for the tribe and later a Spanish mission and fort. *Open daily. Access is by boat only (see Boating).*

# NATURE

The Estero Bay Aquatic Preserve separates the marshy mainland from barrier islands. Its waters and more than 150 isles support all manner of local fauna: manatees, dolphins, seabirds, and fish.

◆ **Corkscrew Swamp Sanctuary.** The National Audubon Society oversees this 11,000-acre wetlands refuge. It protects alligators, nesting wood storks, and the largest stand of mature bald cypress trees in the country. A 1 3/4-mile-long boardwalk allows you to penetrate this ancient habitat, and marsh hiking trails take you through upland environment. *375 Sanctuary Rd., Naples, FL; tel. 941-657-3771. Open daily 7-5 Dec. 1-Apr. 30; 8-5 May 1-Nov. 30. Admission. 21 mi. east of the Tamiami Trail, off Naples-Immokalee Rd.*

◆ **Estero River Tackle and Canoe Outfitters.** Rents and outfits canoes for four-mile trips down the picturesque Estero River, past otters, bird life, and the lush shores of Koreshan Park. *20991 S. Tamiami Trail, Estero, FL 33928; tel. 941-992-4050. Open daily. Admission.*

# TOURIST INFORMATION

◆ **Bonita Springs Area Chamber of Commerce.** *Box 1240, Bonita Springs, FL 33959; tel. 941-992-2943, 800-226-2943; fax 941-992-5011. Open Mon.-Fri. 9-5. Welcome center on the Tamiami Trail, next to the firehouse and across from Pelican Landing development.*
◆ **Lee County Visitor & Convention Bureau.** *2180 W. First St., Suite 100, Fort Myers, FL 33901; tel. 941-338-3500, 800-237-6444. Open Mon.-Fri. 8-5. No visitors center.*

## CHAPTER 16

# North Naples

Northern of Naples lies a little-known stretch of beach shared by nature preserves, hotels, a posh residential area, and the community of Vanderbilt Beach. Visitors can roam seven miles of beach, explore the habitats of exotic birds and marine life, and take their pick of other activities. Just a stone's throw from the area's bike paths, canoe trails, and water sports are fine restaurants, upscale shopping, a teddy bear museum, and a world-class concert hall.

| | |
|---|---|
| Beauty | B+ |
| Swimming | B |
| Sand | B |
| Hotels/Inns/B&Bs | A- |
| House rentals | A |
| Restaurants | A- |
| Nightlife | B+ |
| Attractions | B |
| Shopping | A+ |
| Sports | A |
| Nature | A- |

It is all bookended by two waterfront recreational preserves: Delnor-Wiggins State Recreation Area on the north and Clam Pass Park on the south. Each has unspoiled beaches and a wide variety of wildlife and vegetation.

Although development detracts from the beauty of the beach in the town of Vanderbilt Beach, this fortunately is not true of the fine expanse of beach fronting the 2,100-acre Pelican Bay development. There, the bay separates luxury homes from the beach, which residents reach by private boardwalks. Beachgoers who want to explore the strand are free to walk down from Vanderbilt Beach.

Note: In exploring the territory by car, bear in mind that many of the shops and other points of interest are on two streets which, though they bear similar names, are far apart. One is Gulf Shore Drive in the town of Vanderbilt Beach.

The other is Gulf Shore Boulevard, where the shopping center called Village on Venetian Bay (or simply Venetian Village), is located. To reach this area from Seagate Drive, go south on Highway 41 (Tamiami Trail) for about a mile and turn right onto Park Shore Drive. Go west for about a mile to Gulf Shore Boulevard.

# GULF BEACHES

## DELNOR-WIGGINS STATE RECREATION AREA

These unspoiled sands provide visitors with a rare chance to explore a natural beachscape. Sea oats, cabbage palms, cactus, and sea grapes anchor the dunes. Shells and other wash-ups carpet the water's edge. In summer, the area is a

| Beauty | A |
|---|---|
| Swimming | B |
| Sand | B |
| Amenities | B+ |

popular nesting area for loggerhead turtles, so stay away from the staked-out areas that mark nests. To the east, there's another waterfront on the bay. At the north end, a boardwalk trail leads to an observation tower. There, swift

## HOW TO GET THERE

◆ From I-75 (about 15 minutes from Vanderbilt Beach), take exit 17 and head west on Rte. 846. Cross Hwy. 41 (Tamiami Trail) and contine to where the road ends at the entrance to Delnor-Wiggins State Recreation Area. Enter the park there, or, to reach Vanderbilt Beach, turn left on Gulf Shore Dr. and drive through the town of Vanderbilt Beach to Vanderbilt Beach Rd.

◆ To get to Clam Pass Recreation Area from Rte. 846, turn left on Hwy. 41 and drive south. Turn right on Seagate Dr. and follow it until it ends at the county parking lot next to the Registry Hotel.

waters from Wiggins Pass pose a danger to swimmers but are a boon to fishermen. Nature programs are offered from mid-December through mid-April. *At the intersection of Rte. 846 and Gulf Shore Dr. N.; tel. 941-597-6196. Open 7-sunset.*
*Swimming:* Gulf waters tend to be murky here, but the gently lapping waves and easy slope of the bottom make for good bathing, everywhere except in Wiggins Pass. Water temperatures stay warm throughout the year. Lifeguard on duty.
*Sand:* There's light-tan sand with whole shells and shell hash at the high-tide line. A good spot for shell collectors.
*Amenities:* Rest rooms, changing rooms, outdoor showers, a picnic pavilion, picnic tables, grills, a boat ramp, and a fish-cleaning table.
*Sports:* Fishing is great from Wiggins Pass. Horseshoes, darts, and kite-flying are prohibited.
*Parking:* There are five large lots, all close to the beach. Admission to the park is $3.25 per vehicle; $1 for walk-ins and those on bikes.

## VANDERBILT BEACH

Condo buildup within the town of Vanderbilt Beach detracts from this otherwise pristine strand. Tall buildings encroach upon the beach, which is quite narrow and crowded in parts, especially close to the public access. Beachcombers

| | |
|---|---|
| Beauty | B- |
| Swimming | B |
| Sand | B |
| Amenities | B+ |

will prefer to wander south to Pelican Bay, where there are three miles of beach, with homes on only a small section. *At the junction of Gulf Shore Dr. and Vanderbilt Beach Rd.*
*Swimming:* Warm water all year. Gentle waves and a gradual slope to the bottom.
*Sand:* This narrow beach has light-tan sand stubbled with broken shells at the high-tide line.
*Amenities:* No rest rooms. Outdoor showers are provided. From the public access, you can easily walk to the Ritz-Carlton to get a snack or drink at the beach pavilion (closed in summer). Vanderbilt Inn, about a mile to the north, provides similar amenities.

*Sports:* Sailboats, jet skis, windsurfers, paddleboats, and kayaks may be rented at the Ritz-Carlton or Vanderbilt Inn.
*Parking:* Free parking at a nearby lot and along Vanderbilt Beach Road. There's a drop-off zone at the beach.

## CLAM PASS RECREATION AREA

Getting to this lovely beach is nearly as much fun as being there. The tram ride along a three-quarter-mile boardwalk removes you from the high-rise development on the mainland and provides fine views of the tidal bay, with its hulking

| Beauty | B+ |
| --- | --- |
| Swimming | B |
| Sand | B+ |
| Amenities | B+ |

mangrove trees. The 35-acre park is a natural habitat for raccoons, eagles, hawks, ospreys, and many varieties of fish. The beach, about two-thirds of a mile long, tends to be crowded with Registry Hotel guests, but it's a gem. *Open sunrise-sunset. Take Seagate Dr. to the county parking lot next to the Registry Hotel. (Tram operates 8 to sunset).*
*Swimming:* Good bottom and calm waves make this a favorite of children.
*Sand:* Fine, fluffy, and clean.
*Amenities:* The park has small rest rooms, foot showers, and a snack counter. A stand rents cabanas and chaises and sells beach supplies.
*Sports:* From the parking lot, you can launch a canoe or kayak into a backwaters canoe trail. At the beach, you can rent canoes, kayaks, waterbikes, catamarans, and Windsurfers.
*Parking:* Free parking in the county lot near the entrance to the Registry Hotel. From there, you catch a motorized tram for the beach.

# HOTELS/INNS/B&Bs

L odging on the beach is not abundant, but the options range from grand resorts to humble motels. More hotels and inns line nearby Highway 41 (Tamiami Trail).

♦ **The Ritz-Carlton** (very expensive). When the Ritz came to town in 1985, things changed. Set in a wild mangrove and beach environment, it established   a new standard for service at

Florida resorts. Rooms, restaurants, and public areas are filled with antiques and decorated in soothing tones. Everyone gets a view of the Gulf. Families should consider staying on the top two "club floors," where continental breakfast, snacks, beverages, and after-dinner bites are complimentary. *280 Vanderbilt Beach Rd., Naples, FL 33963; tel. 941-598-3300, 800-241-3333.*

♦ **The Registry Hotel** (very expensive). High-dollar glitz characterizes the towering Registry and its crystalline lobby. Fifty villas border the resort's 15 tennis courts. Another 474 rooms and suites overlook the Gulf. Guests can choose among seven restaurants, three heated pools, Jacuzzis, a health club, and beach sports. A tram takes you to secluded Clam Pass Beach via an estuary tour. The Registry also provides shuttles to its 27-hole golf course nearby. *475 Seagate Dr., Naples, FL 33940; tel. 941-597-3232, 800-247-9810.*

♦ **Vanderbilt Inn on the Gulf** (expensive). Square on the beach, its 147 rooms are clean, roomy, and modern. They and the lobby reflect the current pastel, tropic theme popular in Florida. Rooms with a view of the Gulf are best. The resort has a restaurant, heated pool, and a popular outdoor bar. *11000 Gulf Shore Dr. N., Vanderbilt Beach, FL 33963; tel. 941-597-3151, 800-643-8654.*

# HOUSE RENTALS

Most houses, especially waterfront properties, rent for the full season (mid-December to mid-April) although the minimum required stay is one week. Rates begin at $1,000 per week on a by-the-week basis.

♦ **Bluebill Properties.** *26201 Hickory Blvd., Bonita Springs, FL 33923; tel. 941-597-1102, 800-237-2010. Open daily.*

# RESTAURANTS

The Naples area is known equally well for fine dining and casual fish houses.

♦ **The Dining Room** (very expensive). Whatever the chefs do at the Ritz-Carlton's top restaurant, they do with panache. The menu, which changes from season to season, combines the traditional with the trend-setting. Service is excellent, and the ambience, with classical music in the background, is formal but friendly. Appropriate dress requested. Reservations recommended. *280 Vanderbilt Beach Rd., Naples, FL 33963; tel. 941-598-3300. Closed in summer. In the Ritz-Carlton.*

♦ **The Cocahatchee Bay House** (moderate). There's lots of atmosphere at this little-known hideaway on a protected waterway, where manatees and alligators entertain. Inside you find dark stained mahogany, a brick hearth, casement windows, and shellacked wooden sailboats overhead. The cooking is contemporary, and includes many fine seafood dishes. Try the seafood Chardonnay and, as an appetizer, key-lime grilled shrimp with angel hair pasta. Reservations recommended. *799 Walkerbilt Rd., Naples, FL 33963; tel. 941-591-3837. Open for dinner. From Rt. 846, drive north on Hwy. 41 for about 1/4 mi. Turn left on Walkerbilt Rd.*

♦ **Backstage Tap & Grill** (inexpensive). This small cafe states its theme with playhouse props dangling from the ceiling and Broadway memorabilia encased in table tops. Sit under an umbrella outside or around the stage-like bar inside. The food is nibbly fare and sandwiches; huge jars of pickle chunks grace the tables. *5535 Tamiami Trail N., Naples, FL 33963; tel. 941-598-1300. Open daily for breakfast, lunch, and dinner; no Sun. dinner. At Seagate Dr. in the Waterside Shops.*

# NIGHTLIFE

♦ **Vanderbilt Inn Chickee Bar.** Folk, rock, and other contemporary music set the tone at this outdoor bar, which for decades has been the place for fun and live music. *11000 Gulf Shore Dr. N., Vanderbilt Beach, FL 33963; tel. 941-597-3151. Open daily.*

♦ **Backstage Tap & Grill.** The place for live jazz on weekends. *5535 Tamiami Trail N., Naples, FL 33963; tel. 941-598-1300. Open daily; entertainment Thu.-Sat. At Seagate Dr. in the Waterside Shops.*

♦ **Naples Dinner Theater.** Enjoy a live musical show or comedy with your dinner. *1025 Piper Blvd., Naples, FL 33942; tel. 941-597-6031. Box office open daily.*

♦ **Cobb's Pavilion 10-Plex Theaters.** Ten screens give you a wide selection of films. *833 Vanderbilt Rd., Naples, FL 33963; tel. 941-*

*598-1211. Open daily. At Hwy. 41 in the Pavilion Shopping Center.*
♦ **Philharmonic Center for the Arts.** The pride of the Naples community, it hosts the Naples Philharmonic, the Miami City Ballet, Broadway shows, and art exhibits. *5833 Pelican Bay Blvd., Pelican Bay, Naples, FL 33963; tel. 941-597-1900. Box office open Mon.-Fri. 10-4.*

# ATTRACTIONS

♦ **Teddy Bear Museum of Naples.** This collection includes more than 2,400 gigantic, miniature, antique, and limited-edition bears, plus a signed first-edition copy of A.A. Milne's *Winnie the Pooh. 2511 Pine Ridge Rd., Naples, FL 33942; tel. 941-598-2711. Open Wed.-Sat. 10-5; Sun. 1-5. Also open Mon. 10-5 Dec.-Apr. Admission. From Clam Pass Recreation Area, take Seagate Dr., which becomes Pine Ridge Rd. east of Hwy. 41.*

♦ **King Richard's Fun Park.** Take your pick of fun within this 11-acre amusement kingdom: water bumper boats, batting cages, a castle full of video games, go-cart tracks, a kiddie train, and two 18-hole miniature golf courses. *6780 N. Airport Rd., Naples, FL 33942; tel. 941-598-1666. Open Tue.-Thu. noon-9; Fri.-Sat. noon-10. Admission.*

# SHOPPING

The Pavilion Shopping Center at Vanderbilt Beach Road and Highway 41 (Tamiami Trail) has all sorts of shops. Further south on Highway 41, at Seagate Drive, the lavishly landscaped Waterside Shops has fine gift shops and clothing stores. Good shops may also be found in the Village on Venetian Bay. To reach this area from Seagate Drive, go south on Highway 41 for about a mile and turn right on Park Shore Drive. Follow this west for about a mile to Gulf Shore Boulevard.

♦ **The Nature Company.** The best place for anything related to birds, butterflies, dinosaurs, or rocks. *5475 Tamiami Trail N., Naples, FL 33963; tel. 941-597-4442. Open daily. At Seagate Dr. in the Waterside Shops.*

♦ **Carousel Galleries.** This shop specializes in antique merry-go-round animals, reproductions, and related gifts. *5455 Tamiami Trail N., Naples, FL 33963; tel. 941-495-2574. Open daily. At*

*Seagate Dr. in the Waterside Shops.*

◆ **Kirsten's Boutique Gallery.** This unusual store sells African masks, tribal jewelry, and flowing women's fashions. *5535 Tamiami Trail N., Naples, FL 33963; tel. 941-598-3233. Open daily. At Seagate Dr. in the Waterside Shops.*

# BEST FOOD SHOPS

**SANDWICHES:** ◆ **Gulfshore Gourmet.** *1400 Gulf Shore Blvd. N., Naples, FL 33940; tel. 941-262-8055. Open daily.*

**FRESH PRODUCE:** ◆ **Stallings U-Pick Farm.** *2600 Pine Ridge Rd., Naples, FL 33942; tel. 941-263-1028. Open daily.*

**BAKERY:** ◆ **Naples Cheesecake.** *8050 Trail Blvd., Naples, FL 33963; tel. 941-598-9070. Open daily.*

**ICE CREAM:** ◆ **Breakfast & Cream.** *881 103rd Ave. N., Naples, FL 33963; tel. 941-591-4060. Open Tue.-Sun.*

**WINE:** ◆ **Artichoke & Company.** *4370 Gulf Shore Blvd. N., Naples, FL 33940; tel. 941-263-6979. Open daily. In the Village on Venetian Bay.*

# SPORTS

## FISHING

Fish Wiggins Pass and the bay waters of Delnor-Wiggins Park. Or catch a charter from one of the nearby marinas, some of which also sell fishing licenses.

◆ **Wiggins Pass Marina.** *Wiggins Pass Rd., Vanderbilt Beach, FL 33963; tel. 941-597-3549. Open daily.*

◆ **Vanderbilt Beach Marina.** *179 Commerce St., Vanderbilt Beach, FL 33963; tel. 941-597-7584. Open daily.*

◆ **Park Shore Marina.** *4310 Gulf Shore Blvd. N., Naples, FL 33940; tel. 941-434-6964. Open daily.*

## BOATING

Marinas rent powerboats for half and full days to use in intracoastal waters. Many resorts rent small sailboats, kayaks, and other craft.

◆ **Wiggins Pass Marina.** Rents center-console powerboats and pontoon boats. *Wiggins Pass Rd., Vanderbilt Beach, FL 33963; tel. 941-597-3549. Open daily.*

♦ **Vanderbilt Beach Marina.** Rents pontoon boats. *179 Commerce St., Vanderbilt Beach, FL 33963; tel. 941-597-7584. Open daily.*

♦ **Park Shore Marina.** Pontoon boats, runabouts, and waterski equipment are for rent here. *4310 Gulf Shore Blvd. N., Naples, FL 33940; tel. 941-434-6964. Open daily.*

## BICYCLING

Naples' best biking is on a pathway in Pelican Bay, which incorporates a 580-acre nature preserve. From Pelican Bay, via Crayton Road and Seagate Drive, you can get to Clam Pass Park and Gulf Shore Boulevard, where a bike lane takes you into Old Naples with its beaches and shops. No biking is allowed on the Clam Pass boardwalk, but there are bike racks in the parking lot. To the north, a narrow path follows Vanderbilt Drive south from Bonita Beach Road, down Bluebill Avenue to Delnor-Wiggins Park. There are bike racks at the park and beach entrances, or cyclists may take to the road that winds through the park. Biking is forbidden, however, on the paved path between Bluebill Avenue and Vanderbilt Beach Road.

♦ **Bicycle Shoppe of Naples.** Rentals available. *813 Vanderbilt Beach Rd., Naples, FL 33963; tel. 941-566-3646. Open Mon.-Sat.*

## GOLF

Naples claims more golf courses per capita than any city in the U.S. Its top-rated courses attract major tournaments and professional golfers, including Nancy Lopez, Chi Chi Rodriquez, and Arnold Palmer. Many of the courses are private, but resort guests may receive privileges to play there.

♦ **Naples Beach Golf Club.** An 18-hole resort course open to the public. *851 Gulf Shore Blvd. N., Naples, FL 33940; tel. 941-434-7007. Open daily.*

## TENNIS

♦ **Naples Park Elementary School.** The public can use the two lighted courts here. *685 111th Ave. N., Naples, FL 33940. Open daily.*

♦ **Pelican Bay Community Park.** A number of lighted courts are open to public use. *Vanderbilt Beach Rd., Naples, FL 33963. Open daily.*

# HISTORY

◆ **Naples Trolley Tours.** Originating at the Vanderbilt Inn, the two-hour tour is enlivened by the colorful history and lore of more than 100 points of interest. *Vanderbilt Inn, 11000 Gulf Shore Dr. N., Vanderbilt Beach, FL 33963; tel. 941-262-7300. Open daily. Admission.*

# NATURE

◆ **The Conservancy's Naples Nature Center.** Besides nature walks and boat tours, the Conservancy runs a shelter for injured and orphaned birds. A video monitoring system lets visitors watch without disturbing the healing process. Also within its 13 acres are marine aquariums, a nature store, and a natural science museum with a habitat for live snakes. *1450 Merrihue Dr., Naples, FL 33942; tel. 941-262-0304. Open Mon.-Sat. Admission. From Seagate Dr., take Hwy. 41 south, and turn left on Fleischman Blvd. Turn right on Goodlette Rd. Bear left onto 14th Ave. N., and go one block to the Nature Center.*

# SAFETY TIPS

If you walk on the boardwalk to Clam Pass Beach, wear shoes. Foot splinters are one of the more common injuries of beach-goers.

# TOURIST INFORMATION

◆ **Naples Area Tourism Bureau.** *853 Vanderbilt Beach Rd., Suite 351, Naples, FL 33963; tel. 941-598-3202.*
◆ **Naples Chamber of Commerce.** *3620 Tamiami Trail N., Naples 33940; tel. 941-262-6141. Open Mon.- Fri. 8:30-5.*

## CHAPTER 17

# Bahia Honda Key

T he islands of the Florida Keys dribble off the south end of the peninsula, much as your worldly cares will melt away when you enter their laid-back version of reality. With their stunning natural coral reef and aquarium-clear waters, the Keys encompass a sea-world playground unlike any other in Florida. But what the reef gives to divers and fishermen, it takes away from beachers. The coral barrier softens sand-making waves and leaves the Keys practically beach-starved. The notable exception is Bahia Honda

| | |
|---|---|
| Beauty | A- |
| Swimming | A- |
| Sand | B |
| Hotels/Inns/B&Bs | B+ |
| House rentals | A |
| Restaurants | A- |
| Nightlife | B+ |
| Attractions | B+ |
| Shopping | B |
| Sports | A+ |
| Nature | A+ |

State Park, between Marathon and Big Pine Key in the Lower Keys.

Marathon sits on Vaca Key, named by Spanish explorers for its profuse sea cows, or manatees. It was first settled by pirates and salvagers, later by fishermen from Mystic, Connecticut. Farmers from the Bahamas immigrated, and Marathon became the Keys' first center of Bahamian culture. Many of the old Conch (a term applied to Bahamians who transplanted to the Keys) homes still survive. The town is said to have gotten its name from the breakneck pace at which workers slaved to build Henry Flagler's railroad during the early 1900s.

The Seven Mile Bridge that crosses between Marathon and the Lower Keys is the longest segmental bridge in the world. It was built in 1982 in pieces in Tampa, and shipped to the Keys

South of the bridge, the temperament changes. ⎯ps a notch. Wildlife and vegetation become ⎯. The perfectly gorgeous state park dominates ⎯a Honda Key, protecting its natural beaches, quiet ⎯goons, and lush, tropical foliage.

To the southwest is Big Pine Key, second in size only to Key Largo and cushioned from some of the commercial crassness of nearby Marathon and Key West by its nature preserves. This is home of the tiny, endangered Key deer. Farther southwest, but within 15 minutes of Bahia Honda, the islands of Little Torch Key, Middle Torch Key, Ramrod Key, and Summerland Key provide accommodations and services for water-sports enthusiasts and other visitors. Down at the very end of the chain is legendary Key West—with its sub-cultural nightlife, marvelous restaurants, charming guest houses, unusual shops, and historic attractions. It's about a 45-minute drive (and a whole other world) away.

Whether it's a reflection of the generally laid-back atmosphere or a result of the small size of many communities, many businesses in the Keys claim not to have a specific street address. If you can't find a place even with the mile-marker directions given, your best bet is just to call.

Christmas to Easter is busy for the Keys, but another high sea-

## HOW TO GET THERE

◆ Commuter airplane flights connect Marathon with Miami International and Tampa International airports. From Marathon Airport (about 20 minutes from Bahia Honda Key), follow Hwy. 1 (Overseas Hwy.) southwest about 5 mi., through Marathon to the Seven Mile Bridge. Cross Little Duck Key, Missouri Key, and Ohio Key to get to Bahia Honda Key. The entrance to Bahia Honda State Park is just after mile marker 37, about 1 1/2 mi. from Ohio Key. (Note: Addresses in the Keys are usually given in terms of mile markers, designated "MM," alongside the road.)

son runs from the end of July through Labor Day.

# OCEAN BEACHES
## SANDSPUR BEACH

Despite its prickly name, this beach is the prettier, cleaner, and more secluded of the two main beaches in Bahia Honda State Park. Fringed with dense vegetation and coconut palms, it stretches, long and narrow, along the ocean. At high tide, it

| Beauty | A- |
| --- | --- |
| Swimming | A- |
| Sand | A- |
| Amenities | B |

becomes impassable in spots. The shoreline view is virtually pristine. This is a popular spot for couples; families usually are drawn to Caloosa Beach, where there are more amenities. *Open 8-sunset. The entrance to Bahia Honda State Park is on Hwy. 1, just after mile marker 37. Turn left after entrance gate and follow signs to the beach.*
*Swimming:* Though breezier and more churned up here than at Caloosa Beach, the shallower, clearer waters and smooth ocean bottom make it inviting to swimmers.
*Sand:* Fine, light-colored sand is strewn with lots of seaweed.
*Amenities:* Large, wooden picnic shelters (reserve at ranger station) with grills, rest rooms, outdoor showers. No lifeguards.
*Sports:* Short nature trail. Good snorkeling. Water-sports rentals nearby at Caloosa Beach.
*Parking:* Two parking lots and some roadside parking. The fee to enter Bahia Honda State Park is $3.25 per car, $1 per bicycle or pedestrian, plus 50 cents county surcharge per person.

# BAY BEACHES
## CALOOSA BEACH

Snuggled between the original, historic Flagler Bridge and the newer Seven Mile Bridge, this short, narrow beach has calm waters and concessions—both of which make it popular with families. It lies near the marina and is prettily garnished with

| Beauty | B+ |
| --- | --- |
| Swimming | B+ |
| Sand | B- |
| Amenities | A |

**167**

tall coconut palms and well-kept tropical vegetation. *The entrance gate to Bahia Honda State Park is on Hwy. 1, just after mile marker 37. Turn right after entrance gate and follow signs to the beach.*

*Swimming:* A swimming area is defined by buoys. The water is murkier than you'd expect in the Keys, and the bottom is prickly with shells and has a steep slope. Waters stay warm year-round.

*Sand:* Coarse tan sand is shelly and strewn with seaweed.

*Amenities:* Small cement picnic shelters with grills, rest rooms, outdoor showers, food and beach concessions. No lifeguard.

*Sports:* Water-sports buffs are well-tended. The marina has a boat ramp, charter boats, and fishing guides. (Fishing is good under the bridges from shore.) The dive shop offers equipment rentals and daily snorkel trips to Looe Key National Marine Sanctuary. Snorkeling and windsurfing are good on the other side of the road facing full into the ocean. Kayak and windsurfing rentals available.

*Parking:* Large parking lot that fills up on weekends and in season. The fee to enter Bahia Honda State Park is $3.25 per car, $1 per bicycle or pedestrian, plus 50 cents county surcharge per person.

# HOTELS/INNS/B&Bs

Campgrounds, guest houses, diving and fishing lodges, luxury resorts: Bahia Honda's neighborhood has it all—except ho-hum chain motels. Rates are reasonable, but this could change as environmental restrictions are enforced with new legislation designating all Keys waters as national marine sanctuary.

◆ **Little Palm Island** (very expensive). This sandy, palmy haven seated on an unbridged island has hosted the Trumans, President Kennedy, and the crew of the film *PT-109*, among others. Thatched-roof luxury bungalows and flourishing vegetation give it a South Seas feel. All types of water sports are provided, and meals are served in the award-winning restaurants on the European or American plan. *28500 Overseas Hwy., Little Torch Key, FL 33042; tel. 305-872-2524, 800-343-8567. Resort* *welcome center and dock is located oceanside at the Dolphin Marina, at mile marker 28.5 on Little Torch Key.*

◆ **Banana Bay Resort** (expensive). Pleasantly overgrown with banana trees, palms, and lush Florida landscaping, it holds 60 rooms with refrigerators, plus tennis courts, a pool, a whirlpool, and a man-made beach. Its 50-slip marina includes a ramp and a full menu of water-sports rentals. You can enjoy your continental breakfast poolside. Older units are of concrete block construction; newer ones are rounded stilt structures. *4590 Overseas Hwy., Marathon, FL 33050; tel. 305-743-3500, 800-226-2621; fax 305-743-2670. Bayside, at mile marker 49.5.*

◆ **Bahia Honda State Park** (inexpensive). Three campgrounds hold 80 sites near the Keys' best beaches. The Sandspur Campground has the most secluded wooded sites, near the park's nicest beach. Buttonwood Campground is on the marina side, between two bridges. A few bayside cabins are in the moderate range. *Rte. 1, Box 782, Big Pine Key, FL 33043; tel. 305-872-2353. The entrance to the park is on Hwy. 1, at mile marker 37 on Bahia Honda Key.*

◆ **Big Pine Fishing Lodge** (inexpensive). In a tidy, pretty property at the channel, the fishing-fetished find perfect respite. This combination campground/efficiency resort comes complete with marina, boat rentals, fishing charters, pool, laundry, and bait-and-tackle supplies. Quiet and shady. *Box 430513, Big Pine Key, FL 33043; tel. 305-872-2351. Oceanside, at mile marker 33.*

◆ **Looe Key Reef Resort** (inexpensive). For vacationers more interested in bottom town than bedtime, this diving-focused resort is perfect. It has its own dive center and charters, as well as a tiki bar, a restaurant, a pool, boat docks, and a liquor store. Most of the 23 unfancy rooms front a canal. Rates are higher in lobster season, August to mid-March. *Box 509, Ramrod Key, FL 33042; tel. 305-872-2215, 800-942-5397; fax 305-872-3786. Oceanside, at mile marker 27.5.*

# HOUSE RENTALS

Home rentals are plentiful in Marathon and the Lower Keys. Many are waterfront; some include a boat and other water-oriented amenities. In Marathon, expect to pay $500 to

$3,500 for a week. In Big Pine Key, the range is $400 to $2,000.

◆ **Big Pine Vacation Rentals.** *Rte. 5, Box 89A, Big Pine Key, FL 33043; tel. 305-872-9863, 800-654-9560. Open daily. Bayside, at mile marker 29.5.*

◆ **Century 21-Heart of the Keys.** *12690 Overseas Hwy., Marathon, FL 33050; tel. 305-743-3377, 800-451-4899. Open daily. Bayside, at mile marker 54.5.*

# RESTAURANTS

In the language of Keys cuisine, conch, lobster, and Key lime pie get the most lip service. Although conch collecting has long been banned in Florida, restaurateurs continue to import the product to keep the symbolic reputation alive. Spiny lobster is caught locally; the best time to order one is August to mid-March. Just about every other restaurant claims the best Key lime pie in an ongoing battle to perfect or improve upon the classic recipe of sweetened condensed milk, Key lime juice (which is yellow), and egg yolks.

◆ **Little Palm Island** (very expensive). For a special, romantic evening, reserve a boat ride to and table at this exclusive resort's top-shelf South Seas-style restaurant, which offers classic French and Caribbean cuisine. (You can also go for lunch.) Thursday is "Gourmet Night," featuring a seven-course service. Children must be 12 years or older. *28500 Overseas Hwy., Little Torch Key, FL 33042; tel. 305-872-2551, 305-872-2524; fax 305-872-4843. Open daily for lunch and dinner; Sun. for brunch and dinner. Resort welcome center and boat launch are oceanside at Dolphin Marina, at mile marker 28.5 on Little Torch Key.*

◆ **Mangrove Mama's Restaurant** (moderate). A Keys classic, it peeks out of banana-tree camouflage with a Bahamian wink. Colorful, splattered paint jobs and ultra-casual attitudes set the stage for the finest in this genre you'll find in the area. It's worth the extra drive (about 20 minutes from the beach). The Key lime pie is legendary. The broiled fish sandwich (especially if the day's catch is snapper) beats most fish-house fare. The menu concentrates on seafood, but also offers steaks and ribs. *19991 Overseas Hwy., Sugarloaf Key, FL 33042; tel. 305-*

*745-3030. Open daily for lunch and dinner. Bayside, 17 mi. south-west of Bahia Honda; just over the Sugarloaf Key bridge and near mile marker 20.*

◆ **Shuckers' Raw Bar & Grill** (moderate). Situated near the shrimp docks, its lobster, grouper, and shrimp specialties are as fresh as they can be. Choice of preparation includes Francaise, pan-fried, tempura, and *fra diavolo* styles. Dining room looks out at the docks of Marathon Marina. *725 11th St., Marathon, FL 33050; tel. 305-743-8686. Open daily for lunch and dinner. Oceanside, at Marathon Marina and mile marker 47.5.*

# NIGHTLIFE

Marathon has a reputation as a party town. A lot of the partying goes on after work and around sunset in tiki bars. A derivative of Florida's west coast "chickee" (*CHEEK-ee*) bars, named for the Native American-made thatched roofs that often cover them, a Keys "tiki" bar simply means the bar is outdoors. Often it's just a bar, with no tables, where the entertainment is conversation and nature's gorgeous curtain call. In addition, although it's out of the normal driving radius of a beach in this book, Key West is worth mentioning for its nightlife—on the off-chance that you'll want to drive the 45 minutes it takes to get there from Bahia Honda Key.

◆ **Anglers Lounge.** Local bands play contemporary tunes nightly. Known for its Friday "T.G.I.F." party. *Faro Blanco Resort, 1996 Overseas Hwy., Marathon, FL 33050; tel. 305-743-9018. Open daily. Bayside, at mile marker 48.*

◆ **Looe Key Tiki Bar.** Local bands and lots of diving-experience tales entertain. *Looe Key Reef Resort, Box 509, Ramrod Key, FL 33042; tel. 305-872-2215. Open daily. Live entertainment Wed. and Fri.-Sat.; plus Sun. in winter. Oceanside, at mile marker 27.5.*

◆ **Marathon Community Theatre.** Local actors and actresses perform comedies and musicals. *Box 500124, Marathon, FL 33050; tel. 305-289-0774. Open daily mid-Nov.-mid-Apr. Admission. Performances in Key Colony Beach City Hall at 600 W.*

**171**

*Ocean Dr. in Key Colony Beach. North of Marathon, turn east at the causeway (131st St.) and take your first right.*

# SHOPPING

◆ **Blue Moon Trader.** A complex of fascinating shopping experiences. Crystals, tarot cards, kids' stuff, unusual books, and consignment clothes are sold on the upper two levels. Below, local artists set up headquarters and display their work in winter. *Rte. 5, Box 129, Big Pine Key, FL 33043; tel. 305-872-8864. Open daily. Oceanside, at mile marker 29.7.*

◆ **Edie's Hallmark Shop.** Much more than a card shop, it carries a great selection of local-interest books, as well as local art works. *Big Pine Key Shopping Plaza, Big Pine Key, FL 33043; tel. 305-872-3933. Open daily. Turn north on Key Deer Blvd. The entrance to the shopping center is on your left.*

◆ **Leda Bruce Galleries.** Shows and sells the work of local artists in a variety of media. *Big Pine Key, FL 33032; tel. 305-872-0212. Open Mon.-Sat. Oceanside, at mile marker 30.*

◆ **Sherman's Nautical Emporium.** A one-stop souvenir shop: decorative lobster traps, T-shirts tacky to high-quality, jewelry, home-decor items of all levels, toys, clothes. Look for the sea-life mural on front. *24326 Overseas Hwy., Summerland Key, FL 33042; tel. 305-745-1748; fax 305-745-2012. Open daily. Oceanside, at mile marker 24.*

◆ **Wood Carvings Etc.** An unusual, side-of-the-road place where an artist sells her colorful wood statues, relief plaques, and antiques. *51 Dobie St., Summerland Key, FL 33042; tel. 305-745-2726. Open daily. Oceanside, at mile marker 24.1.*

# BEST FOOD SHOPS

**SANDWICHES:** ◆ **Mark's Gourmet Deli.** *Box 431764, Big Pine Key, FL 33043; tel. 305-872-1230. Open daily. Oceanside, at mile marker 30.*

**SEAFOOD:** For the freshest seafood, explore the seafood markets along the docks at the end of 11th or 15th streets in Marathon. *Days open vary. Turn east at mile marker 48.*

◆ **Monte's Fish Market.** *Hwy. 1, Summerland Key, FL 33042; tel. 305-745-3731. Open daily except Mon. Oceanside, at mile marker 25.*

**FRESH PRODUCE:** ◆ **Garden Gourmet.** *11400 Overseas Hwy., Marathon, FL 33050; tel. 305-289-9425. Open daily. At mile marker 53.*

**BAKERY:** ◆ **Peddler's Bakery.** *Big Pine Key Shopping Plaza, Rte. 7, Box 21, Big Pine Key, FL 33043; tel. 305-872-4725. Open daily except Mon. Off Key Deer Blvd.*

**ICE CREAM:** ◆ **Dip N' Deli.** *Big Pine Key, FL 33043; tel. 305-872-3030. Open daily. Bayside, at mile marker 31.*

**BEVERAGES:** ◆ **Tom Thumb.** *2690 Overseas Hwy., Big Pine Key, FL 33043; tel. 305-872-9498. Open daily 24 hrs. Bayside, at mile marker 31.*

**WINE:** ◆ **Marathon Liquors.** *5101 Overseas Hwy., Marathon, FL 33050; tel. 305-743-6350. Open daily. Bayside, at mile marker 49.*

# SPORTS
## FISHING

The bridges around Bahia Honda attract tarpon and other large game fish. The most coveted catch of the Keys, however, is the elusive bonefish. Fly fishermen are especially beguiled by this easily spooked flats fish. Dolphinfish is another popular catch. Charters are available through Bahia Honda State Park, or you can check out the many marinas. Snorkelers and divers stalk the tasty, clawless spiny lobster August through mid-March.

◆ **Jig's.** Full-service tackle shop with gear, bait, licenses, charters, kayak rentals, and information. *Big Pine Key, FL 33043; tel. 305-872-1040. Open daily. Oceanside, at mile marker 30.5.*

◆ **Neredi Charters.** Fly and light-tackle charters for bonefish, tarpon, sharks, permit, and barracuda. *Box 431954, Big Pine Key, FL 33043; tel. 305-872-4317. Open daily.*

◆ **Sea Boots Charters and Outfitters.** Bonefishing, billfishing, and other backwater excursions, video services, taxidermy, and fishing equipment. *110 Ship Way, Big Pine Key, FL 33043; tel. 305-872-9005, 800-238-1746; fax 305-872-0780. Open Mon.-Sat. Turn north on Ship Way, near mile marker 29.5.*

◆ **Strike Zone Charters.** Taking you in search of marlin, dolphin, wahoo, bonefish, and barracuda in deep water and the back country. *Rte. 5, Box 89A, Big Pine Key, FL 33043; tel. 305-872-9863, 800-654-9560. Open daily. Bayside, at mile marker 29.5.*

## BOATING

The marina at Bahia Honda State Park (*see* Tourist Information) has a boat ramp and offers docking and charter services. Kayak and windsurfing rentals are also available.

◆ **Bud Boats.** Rents a wide variety of boats on a half-day to weekly basis, plus fishing and snorkeling/diving equipment. *Old Wooden Bridge Marina, Rte. 3, Big Pine Key, FL 33034; tel. 305-872-9165, 800-633-2283; fax 305-743-0889. Open daily. Turn north on Key Deer Blvd. (mile marker 30.5). After 1 1/2 mi. turn right on Watson Blvd., which becomes Old State Rd. 4A. Turn right on Bogie Dr.*

◆ **Jay Bird's Powerboats.** Rentals with depth finders, cellular phones, and bimini tops. *Big Pine Key Fishing Lodge, Box 430513, Big Pine Key, FL 33043; tel. 305-872-8500. Open daily. Oceanside, at mile marker 33.*

◆ **Reflections Nature Tours.** Kayak nature tours into Great White Heron National Wildlife Refuge and National Key Deer Refuge. *Box 430861, Big Pine Key, FL 33043; tel. 305-872-2896. Open daily. Tours leave from Parmers Place resort, at mile marker 28.5 on Little Torch Key.*

## DIVING

The Keys are a diver's paradise. The reefs of Looe Key National Marine Sanctuary are some of the region's most spectacular; many of them are in less than 30 feet of water. You'll find dive shops on practically every corner. But they're strict about whom they serve: You must show a diving certification card and a log book documenting recent diving experience. Many offer lobster dive charters, among others.

◆ **Innerspace Dive Shop.** Full-service diving center with charters into Looe Key sanctuary. *Box 430637, Big Pine Key, FL 33034; tel. 305-872-2319, 800-538-2896. Open daily. Oceanside, at mile marker 29.5.*

◆ **Underseas Inc.** PADI instructions, charters, rentals, and sales.

*Box 319, Big Pine Key, FL 33043; tel. 305-872-2700, 800-446-5663. Open daily. Oceanside, at mile marker 30.5.*

## BICYCLING

Bike lanes and paths parallel most of the road along Highway 1 in these parts. Good side trips include the Key Deer refuge, the bridge to Pigeon Key, and Bahia Honda State Park itself.

◆ **Four Star Rentals.** Rents bikes. *Hwy. 1, Big Pine Key, FL 33043; tel. 305-872-2229. Open daily except Sun. Bayside, at mile marker 30.*

## GOLF

◆ **Key Colony Beach Golf & Tennis.** Public course, nine holes, no tee times. *Eighth St., Key Colony Beach, FL 33051; tel. 305-289-1533. Open daily. Admission. Northeast of Marathon, turn east near mile marker 53.5 at Key Colony Beach Causeway (131st St.). Take first right.*

## TENNIS

◆ **Key Colony Beach Golf & Tennis.** Two courts. *Eighth St., Key Colony Beach, FL 33051; tel. 305-289-1533. Open daily. Admission. Northeast of Marathon, turn east near mile marker 53.5 at Key Colony Beach Causeway (131st St.). Take first right.*

# HISTORY

◆ **Flagler Bridge.** In 1905, railroad magnate Henry Flagler was ridiculed for his plan to lay 150 miles of trestle from the mainland to Key West. But he did succeed in 1912, although he never profited from the Keys railroad. The hurricane of 1935 destroyed his dream, and the trestle was converted into Highway 1. Segments of Flagler's bridge remain parallel to the new Seven Mile Bridge. From a trail in Bahia Honda State Park, you can view the Bahia Honda Bridge segment.

◆ **Pigeon Key.** Historically significant for its old Bahamian architecture and early role in the building of the railroad, Pigeon Key is undergoing restoration. A tram takes visitors to the island (or you can walk or bicycle) via the old Seven Mile Bridge, which crosses the minuscule key; there, you can see turn-of-the-century structures. The visitor center occupies a vintage railroad car and includes a gift shop. *Pigeon Key Welcome Center, 1 Knight's Key Blvd., Marathon, FL 33050; tel. 305-289-0025. Open Tue.-Sun. 9-5 in winter; 10-4 in summer. Shuttle departs from visitor center hourly, 10-4. Last shuttle returns from the island at 5. Admission. Oceanside, in Marathon, at the foot of the Seven Mile Bridge. Turn at Knight's Key Park, at mile marker 48.*

# NATURE

**W**ithin 15 minutes of Bahia Honda lie several wildlife refuges, including Looe Key National Marine Sanctuary and Great White Heron Refuge, which harbors namesake species and other rare and endangered birds, such as the bald eagle.

◆ **Museum of Natural History.** The Keys' social and natural history entwine in exhibits devoted to Native Americans, pirates, railroad workers, coral reefs, and Key deer. The Children's Museum portion has touch tanks, a railway station, a reading center, and a canoe. *5550 Overseas Hwy., Marathon, FL 33050; tel. 305-743-9100. Open Mon.-Sat. 9-5; Sun. 12-5. Admission. Bayside, at mile marker 50, 13 mi. north of Bahia Honda.*

◆ **National Key Deer Refuge.** Some 300 of the fragile, dwarf Key deer survive here. You can drive into the 2,300-acre refuge. You're most likely to spot the deer (drive carefully) evenings and mornings. Visit the blue hole (a lake-like sinkhole in the limestone) where alligators, turtles, herons, and fish languish under the observation deck. A trail leads into wildlife habitat. Guided tours in winter. *Box 430150, Big Pine Key, FL 33043; tel. 305-872-2239. Open daily. From Bahia Honda, cross to Big Pine Key and turn right at mile marker 30.5 onto Key Deer Blvd. (Rte. 940). Visitors center in Big Pine Key Shopping Plaza, off Key Deer Blvd.*

# SAFETY TIPS

**F**amiliarize yourself with the dangers of underwater sports. Certain types of corals are harmful when touched or brushed against. (You shouldn't willfully touch any coral; it kills the organisms.) Barracuda are plentiful, but rarely bother snorkelers or divers. It helps to remove shiny jewelry. Never harass them. During certain seasons, jellyfish float on top of the water. Wear wet suits or other protection to dive below them.

# TOURIST INFORMATION

**Y**ou'll see tourist information signs everywhere in the Keys. Your most comprehensive sources are the local chambers of commerce and their welcome centers.

◆ **Bahia Honda State Park.** *Rte. 1, Box 782, Big Pine Key, FL 33043; tel. 305-872-2353. Open daily 8-sunset.*

◆ **Florida Keys & Key West Visitors Bureau.** Call for information (no visitors center). *Box 984, Key West, FL 33041; tel. 305-294-2587, 800-352-5397. Phone line operates 24 hours a day.*

◆ **Greater Marathon Chamber of Commerce.** *12222 Overseas Hwy., Marathon, FL 33050; tel. 305-743-5417, 800-842-9580; fax 305-289-0183. Open Mon.-Fri. 9-5:30; Sat. 9-1. Mile marker 53.5 bayside.*

◆ **Lower Keys Chamber of Commerce.** *Box 430511, Big Pine Key, FL 33043; tel. 305-872-2411, 800-872-3722. Open Mon.-Fri. 9-5; Sat. 9-3. At mile marker 31 oceanside.*

## CHAPTER 18

# Key Biscayne

**J**ust south of downtown Miami, Key Biscayne sits close enough to the mainland to be convenient to swinging South Beach, trendy Coconut Grove, and some of Miami's best attractions. Still, a wide expanse of Biscayne Bay keeps it distanced from big-city madness. It also sits apart— and a bit elevated—from the resorts to the north.

Key Biscayne is steeped in history, visited by famed 16th-century Spanish explorer Ponce DeLeon and featuring a 170-year-old lighthouse. The most talked-about event in

| | |
|---|---|
| Beauty | A+ |
| Swimming | B+ |
| Sand | B+ |
| Hotels/Inns/B&Bs | B |
| House rentals | B+ |
| Restaurants | A- |
| Nightlife | B |
| Attractions | A |
| Shopping | A |
| Sports | A+ |
| Nature | A- |

recent island history is Hurricane Andrew's brutal blow in August 1992. Key Biscayne took the brunt of the fury, and its beaches suffered tragically. The good news is that it's come back better than before. Many now call the storm a blessing in disguise. The island's southernmost beaches, which had been artifically filled and overgrown with Australian pines—to the point where native vegetation was practically nonexistent—were badly hit. But today, the south-end Cape Florida State Recreation Area, along with north-end Crandon Park, is replanted with palms, sea grapes, and other indigenous plants. They are recovering nicely; sands have been replenished.

The ocean around Key Biscayne is calmer, clearer, and warmer than it is around Palm Beach. At the doorstep of the Florida Keys, Key Biscayne shares some of the same clarity as

those famed waters and offers divers and water-sports enthusiasts of all ilk countless opportunities for fun.

Besides at the following two gorgeous beaches, people park
along the causeway to Key Biscayne to enjoy Hobie Beach, a
narrow strip of sand with a reputation for fine windsurfing and
sailing.

# OCEAN BEACHES
## CRANDON PARK

With a healthy green color and nice landscaping, this huge park has it all in the
recreation and amenities department. Big
shady sea grape and fig trees hover over
picnic areas, and coconut and sabal palm
trees adorn the beach and boulevard.

| Beauty | A |
|---|---|
| Swimming | B+ |
| Sand | B+ |
| Amenities | A |

Families come on weekends to picnic and spend the day.
Beachers watch Port of Miami big-ship traffic against the dis-
tant downtown skyline. *4000 Crandon Blvd.; tel. 407-361-5421.
Open 8-sunset. At the north end of Key Biscayne; look for signs on
Crandon Blvd.*
*Swimming:* Warm, calm waters are perfect for swimming and
playing year-round. Signs restrict swimming to guarded areas.
*Sand:* Fine, dusty-gray sand spreads extremely wide, especially
at the south end of the three-and-a-half-mile-long beach.
*Amenities:* At the beach there are rest rooms, showers, a playground, picnic tables, and grills. Lifeguard on duty. In the park,
there are sports facilities, a marina, and restaurants.

## H O W   T O   G E T   T H E R E

◆ From Miami International Airport, take LeJeune Rd. south
to Rte. 836 east (toll). Take Rte. 836 to I-95 south; follow to
Key Biscayne/Rickenbacker Causeway exit 1. Cross over the
Rickenbacker Causeway (toll) to Virginia Key and continue
along Crandon Blvd. to Key Biscayne.

*Sports:* The marina rents boats and offers diving charters. An 18-hole golf course, lighted driving range, baseball fields, soccer field, bike path, and 17 tennis courts are located in the park. Volleyball nets on the beach. Jet Ski and windsurfing concessions nearby on the causeway.

*Parking:* Four large, paved parking lots charge $3 for a day of parking; $6 for RVs and buses.

## BILL BAGGS CAPE FLORIDA RECREATION AREA

Hurricane Andrew decimated this 900-acre park in 1992. Some consider the leveling of its once-trademark Australian pines (casuarinas) a stroke of luck. The park's been replanted with native vegetation, which the exotic pines tended to

| | |
|---|---|
| Beauty | A- |
| Swimming | B+ |
| Sand | B+ |
| Amenities | B+ |

smother. It still looks somewhat stark, however. The battered, historic Cape Florida Lighthouse (South Florida's oldest structure) is expected to reopen in 1996. The beach looks great and has a nice view. It is popular with urban weekenders, who unfortunately leave their litter. *1200 Crandon Blvd.; tel. 407-361-5811. At the south end of Key Biscayne.*

*Swimming:* A sandbar offshore keeps waters lagoon-calm. The swimming area is roped off. Waters are warm; the bottom is sandy and shallow.

*Sand:* Fine, gray sand covers a wide beach edged in low dunes anchored by sea grape trees, railroad vines, and sea oats.

*Amenities:* Rest rooms, outdoor showers, boardwalks, picnic shelters with grills at south end, food and beach concessions, plus a historic site. No lifeguard.

*Sports:* Foot and bike paths wind through the park. Fishermen favor the bay side. No sports concessions.

*Parking:* Several paved parking lots. Parking is free, but it costs $3 per car, or $1 per biker or pedestrian, to enter the park.

# HOTELS/INNS/B&Bs

◆ **Mayfair House** (very expensive). Classically baroque and individual in style, it is the ultimate in luxury. Its 182 suites feature balconies and Japanese spa tubs. The lobby and dining room are richly dressed in dark wood and artistically embellished. It connects to a deluxe shopping center. *3000 Florida Ave., Coconut Grove, FL 33133; tel. 305-441-0000, 800-433-4555. On the mainland, head south of Rickenbacker Causeway on Bayshore Dr. Turn right on McFarlane Rd., and left on Grand Ave. Florida Ave. is one block north.*

◆ **Sonesta Beach Resort** (very expensive). A newly restored destination resort complete with all the pertinent amenities: 300 rooms and suites, great restaurants, pool, Jacuzzi, tiki bar, tennis, kids' program, shops, fitness center, and gorgeous beach. Ask for an ocean-view room, from which you can watch beach and ship action. Avoid rooms ending in 01, 02, and 04: They're close to the elevator and noisy. *350 Ocean Dr., Key Biscayne, FL 33149; tel. 305-361-2021, 800-766-3782; fax 305-361-3096. From Crandon Blvd., turn east on East Dr., which merges with Ocean Dr.*

◆ **Silver Sands Beach Resort** (expensive). Recovering nicely from the 1992 hurricane's demolishing blow, its 53 minisuites and cottages are newly outfitted with kitchenettes and tropical accoutrements. Cottages and oceanfront units are nicest, but run in the very expensive range. Prettily landscaped, the property follows the beach and has a swimming pool and beach bar. *301 Ocean Dr., Key Biscayne, FL 33149; tel. 305-361-5441; fax 305-361-5477. From Crandon Blvd., turn east on East Dr. and follow it to Ocean Dr.*

◆ **Hampton Inn** (moderate). For more-affordable lodging, drive just off the island to this well-run franchise hotel. Rates include continental breakfast. Swimming pool. *2500 Brickell Ave., Miami, FL 33129; tel. 305-854-2070, 800-426-7866; fax 305-854-2070.*

# HOUSE RENTALS

There are homes to rent seasonally on Key Biscayne, but like other lodging options, they're high-end. Rates start at $2,000 a month, and the sky's the limit. All rentals for a period of less than six months are taxed at 12 1/2 percent.

◆ **Key Biscayne Realty.** *22 Crandon Blvd., Key Biscayne, FL 33149; tel.*

*305-361-0179, 305-361-8800. Open Mon.-Sat.; 24-hr. phone.*

# RESTAURANTS

◆ **Purple Dolphin** (expensive). Ask for a seat in the atrium when you make reservations. The menu perfects fine continental and "Floribbean" (regional, with Cuban and Caribbean influences) cuisine. Try the beef medallions or the grilled shrimp and scallops with risotto: Both are magnificent. Friday's all-you-can-eat seafood buffet is popular. On Wednesday, "Italian night," you design your own dishes and are entertained by opera singers. *Sonesta Beach Resort, 350 Ocean Dr., Key Biscayne, FL 33149; tel. 305-361-2021. Open daily for breakfast, lunch, and dinner.*

◆ **Rusty Pelican** (expensive). A sweeping view of Biscayne Bay lightens the otherwise dark wood-and-rock interior. It looks casually ramshackle from the outside, but inside it's actually dressy. Wandering minstrels entertain. On Sundays, crowds wait in line for the sumptuous brunch buffet. House specialties include veal saltimbocca and curried shrimp or chicken. *3201 Rickenbacker Causeway, Key Biscayne, FL 33149; tel. 305-361-3818. Open Mon.-Sat. for lunch and dinner; Sun. for brunch and dinner.*

◆ **Café Tu Tu Tango** (moderate). Sheer success at presenting a fresh approach to dining has propelled this Coconut Grove original to two spin-offs elsewhere in the United States. Food is served tapas-style, which means in appetizer portions—to allow eclectic grazing through a menu filled with internationally inspired finger foods. Try the *ropa vieja* pizza for a taste of local Cuban-infused nouvelle cuisine. The decor's theme is "starving artist": The loftlike setting features brush pots holding flatware, wooden palettes holding pizzas, and local artists painting daily. Ask for a porch table so you can watch the action. *3015 Grand Ave., Coconut Grove, FL 33133; tel. 305-529-2222. Open daily for lunch and dinner. In the CocoWalk shopping/entertainment complex. From the Rickenbacker Causeway, head south on Bayshore Dr. Turn right on McFarlane Rd. and left on Grand Ave.*

◆ **Señor Frog's** (moderate). This restaurant serves all the Mexican classics, and some of its own homemade specialties, in fine style. The combination platters are a good way to sample the variety. Recommended: the *carne asada* and the custard. The garden patio is most relaxing. *3008 Grand Ave., Coconut Grove, FL 33133; tel. 305-448-0999. Open daily for lunch and dinner. Take Bayshore Dr. south off Rickenbacker Causeway. Turn right on McFarlane Rd. and left on Grand Ave.*

# NIGHTLIFE

The best nightlife lies off the island. The celebrated after-dark scene in Miami South Beach (*see* Chapter 19) is less than a half-hour away. Coconut Grove, about seven miles from Key Biscayne, is closer and a bit tamer.

◆ **Coconut Grove Playhouse.** This historic Spanish rococo-style movie theater was refurbished to stage comedies, innovative productions, and world premieres featuring major-name actors. *3500 Main Hwy., Coconut Grove, FL 33133; tel. 305-442-4000. Open daily; closed in summer. Call for schedule. Admission. From Rickenbacker Causeway, head south on Bayshore Dr. Turn right on McFarlane Rd. and left on Main Hwy.*

◆ **CocoWalk.** A shopping/entertainment complex containing a sports bar, comedy club, dance club, and eight-screen movie theater. *3015 Grand Ave., Coconut Grove, FL 33133; tel. 305-444-0777. Open daily 24 hours. Head south of Rickenbacker Causeway on Bayshore Dr. Turn right on McFarlane Rd. and left on Grand Ave.*

◆ **Hungry Sailor.** Part English pub, part Caribbean rum shop, it features rock and reggae bands behind a somewhat rundown storefront. A nightlife classic. *3064 Grand Ave., Coconut Grove, FL 33133; tel. 305-444-9359. Open daily. Head south from Rickenbacker Causeway on Bayshore Dr. Turn right on McFarlane Rd. and left on Grand Ave.*

◆ **Monty's.** Calypso bands, DJs, and fire-eaters entertain in lively fashion in a tropical bayfront setting. *2550 S. Bayshore Dr., Coconut Grove, FL 33133; tel. 305-858-1431. Open daily. From the Rickenbacker Causeway, head south on Bayshore Dr.*

◆ **Tobacco Road.** Miami's oldest bar. Pub-crawlers love it for its blues, jazz, and name-band live entertainment. Serious Scotch drinkers are devoted to its menu of single-malt whiskeys. Then there's its renowned chili. Funky and always fun. *626 S. Miami Ave., Miami, FL 33131; tel. 305-374-1198. Bar/club open daily. Open Mon.-Fri. for lunch; daily for dinner. Admission. One block west of Hwy. 1.*

# ATTRACTIONS

♦ **Miami Seaquarium.** Home of TV-star Flipper, it also keeps more than 10,000 other marine creatures—including a killer whale, sharks, manatees, sea turtles, and crocodiles, not to mention exotic birds and tropical reptiles. There are continuous performances, as well as a tidal pool exhibit. *4400 Rickenbacker Causeway, Key Biscayne, FL 33149; tel. 305-361-5705. Open daily 9:30-6. Admission. On Virginia Key, where Crandon Blvd. becomes Rickenbacker Causeway.*

♦ **Museum of Science.** Extensive hands-on exhibits, a renowned planetarium, a wildlife center, an aviary, and a natural history center are among the offerings. *3280 S. Miami Ave., Miami, FL 33129; tel. 305-854-4247. Open daily 10-6. Box office closes at 5. Admission. On the mainland, head south of Rickenbacker Causeway on Hwy. 1. Take a left on Miami Ave.*

♦ **Vizcaya Museum and Gardens.** Miami's cultural pride: an Italian Renaisssance-style castle with spectacular architectural features, art, and furnishings from the 15th through the 19th centuries. Industrialist James Deering built it and created the ten acres of formal gardens and fountains. Go there for a peaceful, tropical respite from the city. *3251 S. Miami Ave., Miami, FL 33129; tel. 305-250-9133. Open daily 9:30-4:30. Admission. Turn south on Hwy. 1, west of the Rickenbacker Causeway. Take a quick left on Miami Ave.*

# SHOPPING

Key Biscayne has some interesting shops, but the best local shopping lies a few minutes off-island in trend-setting Coconut Grove. Once a hippie haven, then abandoned, it has perked up nicely in recent decades with renowned restaurants and wonderfully browsable shopping centers. The most popular are CocoWalk, at Virginia Street and Grand Avenue, and the Mayfair Shops nearby.

◆ **Island Shop.** Gifts for the home and the person, including Crabtree & Evelyn toiletries, Portmeiron dishware, and Crane stationery. *Key Biscayne Shopping Center, 654 Crandon Blvd., Key Biscayne, FL 33149; tel. 305-361-1389. Open Mon.-Sat.*

◆ **J. W. Cooper.** Here's where to buy your genuine alligator-hide cowboy boots and belt and other Western apparel. *CocoWalk, 3015 Grand Ave., Coconut Grove, FL 33133; tel. 305-441-1380. Open daily.*

◆ **Maya Hatcha.** A holdover from the Grove's hippie days, it sells incense, New Age stuff, free-spirited clothes, and Oriental and South American objets d'art. *3058 Grand Ave., Coconut Grove, FL 33133; tel. 305-446-0921. Open daily. Head south on Bayshore Dr. from Rickenbacker Causeway. Turn right on McFarlane Rd. and left on Grand Ave.*

◆ **Tabaqueria.** Watch cigars being hand-rolled while you shop for fine tobacco products. *3390 Virginia St., Suite 670, Coconut Grove, FL 33133; tel. 305-446-4003. Open daily. Inside the Mayfair House hotel.*

◆ **Valerio Antiques.** Specializing in lamps, furniture, glassware, and art. *Mayfair Shops, 3390 Mary St., Suite 136, Coconut Grove, FL 33133; tel. 305-448-6779. Open daily.*

◆ **Yaga Ragz.** Color-splashed cool rayon and cotton fashions for men and women, dreadlock tams, sunglasses, jewelry. *CocoWalk, 3015 Grand Ave., No. 110, Coconut Grove, FL 33133; tel. 305-442-0656. Open daily.*

# BEST FOOD SHOPS

**SANDWICHES:** ◆ **Stefano's Deli.** *24 Crandon Blvd., Key Biscayne, FL 33149; tel. 305-361-7007. Open daily.*

**SEAFOOD:** ◆ **Chief's Seafood.** *328 Crandon Blvd., Key Biscayne, FL 33149; tel. 305-361-2499. Open daily.*

**FRESH PRODUCE:** ◆ **Winn-Dixie.** *604 Crandon Blvd., Key Biscayne, FL 33149; tel. 305-361-8261. Open daily.*

**BAKERY:** ◆ **La Boulangerie.** *328 Crandon Blvd., Key Biscayne, FL 33149; tel. 305-361-0281. Open daily.*

**ICE CREAM:** ◆ **Alaska Yogurt.** *328 Crandon Blvd., Suite 110, Key Biscayne, FL 33149; tel. 305-361-8282. Open daily.*
**BEVERAGES:** ◆ **Stefano's Package Store.** *24 Crandon Blvd., Key Biscayne, FL 33149; tel. 305-361-7007. Open daily.*
**WINE:** ◆ **Stefano's Package Store.** *24 Crandon Blvd., Key Biscayne, FL 33149; tel. 305-361-7007. Open daily.*

# SPORTS
## FISHING

◆ **Chief's Seafood.** Sells bait. *328 Crandon Blvd., Key Biscayne, FL 33149; tel. 305-361-2499. Open daily.*
◆ **Reel Time Sport Fishing.** Fishing charters. *2560 S. Bayshore Dr., Coconut Grove, FL 33133; tel. 305-856-5605. Open daily.*

## BOATING

◆ **Biscayne America Company.** Custom boating, fishing, and sailing excursions for groups of any size. *Mailing address: 9401 S.W. 78th St., Miami, FL 33130; tel. 305-857-9000; fax 305-857-9000. Open daily. At Dinner Key Marina. Take Bayshore Dr. south of Rickenbacker Causeway.*
◆ **Celebration Excursions of Miami.** Cruises aboard a 92-foot luxury yacht depart from Coconut Grove for lunch, dinner, or cocktails. *3239 W. Trade Ave., Suite 9, Coconut Grove, FL 33133; tel. 305-445-8456; fax 305-442-9784. Open daily.*
◆ **Club Nautico.** Rents boats for skiing, sightseeing, and fishing. *Crandon Marina, 5420 Crandon Blvd., Key Biscayne, FL 33149; tel. 305-361-9217. Open daily.*
◆ **Flyer Sailing Tours.** Sunset and full-day sailing excursions aboard a 65-passenger catamaran. *Miami Seaquarium Yacht Basin, 4400 Rickenbacker Causeway, Miami, FL 33149; tel. 305-361-3611. Open daily.*
◆ **Sailboats of Key Biscayne.** Sailing school, rentals. *4000 Crandon Blvd., Key Biscayne, FL 33149; tel. 305-361-0328. Open daily. At Crandon Marina.*

## SURFING

The Miami area is not really known for its surfing, but rough days bring out the board-toters anyway, particularly to either end of Key Biscayne.

◆ **Catch A Wave.** Surfing equipment and boards for sale. *2990 McFarlane Rd., Coconut Grove, FL 33133; tel. 305-569-0339. Open daily. Head south on Bayshore Dr. from Rickenbacker Causeway. Turn right on McFarlane Rd.*

## DIVING

Diving and snorkeling charters typically take you to the rich marine life waters in Biscayne National Park, south of Key Biscayne in Biscayne Bay. Not far from the island also lies an artificial reef created from a 727 aircraft.

◆ **Diver's Paradise.** Introductory and full certification courses; charters to wrecks and reefs. *Crandon Marina, 4000 Crandon Blvd., Key Biscayne, FL 33149; tel. 305-361-3483. Open daily.*

## BICYCLING

Bike paths line Crandon Boulevard and loop through Bill Baggs Cape Florida State Recreation Area on the island. There are more bike trails in David T. Kennedy Park on Bayshore Boulevard, between Key Biscayne and Coconut Grove on Bayshore Drive.

◆ **Spokes.** Rents quality biking gear. *3488 Main Hwy., Coconut Grove, FL 33133; tel. 305-529-1688. Open daily.*

## GOLF

◆ **Links at Key Biscayne.** Championship 18 holes and lighted driving range in Crandon Park. *6700 Crandon Blvd., Key Biscayne, FL 33149; tel. 305-361-9129. Open daily. Admission.*

## TENNIS

◆ **Calusa Park Tennis Center.** *Crandon Blvd., Key Biscayne, FL 33149; tel. 305-361-2215. Open daily. Admission.*

◆ **Tennis Center at Crandon Park.** The new octagon-shaped stadium hosts the Lipton Championships. The public can play on the center's 17 hard, 8 clay, and 2 grass courts. *7300 Crandon Blvd., Key Biscayne, FL 33149; tel. 305-365-2300. Open daily. Admission.*

# HISTORY

◆ **Cape Florida Lighthouse.** Built in 1825, it's the oldest structure in South Florida. Hurricane Andrew badly battered it in 1992, so it's not tourable now, but renovations are being done. Projected completion date is 1996. *Cape Florida State Recreation Area, 1200 Crandon Blvd., Key Biscayne, FL 33149; tel. 305-361-5811. Admission.*

◆ **The Barnacle.** Tour the unusual 1891 cone-shaped home of a Coconut Grove founding father, Commodore Ralph Middleton Munroe. *3485 Main Hwy., Coconut Grove, FL 33133; tel. 305-448-9445. Open Fri.-Sun. 9-4; tours at 10, 11:30, 1, and 2:30. Call for group tours Mon.-Thu. Admission. Across from Coconut Grove Playhouse. Head south of Rickenbacker Causeway on Bayshore Dr. Turn right on McFarlane Rd. and left on Main Hwy.*

# NATURE

◆ **Marjory Stoneman Douglas Biscayne Nature Center.** A research and educational facility concerned with loggerhead turtles, it gives beach and facility tours by prior arrangement. *4000 Crandon Blvd., Key Biscayne, FL 33149; tel. 305-642-9600. Open by appointment. In Crandon Park.*

# SAFETY TIPS

The $1 toll at the Rickenbacker Causeway and parking/entry fees at the beaches abate the presence of less-savory types at Key Biscayne beaches. Nonetheless, they are part of a big city with big-city problems, some of which the media has overblown. Do be careful, in any case, on and off the island. Lock your car at the beach. Travel only familiar roads after dark, and resist antagonizing drivers in other cars.

# TOURIST INFORMATION

◆ **Coconut Grove Chamber of Commerce.** *2820 McFarlane Rd., Coconut Grove, FL 33133; tel. 305-444-7270; fax 305-444-2498. Open Mon.-Fri. 9-5.*

◆ **Greater Miami Convention & Visitors Bureau.** *701 Brickell Ave., Suite 2700, Miami, FL 33131; tel. 305-539-3063, 800-283-2707; fax 305-539-3113. Open Mon.-Fri. 8:30-6. Downtown, on Hwy. 1.*
◆ **Key Biscayne Chamber of Commerce.** *604 Crandon Blvd. #205, Key Biscayne Shopping Center, Key Biscayne, FL 33149; tel. 305-361-5207; fax 305-361-9411. Open Mon.-Fri. 9-2.*

## CHAPTER 19

# Miami South Beach

**M**iami is a montage of human elements, most strongly influenced by the New York and Jewish visitors of its earliest heyday in tourism, and by the Caribbean and Hispanic influx of more recent times.

The islands of Miami Beach are a microcosm of Miami culture. Like an urbanite struggling to stand out among the throngs by dressing and acting outrageously, South Beach, at the southern end of Miami Beach, has of late adopted a personality and reputation all its own: ultra-fashionable, yet attainable. A collision of the

| | |
|---|---|
| Beauty | A- |
| Swimming | B |
| Sand | B |
| Hotels/Inns/B&Bs | A |
| House rentals | D |
| Restaurants | A- |
| Nightlife | A+ |
| Attractions | A |
| Shopping | A+ |
| Sports | A+ |
| Nature | C- |

chic and the decadent, SoBe (as it's called) takes from the richness of old beach development and the slickness of the new. Its age and glorious past give it dimension.

Developed in the 1930s as a haven for the winter-weary, it declined in intervening years. The glamorous headed north to Miami Beach's more recently developed resorts, such as Fontainebleau and Eden Roc. South Beach and its Art Deco treasures were earmarked for the bulldozer until preservationists and painters stepped in to turn the neighborhood into a fantasy land at the edge of the ocean—and of reality.

On fast-paced Ocean Drive, fashion models, movie stars, drag queens, rollerbladers, and the merely curious make the scene from noon 'til dawn. Low-rise Art Deco hotels hold shops, recording studios, sidewalk cafes, and bars at street level. In early morning, street people come to sift through the trash bins for treasures to add to their shopping-cart homes. Washington Avenue keeps the midnight momentum going with its night-clubs and more affordable restaurants. Española Way intersects with Washington, adding its Spanish flavor to the neighbor-hood. Lincoln Road resurrects SoBe's reputation for shopping. All lie contained within the square-mile designated Art Deco Historic District that has propelled South Beach's reputation to a status compared variously to St. Tropez, SoHo, Tangier, and L.A.'s Venice Beach. Don't come for a quiet, relaxing resort vacation. Come for seductive, swinging, trendy fun. It's like spring break for grown-ups.

# OCEAN BEACHES
## PIER/SOUTH POINTE PARK

This urban park actually encompasses two beaches that flank the Miami Beach Pier on this southernmost, less fashionable end of South Beach. Despite its urban locale, the park is green with sea grape trees and grass. Around it, low-profile buildings dis-

| | |
|---|---|
| Beauty | A- |
| Swimming | B |
| Sand | B |
| Amenities | A- |

## HOW TO GET THERE

◆ From Miami International Airport, take LeJeune Rd. south to Rte. 836 east (toll), to merge with I-395. This becomes Rte. A1A and crosses MacArthur Causeway to South Beach. Continue east on Rte. A1A as it becomes Fifth St.; follow Fifth to Ocean Dr. At Ocean Dr., turn right to reach the quiet part of South Beach; left to head into the traffic jam known as SoBe. (Because traffic moves at a crawl most of the day, and parking is hard to come by, many visitors take taxis in and out of South Beach.)

tort the view slightly, but the park is kept clean. The park extends around the island's south end to the fishing pier and South Pointe Park, providing a good vantage point for watching cruise ships enter and leave. Much quieter here than to the north. *Open 5-midnight. South of Fifth St. on Ocean Dr., and around the island's south end via Biscayne St.*

*Swimming:* Slurping waves roll gently, but the bottom is fairly steep. Water temperatures average 74 degrees year-round.

*Sand:* The beach is long and quite wide, and covered with coarse, salt-and-pepper sand. Coconuts, small sticks, shells, and other natural debris.

*Amenities:* Rest rooms, outdoor showers, lifeguards, restaurants. At South Pointe, there are picnic shelters, grills, playground, exercise course. Shops and hotels nearby.

*Sports:* The fishing pier at the end is a popular spot from which to cast. Water-sports rentals nearby.

*Parking:* Meters on Ocean Drive run 15 minutes for 25 cents; three hour maximum. $3-per-day parking lot at South Pointe Park (entrance on Biscayne Street).

## SOUTH BEACH

Also known as Lummus Park, this stretch of spacious beach between Fifth and 14th streets has been crowned the St. Tropez of Florida. Everyone—families, topless European models, Jewish grandmothers—meets on the sand. The backdrop is

| | |
|---|---|
| **Beauty** | B+ |
| **Swimming** | B |
| **Sand** | B |
| **Amenities** | A+ |

candy-store pretty: a picturesque lineup of pastel Art Deco buildings. The seaward view looks upon Port of Miami's ship traffic. The wide beach has a Caribbean flavor, with lifeguard shacks painted in festive colors. Play areas are set up in a wide sand court off the beach. At Eighth Street is Asher Beach, a segment of South Beach set off by Asher sculptures—a gift from the people of Israel to the people of South Beach. There's a covered sitting pavilion here, where people read and loiter. *On Ocean Dr. between Fifth and 14th Sts.*

*Swimming:* The water is clear and calm, but a bit deep right off the beach. Tar balls are a problem in this area.

*Sand:* Yards and yards of coarse grayish sand varies from hard-packed toward the land, to deep and plush toward the sea. Low dunes are covered with sea grasses. Shells and seaweed wash up at the water line. Wear shoes; the sand gets very hot.

*Amenities:* Rest rooms, outdoor showers, playgrounds, food and beach concessions, lifeguards.

*Sports:* Rollerblading is SoBe's trademark sport. They not only skate along the wide sidewalks on the beach, but down the center line of streets. Volleyball nets are everywhere. So are water-sports rentals: wave runners, Windsurfers, paddleboats, parasailers, sailboats, and other toys. Joggers like the hard-packed western edge of the beach.

*Parking:* Parking is a real problem. Metered spots on Ocean Drive stay filled. Municipal lots charge $4 to $6 per day. Try those at 13th and 16th Streets off Ocean Drive.

# HOTELS/INNS/B&Bs

In the past decade, South Beach's reputation has risen: It is now considered an artsy, singular, swinging kind of place. It all happened because of a movement to restore the beachfront's seedy Art Deco buildings, which had fallen from grace to become little more than flophouses. With their radial corners, porthole windows, neon signs, and artistic embellishments, they begged for salvation. The result was stunning: a kingdom of candy-land colors that magically transformed the neighborhood into top-trend. All listings on Ocean Drive are across the street from the beach.

◆ **Casa Grande** (very expensive). Pure luxury with European overtones in its studios and one- and two-bedroom suites. Mini-bar and coffee service in every room. *834 Ocean Dr., Miami Beach, FL 33139; tel. 305-672-7003, 800-688-7678; fax 305-673-3669.*

◆ **Cavalier** (expensive). African batiks cover furniture and accent walls, the paint job looks like a crayon factory explosion, and the furniture and facade are straight out of the 1930s. Cavalier is a class act, with more amenities and service than at some of the older Art Deco hotels. Ask for an oceanfront studio: They're a bit more expensive than the regular rooms, but the beach view

**193**

is worth it. *1330 Ocean Dr., Miami Beach, FL 33139; tel. 305-534-2135, 800-688-7678; fax 305-531-5543.*

◆ **Colony Hotel** (expensive). One of Ocean Drive's grande dames, it defines its Art Deco sleekness with polished marble, aluminum, and neon. All top chic, with better service than you find at many of its counterparts. 36 rooms. Continental breakfast included; American plan available. *736 Ocean Dr., Miami Beach, FL 33139; tel. 305-673-0088, 800-226-5669.*

◆ **Leslie** (expensive). Bright yellow and white on the outside, inside the rooms do a Caribbean routine with Jell-O colors and perky designs. It has a youthful spirit that spills into its sidewalk cafe. Each of its 44 rooms comes with minibar, TV, VCR, and cassette player. Built in 1937, it's a standout in the Art Deco Historic District. *1244 Ocean Dr., Miami Beach, FL 33139; tel. 800-688-7678, 305-534-2135; fax 305-531-5543.*

◆ **Penguin Hotel** (moderate). A bit out of the flurry of things on Ocean Drive, it offers Art Deco ambience with no frills. Its 44 beach-view rooms are small but clean and modern. Complimentary breakfast. *1418 Ocean Dr., Miami Beach, FL 33139; tel. 305-534-9334, 800-235-3296; fax 305-672-6240.*

◆ **Clay Hotel & Hostel International** (inexpensive). The best deal on South Beach: Near the galleries and shops of Española Way, and full of historic memories and Spanish architecture. Hostel nonmembers welcome. *1438 Washington Ave., Miami Beach, FL 33139; tel. 305-534-2988; fax 305-673-0346.*

# RESTAURANTS

On Ocean Drive, sidewalk cafes spill from Art Deco hotels chock-a-block. Most of these are so-so, and come and go with the whims of the flighty clientele. A few persevere. They are reasonably priced for the most part, but the service leaves something to be desired. Much of the service staff consists of would-be models waiting to be discovered. On the positive side, the experience is fraught with the sheer entertainment of people-watching and being seen. For something more down-to-earth, get off the strip. Most places add service gratuities to the check.

Miami is the birthplace of the state's so-called "Floribbean" cuisine, a zesty marriage of island and peninsula food traditions. For the region's best restaurants, including Mark's Place, Chef Allen's, and Yuca, you have to go outside of South Beach.

◆ **Larios on the Beach** (moderate). Partly owned by Miami singer Gloria Estefan, this is the latest oh-so-trendy spot to be seen. Classic Cuban is the theme. *820 Ocean Dr., Miami Beach, FL 33139; tel. 305-532-9577. Open daily for lunch and dinner.*

◆ **News Cafe** (moderate). One that has endured at the top of the SoBe popularity list, it serves a wide range of fashionable dishes alfresco, outside an indoor newsstand. Specialties range from *paté au poivre* to cold meatloaf plate. Fine wines, cognacs, scotches, ports, and sherries. Good place to go for breakfast, when it's easiest to get a table there. *800 Ocean Dr., Miami Beach, FL 33149; tel. 305-531-0392. Open daily, 24 hours, for breakfast, lunch, and dinner.*

◆ **Puerto Sagua** (moderate). For a genuine Cuban restaurant experience, sit at the counter or in the spacious dining room at Puerto Sagua. The extensive menu offers Cuban sandwiches (ham, pork, and cheese on Cuban bread) and traditional dinners. Seafood is its specialty; some dishes are in the expensive range. *700 Collins Ave., Miami Beach, FL 33139; tel. 305-673-1115. Open daily for breakfast, lunch, and dinner.*

◆ **Tap Tap Haitian Restaurant** (inexpensive). Grilled conch, fish, and chicken, and authentic folk stews of goat, chicken, or vegetables dominate the menu of South Beach's colorful corner of Haitian culture. *819 Fifth St., Miami Beach, FL 33139; tel. 305-672-2898. Open daily for lunch and dinner; closed Mon. Jul.-Aug.*

# NIGHTLIFE

The question is: Where *isn't* there nightlife in South Beach? Washington Avenue, in particular, comes to life after midnight, as the mobs make their way to the current top clubs. Some cater to gays, some to X-rated fantasies; many specialize in alternative rock and the music of South Beach, defined by resident recording studios as a cross-breed of Caribbean, Latin, and funk. *For up-to-date entertainment information, call 305-358-*

*8000, ext. 9393, or 800-237-0939.*

◆ **Bayside Marketplace.** Street performers, bandstand musicians, and nightclubs such as Hard Rock Cafe draw nightlifers. *401 Biscayne Blvd., Miami, FL 33132; tel. 305-577-3344. Open daily. Less than 5 mi. from South Beach. Cross MacArthur Causeway back to the mainland and exit onto Hwy. 1 south.*

◆ **Club Amnesia.** Known for its avant-garde Mediterranean decor and open-sky discotheque, it also hosts live contemporary and alternative musicians. *136 Collins Ave., Miami Beach, FL 33139; tel. 305-531-5535. Open daily except Mon. and Wed. Admission.*

◆ **Colony Theatre.** A 1930s original, reopened in 1986 as a center for theater, dance, and music. *1040 Lincoln Rd., Miami Beach, FL 33139; tel. 305-674-1026. Information line open daily 24 hours; call for performance schedule. Admission.*

◆ **Jackie Gleason Theatre of the Performing Arts.** Stages Broadway hits, as well as visiting performances. *1700 Washington Ave., Miami Beach, FL 33139; tel. 305-673-7300. Box office open Mon.-Fri. Performance schedule varies. Admission.*

◆ **Mango's Cafe.** The partying spills into the street. A Cuban-spiced band entertains. *900 Ocean Dr., Miami Beach, FL 33139; tel. 305-673-4422. Open daily.*

# ATTRACTIONS

◆ **Bass Museum of Art.** Paintings, sculptures, textiles, objets d'art, and ecclesiastic pieces. *2121 Park Ave., Miami Beach, FL 33139; tel. 305-673-7533. Open Tue.-Sat. 10-5; Sun. 1-5. Admission.*

◆ **Holocaust Memorial.** *1933-1945 Meridian Ave., Miami Beach, FL 33139; tel. 305-538-1663. Open daily 9-9. Across from the Miami Beach Chamber of Commerce at the Dade Blvd. bridge.*

# SHOPPING

As a shopping arena, South Beach reassumes its early 1930s position as Florida's best. Lincoln Road Mall is blocked for pedestrians. Its scope ranges from discount dollar stores to electronics shops to fine art galleries (the west end). Shops along lovely Ocean Boulevard and its side streets reflect its fashion-model status. Washington Avenue has more-pedestrian wares to offer. Just off the island, Bayside Marketplace, on Biscayne Boulevard (Highway 1) just south of MacArthur Causeway, parades its festive atmosphere of shopping and entertainment along the waterfront. Parking is at a premium no matter where you shop in the area.

◆ **Art By God.** Museum-like collection of things from the ground. Spend as little as $1 for a quartz rock, or as much as $45,000 for the skeleton of an extinct cave bear. Fossils, onyx carvings, Mayan artifacts, and fossilized bones. *Bayside Marketplace, 401 Biscayne Blvd., Miami, FL 33132; tel. 305-573-3011. Open daily.*

◆ **Ba-Balú.** Española Way is the heart of South Beach's Cuban community. Ba-Balú sells cigars, Cuban coffee, and Cuban nationalist souvenirs. *432 Española Way, Miami Beach, FL 33139; tel. 305-538-0679. Open daily.*

◆ **Barbara Gillman Gallery.** The most renowned art showroom on Lincoln Road. Its exhibits are permanent and temporary, representing a variety of media and styles. *939 Lincoln Rd., Miami Beach, FL 33139; tel. 305-534-7872. Open daily. Closed Sun.-Mon. Jun.-Oct.*

◆ **Books & Books.** Good selection of books about Art Deco, Cuba, Miami, and art, as well as for kids. Also sells pastries and espresso. *933 Lincoln Rd., Miami Beach, FL 33139; tel. 305-532-3222. Open daily.*

◆ **Heres Gift Center.** Symbolic of South Beach's mesh of the tacky and the tasteful, it is stuffed with glittering kitsch souvenirs, Oriental objets d'art, and fine porcelain. *437 Lincoln Rd., Miami Beach, FL 33139; tel. 305-532-7633; fax 305-673-3633. Open Sun.-Fri.*

◆ **Island Trading Company.** Imported fashions, fabrics, music, and home-decor art, including African batiks. *1332 Ocean Dr., Miami Beach, FL 33139; tel. 305-673-6300. Open daily. At the Netherlands Hotel.*

◆ **Silvery Moon.** Incense, jewelry, cards, and New Age paraphernalia. *825 Washington Ave., Miami Beach, FL 33139; tel. 305-532-1824. Open daily.*

◆ **South Florida Art Center.** This complex established Lincoln

Road as Miami's emerging-artists quarter by offering affordable studio and gallery space. It still anchors the visual arts in South Beach with permanent and changing displays. *924 Lincoln Rd., Miami Beach, FL 33139; tel. 305-674-8278. Call for hours.*

# BEST FOOD SHOPS

**SANDWICHES:** ◆ **Compass Market.** *860 Ocean Dr., Miami Beach, FL 33139; tel. 305-673-5890. Open daily.*

**SEAFOOD:** ◆ **Dockside Fresh Fish.** *1020 MacArthur Causeway, Miami Beach, FL 33132; tel. 305-377-3474. Open daily.*

**FRESH PRODUCE:** ◆ **Fernandez Fruit Corporation.** *1407 Washington Ave., Miami Beach, FL 33139; tel. 305-531-6403. Open daily.*

**BAKERY:** ◆ **Lyon Freres èt Compagnie.** *600 Lincoln Rd., Miami Beach, FL 33139; tel. 305-534-0600. Open daily.*

**ICE CREAM:** ◆ **TCBY.** *1052 Ocean Dr., Miami Beach, FL 33139; tel. 305-534-8989. Open daily.*

**BEVERAGES:** ◆ **Compass Market.** *860 Ocean Dr., Miami Beach, FL 33139; tel. 305-673-5890. Open daily.*

**WINE:** ◆ **Lyon Freres èt Compagnie.** *600 Lincoln Rd., Miami Beach, FL 33139; tel. 305-534-0600. Open daily.*

# SPORTS

## FISHING

◆ **Reward II Drift Fishing.** Fishing charters. *300 Alton Rd., Miami Beach Marina, Miami Beach, FL 33139; tel. 305-372-9470. Open daily. South of MacArthur Causeway.*

◆ **Ship & Shore Marine Store.** Sells fishing licenses and tackle. *541 West Ave., Miami Beach, FL 33139; tel. 305-534-4137. Open daily. North of MacArthur Causeway on West Ave.*

◆ **Watson Island Fuel & Fishing Supplies.** Fishing tackle and bait. *1050 MacArthur Causeway, Miami Beach, FL 33132; tel. 305-371-2378. Open daily.*

## BOATING

◆ **Beach Boat Rentals.** Rent a powerboat for just an hour or a day. *2380 Collins Ave., Miami Beach, FL 33139; tel. 305-534-4307. Open daily except Wed.*

◆ **Cigarette Powerboat Charter.** Take a fast ride through local waterways on high-performance powerboats. *401 Ocean Dr., Suite 1104, Miami Beach, FL 33139; tel. 305-532-7223. Open daily. Boats leave from Miami Beach Marina at 300 Alton Rd.*

◆ **Island Queen Sightseeing Tours.** Gawk at the homes of the local illuminati and national stars, and the cruise ships in port. *Bayside Marketplace, 401 Biscayne Blvd., Miami, FL 33132; tel. 305-379-5119; fax 305-372-0186. Open daily.*

◆ **Kozy Charters.** Gaff-rigged schooner charters for lunch, snorkeling, and blue-water sailing. Complimentary bar. Reservations required. *344 Alton Rd., Box 6, Miami Beach, FL 33931; tel. 305-653-0591; fax 305-653-0597. Open daily.*

◆ **Romantic Gondola Rides.** *Gondola Adventures, Bayside Marketplace, 401 Biscayne Blvd., Miami, FL 33132; tel. 305-573-1818. Open daily.*

◆ **Schooner Heritage of Miami.** Tall-ship excursions past the homes of Miami Beach-area stars, including Sylvester Stallone, Madonna, and Bruce Willis and Demi Moore. *Bayside Marketplace, 401 Biscayne Blvd., Miami, FL 33132; tel. 305-442-9697. Open daily Sep.-May.*

◆ **Water Taxi.** Transports you by water throughout Miami, Miami Beach, Coconut Grove, and Key Biscayne. Taxis pick up at major hotels, attractions, marinas, and parks. *651 Seabreeze Rd., Ft. Lauderdale, FL 33316; tel. 305-467-6677. Open daily; call for schedule.*

## SURFING
◆ **X-Isle Surf Shop.** Surfboards and gear. *437 Washington Ave., Miami Beach, FL 33139; tel. 305-673-5900. Open daily.*

## BICYCLING
The Miami Design Preservation League sponsors Sunday morning bicycling tours of the Art Deco Historic District. The wide sidewalk along the beach is perfect for bicycling.

◆ **Cycles on the Beach.** Besides renting bicycles, this shop hosts a South Beach historic area bike tour every Sunday at 10:30. *1421 Washington Ave., Miami Beach, FL 33139; tel. 305-673-2055, 305-672-2014. Open daily.*

**199**

## GOLF

◆ **Bayshore Golf Course.** 18 holes with lighted driving range, putting green, pro shop, and restaurant. *2301 Alton Rd., Miami Beach, FL 33139; tel. 305-673-1576. Admission.*

## TENNIS

◆ **Bayshore Golf Course.** The golf course also has two tennis courts available on a first-come, first-served basis at no charge. *2301 Alton Rd., Miami Beach, FL 33139; tel. 305-673-1576. Open daily.*

◆ **Flamingo Park.** 19 clay courts (15 lighted) open to the public. *Jefferson Ave. and 12th St., Miami Beach, FL 33139; tel. 305-673-7761. Open daily. Admission.*

## IN-LINE SKATING

In-line skating is the emblematic sport of South Beach. Several places rent skates.

◆ **Skate 2000.** In-line skate rentals and instruction. *1200 Ocean Dr., Suite 102, Miami Beach, FL 33139; tel. 305-538-8282. Open daily. At 12th St.*

# HISTORY

Several organizations host historic walking tours of South Beach's Art Deco Historic District, a square mile of 800 circa-1930 buildings restored to pastel- and primary-color perkiness in the past few years. Most of these architectural gems have been reincarnated as hotels. For information, call the Miami Design Preservation League (*see* Tourist Information).

# SAFETY TIPS

You're in the big city, where crime is almost as bad as you've heard. Do all the right things and you'll be okay: Keep hotel and car doors locked, don't carry valuables, don't travel alone at night. While driving, stay in well-lighted areas, and resist being aggressive or confrontational. Stay in your car if you have problems.

# TOURIST INFORMATION

◆ **Greater Miami Convention & Visitors Bureau.** *701 Brickell Ave., Suite 2700, Miami, FL 33131; tel. 305-539-3000, 800-283-2707; fax 305-539-3113. Also operates a Visitors Center at Bayside Marketplace, 401 Biscayne Blvd., Miami, FL 33130; tel. 305-539-2982, Headquarters open Mon.-Fri. 8-6. Visitors Center open daily 9-5:30.*

◆ **Miami Beach Visitor Information Center.** *1920 Meridian Ave., Miami Beach, FL 33139; tel. 305-672-1270; fax 305-538-4336. Open Mon.-Fri. 8:30-6; Sat. 10-4. Lincoln Rd. information kiosk open Mon.-Fri. 9:30-4. Center is on Meridian Ave. at Dade Blvd. Bridge. Information kiosk is in Lincoln Rd. pedestrian mall at Washington Ave.*

◆ **Miami Design Preservation League.** Information on the Art Deco Historic District. The League operates an Art Deco Welcome Center at Ocean Front Auditorium on the beach. *1001 Ocean Dr., Miami Beach, FL 31339; tel. 305-531-3484 (Welcome Center), 305-672-2014 (League office); fax 305-672-4319. Welcome Center open daily 11-6. League office open Mon.-Fri. 9-5.*

## CHAPTER 20

# North Palm Beach

N orth of gold-plated Palm Beach, the coastline keeps its privileged air while reverting to the gentle peace of nature. At its southern extreme, it starts out somewhat pedestrian, with Riviera Beach's early-Florida personality. John D. MacArthur Park then reasserts nature's dominance with 225 acres of away-from-it-all beach, estuaries, and pristine loveliness. Juno Beach and Jupiter, at Palm Beach County's northernmost doorstep, associate themselves with Burt Reynolds, bluff-edged beaches, marina pas-

| | |
|---|---|
| Beauty | A- |
| Swimming | B |
| Sand | B+ |
| Hotels/Inns/B&Bs | B |
| House rentals | C |
| Restaurants | B+ |
| Nightlife | A |
| Attractions | A- |
| Shopping | A |
| Sports | A |
| Nature | B+ |

times, and quiet exclusivity. Route A1A threads the diverse communities of North Palm together in a lazy, scenic way. Seaside, it invites a slow, island attitude with a careful injection of metropolitan sophistication.

Its beaches are popular and fairly developed, but special in the way they spread wide or hide beneath ridges. Where A1A merges with Highway 1, strip malls wall the corridor and culture flips the coin to expose the other side of Palm Beach County vacationing. Tourist services leave you lacking nothing, and all restaurants are within a short drive of the beaches.

On the scale of urbanization, North Palm Beach lies, as it does geographically, between Fort Lauderdale and Hutchinson Island. Thankfully, its beaches and freeways are less crowded than many points south.

# OCEAN BEACHES
## JUPITER BEACHES

These beaches are fairly well-developed, and there's ongoing restoration work. Casuarinas provide shade in parts; sea grapes make pretty fringes.

| Beauty | B+ |
|---|---|
| Swimming | B+ |
| Sand | A |
| Amenities | A |

*Swimming:* Jupiter Beach Park's jetty keeps waters calm, but there are drop-offs. Swimming is prohibited in the Jupiter Inlet. Small waves and a gentle underwater slope please swimmers at Carlin Park.

*Sand:* Tawny and fine, replenished sand spreads a very wide, soft blanket at Carlin, which is scattered with shell fragments. Medium-sized dunes surround; the beach slopes rather steeply into the water from the high-tide mark. Jupiter Beach Park has lower dunes and a wide beach at its south end.

*Amenities:* Jupiter Beach Park's rest rooms, showers, lifeguards, and picnic areas are mostly concentrated at its southern end. Carlin Park has rest rooms and outdoor showers, a food concession, playgrounds, a baseball field, lots of picnic shelters with grills, and lifeguards.

*Sports:* Fishermen cast into the pass from the jetty and small pier at Jupiter Beach Park. Water sports are close by at the marina near Jupiter Beach Park.

*Parking:* Plenty of free parking along the beach and across the street.

## HOW TO GET THERE

◆ From Palm Beach International Airport, go east on Southern Blvd. (Hwy. 98) to I-95 and head north. Take exit 55 and turn right onto Blue Heron Blvd. (Rte. 708). It becomes Rte. A1A when it crosses the Riviera Bridge onto Singer Island; as A1A curves north, it passes Riviera Beach. Continue north along A1A (which merges with Hwy. 1 at times) to reach the other beaches.

## Jupiter Beach Park

A restoration project is working to improve this beach, which is currently less developed than Carlin Park. *Off Rte. A1A on Jupiter Beach Rd., just north of Rte. 706 (Indiantown Rd.).*

## Carlin Park

A full-service beach park where special events are staged both indoors, at the civic center, and outdoors. It's popular with weekending metropolites. The view to the north is pristine, but it's condo-cluttered to the south. The garbage smells up the picnic areas after busy weekends. *On A1A, just south of Rte. 706 (Indiantown Rd.).*

## JUNO BEACH BEACHES

Along a two-mile-long run of beach, several private and public foot accesses accommodate residents of the development on Route A1A. Some people park their cars roadside and use the foot entrances, despite signs warning "No

| Beauty | A- |
|---|---|
| Swimming | B |
| Sand | B+ |
| Amenities | A |

Parking." I watched a police car drive right by them without issuing tickets, but you're taking a chance nonetheless. There are also a couple of accesses with parking and rest rooms across the street. The two accesses listed below offer more-extensive amenities and better parking.

*Swimming:* Surf gets two to three feet high—and higher. At Juno Beach, rocks near the shore pose a danger.

*Sand:* The beach grows narrow in some spots, with hard-packed sand.

*Amenities:* Parks have facilities across Route A1A: rest rooms, showers, picnic shelters, and small playground areas. Lifeguards are on duty at times. Across Highway 1 from Loggerhead's parking, you'll find a strip of restaurants and shops.

*Sports:* Loggerhead is a good park for active beachers. It has a nature trail and tennis courts across the road from the beach. Surfing can be good anywhere when the waves are cooperating.

*Parking:* Lots of free paved parking across the street (Route A1A). Some angle-in parking along beach side of road. The entrance to the Loggerhead Beach parking lot and facilities is a block west of the beach access, on Highway 1.

## Juno Beach Park

High, grassy dunes hide beachers from traffic noise and views, though some buildings are visible to the south. It's less developed than Loggerhead Beach. *Located at 14775 Rte. A1A. Open 8-sunset.*

## Loggerhead Beach

Named for the turtles that nest in abundance here come summer, it takes its wildlife protection role seriously with nest-monitoring, a nature trail, and a wildlife education center. The park is large, with lots of picnic facilities (including grills) and carefully tended landscaping. On the beach, the sand apron widens here. Skirting a sheltering high dune ridge, the beach has a protected feel to it. *Large parking lot at 1200 Hwy. 1.*

## JOHN D. MACARTHUR PARK

For solitude and natural beauty, this is the champion beach of Florida's middle Atlantic beaches. To get to the beach, you walk or take a tram across a 1,600-foot boardwalk. Birds are rife amongst the mangroves. Nature trails lead to the

| Beauty | A+ |
| --- | --- |
| Swimming | B+ |
| Sand | B |
| Amenities | A- |

beach, with signs identifying native flora and fauna: golden orb spiders, gumbo limbo trees, Jamaica caper, and mastic trees. *Open 8-sunset. On Rte. A1A north of Palm Beach Shores.*

*Swimming:* The Atlantic's waves can be active so beware, unless you're a strong swimmer. (You can't swim in Lake Worth or Lake Worth Cove because there's no beach access.)

*Sand:* Left to nature's whims, this 8,000-foot-long beach changes regularly. Recently, it's been gnawed away by storms.

*Amenities:* Dune crossovers and showers on the beach; nature center, picnic areas, and rest rooms across the boardwalk bridge from the beach.

*Sports:* Fish in the Atlantic, Lake Worth, or Lake Worth Cove. Nature trails. No nearby water-sports concessions.

*Parking:* Admission to park is $3.25 per car; $1 per bicycle or pedestrian. Parking is free and ample.

## RIVIERA BEACH

One of the area's first public beaches, it is representative of how early beaches were developed: with beach strip malls and a hedonistic philosophy. A pink cement barrier separates an open sand courtyard from the street and shops. There's a vol-

| Beauty | B- |
| --- | --- |
| Swimming | B |
| Sand | B |
| Amenities | A |

leyball net and a broken swing set inside the courtyard. At the beach, water-sport and beach-rental concessions introduce the extremely wide sand skirt. The main beach is a hive of activity, but just to the south things are quieter and less crowded. *Open sunrise to sunset. On the southern portion of Singer Island, near intersection of Rte. A1A and Ocean Ave.*

*Swimming:* Calm, warm waters are good news for swimmers, but the bottom tapers off fairly quickly.

*Sand:* Medium dunes and coarse, tan sand make up the wide beach.

*Amenities:* Lifeguards, rest rooms, outdoor showers, and beach rentals on the beach. Restaurants, bars, and shops nearby.

*Sports:* You can rent Boogie and skim boards from a beach concession.

*Parking:* Limited metered parking along the street at 25 cents for 15 minutes; ten-hour maximum. Don't park in the mall lot to go to the beach: Policemen watch, and ticket those who do.

# HOTELS/INNS/B&Bs

**N**orth Palm Beach County's hotels are mostly of the chain variety, with some mom-and-pops and destination resorts thrown in for good measure. Rates are high-end: Ask about packages for more-economical options—especially if you're an avid golfer.

◆ **Embassy Suites** (very expensive). Families will love it here. The suites accommodate them with a bedroom and kitchen. The kids' program is top-notch, with outdoor activities, dinner parties, field trips, and a great indoor playroom. A restaurant with free short-order breakfast, and bar with free happy hour drinks figure into the cost. Its 257 suites maintain a low, pink profile along Singer Island's south-end secluded beach. To fill out your vacation schedule, there's tennis, a health club, water sports, and fishing charters. *181 Ocean Ave., Palm Beach Shores, FL 33404; tel. 407-863-4000.*

◆ **PGA National Resort & Spa** (very expensive). Home of the Professional Golfers Association, the resort community boasts a European spa, 19 tennis courts, and a lake beach, as well as its five 18-hole golf courses. Earthy tones decorate the 150-acre resort's 335 large guest rooms, 59 of them suites. There are also 85 two-bedroom suites with kitchens. *400 Ave. of the Champions, Palm Beach Gardens, FL 33418; tel. 407-627-2000, 800-633-9150; fax 407-622-0261.*

◆ **Comfort Inn** (moderate). Targeted at business travelers, it is also a reasonably priced option for vacationers. There are eighty-eight nicely decorated rooms. The best ones have king-size and sofa beds. Complimentary continental breakfast, free local calls, exercise room. *11360 Hwy. 1, Palm Beach Gardens, FL 33410; tel. 407-624-7186, 800-228-5150. At PGA Blvd.*

◆ **Jonathan Dickinson State Park** (inexpensive). Campers at its 135 wooded sites have access to the park's unique ecosystem and nature offerings: boat tours, canoe rentals, fishing, hiking, and observation tower. Cabins are also available. *16450 S.E. Federal Hwy., Hobe Sound, FL 33455; tel. 407-746-1466. On Hwy. 1, 6 mi. north of Rte. 706.*

# HOUSE RENTALS

Condominium rentals are more common than home rentals. In season, you'll have difficulty trying to rent either for shorter than a three-month period. Rates for homes and condos are between $2,000 and $3,000 per month.

◆ **Home Property Management**. *4360 Northlake Blvd., Palm Beach Gardens, FL 33410; tel. 407-624-4663. Open Mon.-Fri.*

# RESTAURANTS

◆ **Harpoon Louie's** (expensive). A legend in these parts, its many dining rooms overlook the water and picturesque Jupiter Lighthouse. Sit on the porch when it's seasonable. The menu has a Caribbean bearing. The grilled Jamaican chicken and pasta is marvelous. *1065 N. Rte. A1A, Jupiter, FL 33477; tel. 407-744-1300. Open daily for lunch and dinner. At the intersection of Hwy. 1 and Rte. A1A.*

◆ **Crab Pot** (moderate). One of a dying breed of authentic old Florida fish houses, it serves up a cool view of the Intracoastal Waterway in an unpretentious setting. The accent is on crab, some of which will get you into the expensive price range. Sit outdoors if you can. Order the Chesapeake crab soup, and douse it with the bottle of sherry on the table. Catfish, scallops, crab cakes (very good), shrimp, fresh catches, steak, and raw bar items complete the extensive menu. *386 E. Blue Heron Blvd., Riviera Beach, FL 33404; tel. 407-844-2722. Open daily for lunch and dinner.*

◆ **Jupiter Crab Company** (moderate). Tropical birds "greet" you. Bottled beers come in ice buckets. The view is of sand dunes from the east room, where you're eye level with sea oats. The extensive menu features seafood and ribs. *Embassy Suites Hotel, 181 Ocean Ave., Palm Beach Shores, FL 33404; tel. 407-863-4000. Open daily for breakfast (hotel guests only), lunch, and dinner; Sun. for brunch. At the Embassy Suites resort on Rte. A1A, Singer Island.*

# NIGHTLIFE

◆ **Burt Reynolds Institute for Theater Training.** Name movie stars take the stage with local actors. *304 Tequesta Dr., Tequesta, FL 33469; tel. 407-743-7458. Call for show times. Admission.*

◆ **Jupiter Theatre.** Nationally famous comedians and magicians and Broadway musicals fill the bill. *1001 E. Indiantown Rd., Jupiter, FL 33477; tel. 407-746-5566; fax 407-575-4766. Open daily Nov.-May. Admission. At Indiantown Rd. and Rte. A1A.*

◆ **Palm Beach County Cultural ArtsLine.** Call for the up-to-date schedule of theater and other cultural events in the county. *1555 Palm Beach Lakes Blvd., #900, West Palm Beach, FL 33401; tel. 407-471-2901, 800-882-2787.*

◆ **Panama Hattie's.** The place to go for reggae on weekends. *11511 Ellison Wilson Rd., North Palm Beach, FL 33408; tel. 407-*

*627-1545. Open daily. Off PGA Blvd.*

◆ **Water Taxi.** Party on a five-hour bar-hop cruise along the Intracoastal Waterway from North Palm Beach to Jupiter. Boat departs from Panama Hattie's restaurant and bar. *11511 Ellison Wilson Rd., North Palm Beach, FL 33408; tel. 407-775-2628. Call for times. Admission. Off PGA Blvd.*

# ATTRACTIONS

◆ **Burt Reynolds Ranch Studios.** Pet llamas, emus, miniature horses, goats, and other farm and exotic animals in the mini-petting zoo. Tours take you through movie studios with stage sets and props from the movie *Smokey & the Bandit* and the TV series *B. L. Stryker*. *16133 Jupiter Farms Rd., Jupiter, FL 33478; tel. 407-746-0393. Open daily 10-5. Admission.*

# SHOPPING

Grand malls and incessant strip centers vie for your spending dollars throughout the area. You'll find it all, from prestige clothing shops to Wal-Mart. For something with more character, head to the stubbornly small-town arena of Hobe Sound, about 15 minutes north of Jupiter on Route A1A, close to the nature center. This thin slice of shopping has the unusual in gifts, art, and antiques. If you're looking for world-class shopping, get in the car and make the 30-minute trip south to Palm Beach's famed Worth Avenue, and shop (theoretically, anyway) with the stars.

◆ **Native Hands Gallery.** Native American stuff: books, tapes, headdresses, arrowheads, sand paintings, jewelry, pipes, clothing. *Courtyard Plaza #1, 11970 S.E. Dixie Hwy., Hobe Sound, FL 33455; tel. 406-546-1400, 800-813-4263. Open daily except Sun.*

◆ **On A Whim Gallery.** Fanciful hand-painted wood items, decorative dolls, kids' gifts, and a book shop specializing in Florida classics. *12000 S.E. Dixie Hwy., Hobe Sound, FL 33455; tel. 407-546-1155. Open Mon.-Sat. Closed Mon. in summer.*

◆ **Past & Present.** Antique furniture, tableware, needlepoint rugs, and more. *11960 S.E. Dixie Hwy., Hobe Sound, FL 33455; tel. 407-546-2727. Open daily. Closed in summer.*

◆ **The Doll Adventure.** Dolls, dollmaking supplies, doll clothing, custom-made dolls, and doll repairs. *Driftwood Plaza, 2129 Hwy. 1, Jupiter, FL 33469; tel. 407-575-4292. Open Tue.-Sat.*

# BEST FOOD SHOPS

**SANDWICHES:** ◆ **Mother Nature's Pantry.** *2411 N. Ocean Blvd., Singer Island, Riviera Beach, FL 33404; tel. 407-845-0533. Open daily.*

**SEAFOOD:** ◆ **Island Seafood Market.** *1420 Broadway, Riviera Beach, FL 33404; tel. 407-863-3474. Open daily except Sun.*

**FRESH PRODUCE:** ◆ **52nd Street Farm Market.** *4077 Lake Worth Rd., Lake Worth, FL 33461; tel. 407-433-8747. Open daily.*

**BAKERY:** ◆ **Ralph's Place.** *4016 Broadway, W. Palm Beach, FL 33407; tel. 407-848-7858. Open daily.*

**ICE CREAM:** ◆ **David's Ice Cream.** *2427A N. Ocean Ave., Singer Island, FL 33404; tel. 407-845-1148. Open daily.*

**BEVERAGES:** ◆ **Grator Gator Food Market.** *1245 E. Blue Heron Blvd., Riviera Beach, FL 33404; tel. 407-844-0733. Open daily.*

**WINE:** ◆ **Jupiter Square Liquors.** *103 S. Hwy. 1, Jupiter, FL 33477; tel. 407-743-5500. Open daily. On Hwy. 1 at Indiantown Rd.*

# SPORTS

## FISHING

A variety of sailfish and other game catches swim the open waters as well as the backwaters of this sportsperson's haven. Buy your fishing license at any K-Mart store. (Licenses are provided on charter boats.)

◆ **Blue Heron Fleet Drift Fishing.** Fishing charters. *Rte. A1A and Hwy. 1, Jupiter, FL 33477; tel. 407-747-1200. Open Tue.-Sun.*

◆ **Sailfish Marina.** Deep-sea charters specializing in sailfish, dolphin, and kingfish. *98 Lake Dr., Palm Beach Shores, FL 33404; tel. 407-844-1724. Open daily.*

◆ **Seagate Marina Ships Store.** Sells bait and tackle. *18701 S.E. Federal Hwy., Tequesta, FL 33469; tel. 407-746-2600. Open daily. North of Jupiter on Hwy. 1.*

## BOATING

◆ **Adventure Times Kayaking.** Guided outings in local waterways; sales, rentals and instruction. *1372 N. Killian Dr., Lake Park, FL 33403; tel. 407-881-7218. Store open Tue.-Sat.; outings Tue.-Sun. 1 block south of N. Lake Blvd.; just south of N. Palm Beach.*

◆ **Jupiter Hills Lighthouse Marina.** Rents boats. *18261 S.E. Federal Hwy., Tequesta, FL 33469; tel. 407-744-0727. Open daily.*

◆ **Jupiter Seasport Marina.** Rents boats. *1095 N. Rte. A1A, Jupiter, FL 33477; tel. 407-575-0006. Open daily.*

◆ **Louie's Lady.** Cruise past million-dollar homes on this double-decker excursion boat. Some tours include breakfast or lunch. *Hwy. 1 and Rte. A1A, Jupiter, FL 33477; tel. 407-744-5550. Open daily. Closed Mon. in summer. Located at the docks of Harpoon Louie's restaurant.*

◆ **Loxahatchee River Adventures.** Take a guided ecological pontoon cruise on the wild and scenic Loxahatchee River. *16450 S.E. Federal Hwy., Jonathan Dickinson State Park, Hobe Sound, FL 33455; tel. 407-746-1466, 800-746-1466. Open daily.*

◆ **Palm Beach Water Taxi.** Tours of Palm Beach mansions, Peanut Island, Lost Tree Village (home of Jack Nicklaus), and other area sights. *Sailfish Marina, 98 Lake Dr., Palm Beach Shores, FL 33404; tel. 407-844-1724. Open daily. Tours depart from Sailfish Marina on Singer Island and from Riviera Beach Marina across the bridge.*

◆ **Star of Palm Beach.** Sightseeing, lunch, dinner, brunch, and party cruises on a 300-passenger paddlewheel boat that plies the Intracoastal Waterway, past the storied mansions of Palm Beach. *900 E. Blue Heron Blvd., Singer Island, FL 33404; tel. 407-848-7827. Open daily.*

## SURFING

Surfing gets better up the coast, but still finds an avid audience in the North Palm Beach area. For up-to-date surfing reports, call 407-744-8805. Surf shops are everywhere.

◆ **Ocean Magic Surf & Sport.** Sells surfboards, wet suits, and other equipment. *103 S. Hwy. 1, Jupiter, FL 33477; tel. 407-744-8925. Open daily.*

## DIVING

The Palm Beach area is known for its wreck and drift dives. The area also abounds in reefs and ledges populated by tropical fish and logger-head turtles. There are plenty of dive shops in the area that can take you to local sites and teach certification courses. Some hotels offer resort courses, which allow you to go down with your instructor only.
◆ **Dive USA.** *1201 N. Ocean Blvd., Singer Island, FL 33404; tel. 407-844-5100. Open daily.*

## BICYCLING

Bike paths follow the road at various places along the beach. There are bike trails through Jonathan Dickinson State Park.
◆ **Tequesta Bicycle.** Rents 3- and 10-speeds. *300 N. Old Dixie Hwy., Jupiter, FL 33458; tel. 407-746-9191. Open daily except Sun.*

## GOLF

Home to the Professional Golfers Association (PGA), the area is closely aligned with the sport. The county holds more than 145 courses. Palm Beach County's Golf-A-Round program lets resort guests sample the links at more than 100 participating properties (for information about the program, contact the county's Convention and Visitors Bureau; *see* Tourist Information).
◆ **North Palm Beach Country Club.** A semiprivate course with 18 holes. *951 Hwy. 1, North Palm Beach, FL 33408; tel. 407-626-4345. Open daily. Admission.*

## TENNIS

North Palm Beach County hosts several major tennis tournaments, including the Virginia Slims and Pringles Light celebrity tournaments.
◆ **Loggerhead Park.** Four lighted tennis courts with stadium seating. *Hwy. 1, Juno Beach, FL 33408. Open daily.*

# HISTORY

◆ **DuBois Home.** The circa-1890 home of a pioneer family, it displays period furnishings and dress. Donations accepted. *DuBois Park, Jupiter, FL 33477; tel. 407-747-6639. Open Wed. and Sun. 1-4. Admission.*

◆ **Florida History Center & Museum.** Hosts permanent and changing exhibits on general local history and how it has been shaped by nature. *Burt Reynolds Park, 805 N. Hwy. 1, Jupiter, FL 33477; tel. 407-747-6639. Open Tue.-Fri. 10-5; Sat.-Sun. 1-5. Admission.*

◆ **Jupiter Inlet Lighthouse.** This, the oldest existing structure in the county, is listed on the National Historic Register. There's a small museum at the base (a branch of the Florida History Center & Museum) to visit, and you can climb to the top, if you're 48 inches or taller. *Hwy. 1 and Alt. Rte. A1A, Jupiter, FL 33477; tel. 407-747-6639. Open Sun.-Wed. 10-4. Admission.*

# NATURE

◆ **Blowing Rocks Preserve.** This 73-acre refuge for natural vegetation gets its name from the occasional geyserlike spurts it emits along its 4,000 feet of rocky shoreline. The refuge sponsors guided tours and sea turtle watches. Good snorkeling. Donation requested. *Beach Rd., Jupiter Island, FL; tel. 407-747-3113 (preserve), 407-575-2297 (Nature Conservancy). Open daily 6-5. 2.5 mi. north of intersection of Beach Rd. and Alt. Rte. A1A on Jupiter Island.*

◆ **Hobe Sound National Wildlife Refuge.** Hosts environmental education programs, exhibits, camps, nature walks, and sea turtle walks. Four miles of beach reachable only by boat or footpath. *Hobe Sound Nature Center, 13640 S.E. Federal Hwy., Hobe Sound, FL 33455; tel. 407-546-2067. Open Mon.-Fri. 9-3. Admission.*

◆ **John D. MacArthur Beach State Park.** Escape the hustle of the Palm Beach area at this natural gem of 225 land acres. (It contains an additional 535 acres of submerged land.) Acquaint yourself with the coast's natural world in the well-designed nature center, which includes aquariums, stuffed-wildlife exhibits, historical background, and interpretive video. Outside, there's a butterfly garden and a 1,600-foot boardwalk across Lake Worth Cove (tram service available). Between it and the beach, a self-guided nature trail takes up the lesson. *10900 Rte. A1A, North Palm Beach, FL 33408; tel. 407-624-6950, 407-624-6952. Park open daily 8-sunset. Nature center open Wed.-Mon. 9-5. Admission.*

◆ **Jonathan Dickinson State Park.** Explore estuarine and forested environments on foot, bike, canoe (rentals available), and pontoon tours. The immense, 1,000-acre park hosts rare wildlife species such as deer, southern bald eagles, and Florida scrub jays. *16450 S.E. Federal Hwy., Hobe Sound, FL 33455; tel. 407-546-2771. Open daily. Admission. On Hwy. 1, 6 mi. north of Rte. 706.*

◆ **Marinelife Center of Juno Beach.** Facilities at the beach parking lot, across Route A1A from the beach, introduce you to maritime fauna and flora with a nature trail and indoor educational displays on sea turtles, shells, crabs, and sharks. The center monitors sea turtle nesting activities at the beach. Donations appreciated. *12400 Hwy. 1, Loggerhead Park, Juno Beach, FL 33408; tel. 407-627-8280. Open Tue.-Sat. 10-4; Sun. 12-3.*

◆ **Peanut Island.** A small river island undergoing procedures to make it a protected park, it is accessible only by boat (*see* Boating). It has both historic and natural value. The bunker built for President Kennedy during the Cuban missile crisis still exists on one end. Local nature charters go there to observe and interpret indigenous marine life. *Open daily.*

# SAFETY TIPS

Palm Beach County is largely metropolitan, and suffers the inherent problems with crime. The beach neighborhoods are the most upscale and the safest, but it still behooves travelers to take precautions. Avoid going out at night alone. Lock your car and stow your valuables, particularly in lower-income areas such as Riviera Beach and along secluded stretches.

# TOURIST INFORMATION

◆ **Jupiter-Tequesta-Juno Beach Chamber of Commerce.** *800 N. Hwy. 1, Jupiter, FL 33477; tel. 407-746-7111; fax 407-746-7715. Open Mon.-Fri. 8-4:15.*

◆ **Northern Palm Beaches Chamber of Commerce.** *1983 PGA Blvd. #104, Palm Beach Gardens, FL 33408; tel. 407-694-2300. Open Mon.-Thu. 9-5; Fri. 9-4.*

◆ **Palm Beach County Convention & Visitors Bureau.** *1555 Palm Beach Lakes Blvd., Suite 204, West Palm Beach, FL 33401; tel. 407-471-3995, 800-833-5733; fax 407-471-3990. Open Mon.-Fri. 8:30-5.*

## CHAPTER 21

# Hutchinson Island

Hutchinson Island is one of the true treasures of Florida's so-called Treasure Coast. The name originally applied to the gold spilled when Spanish fleets of yore went to the bottom. Today it implies the wealth of natural settings still unscathed by urban sprawl.

Travelers heading north from Miami find their first respite from metro madness at 16-mile-long Hutchinson Island. It's relatively quiet during the week, but the beaches fill up on weekends when urbanites flock here to picnic in Hutchinson's parks and surf in its frothy water.

| | |
|---|---|
| Beauty | A |
| Swimming | B |
| Sand | B+ |
| Hotels/Inns/B&Bs | B |
| House rentals | D |
| Restaurants | A- |
| Nightlife | A- |
| Attractions | A- |
| Shopping | A- |
| Sports | A |
| Nature | A |

Hutchinson offers the visitor a well-rounded list of attractions. The island, divided among the three mainland communities of Stuart, Jensen Beach, and Fort Pierce, boasts several interesting museums. They relate the island's past roles as pineapple plantation, safe refuge for shipwreck victims, and World War II training ground. Across the scenic Indian River, the mainland downtown areas of the three towns satisfy sightseers with attractions both cultural and natural. Downtown Stuart has a special appeal with its quirky historic veneer and offbeat shops.

Hutchinson Island provides both good and bad lessons in beach development. Tourism keeps a low profile in the southern part, and much of the area resists exploitation. To the north, stretches of residential development smother natural beauty, but there are still pockets of unspoiled beach. Tackiness reigns, however, at the island's north end, which is not covered in this book. Part of the town of Fort Pierce, it is rife with honky-tonk motels and sardine-tight commercial development. (Fort Pierce's more pristine beaches on North Hutchinson Island are described in the Fort Pierce chapter.)

# OCEAN BEACHES
## STUART BEACHES

High dunes topped with sea grapes, grasses, silver buttonwood, and other native plants separate the beaches from their parks, creating a pleasant barrier between the broad stretch of sand and man-made amenities. Board walkovers with steps lead down to sands the color of café au lait.

| | |
|---|---|
| Beauty | A |
| Swimming | B |
| Sand | B |
| Amenities | A |

Although lifeguards are on hand only during peak periods, posted notices report on water and air temperatures and surf conditions. They also warn about possible swimming dangers, such as submerged rocks, dangerous waters, deep holes, Portuguese men-of-war, and sea lice (*see* Safety Tips). *Parks and*

## HOW TO GET THERE

◆ From Palm Beach International Airport (an hour from Hutchinson Island), go east on Southern Blvd. (Hwy. 98) to I-95 and head north for about 40 mi. Take exit 61 and turn right onto Kanner Hwy. (Rte. 76). Turn right on Cove Rd. Continue for 2 1/2 mi. and turn left onto Old Dixie Hwy. (Rte. A1A). After 5 1/2 mi., veer right at a confusing intersection where Ocean Blvd. enters. Remain in the right lane and continue on Rte. A1A for 4 1/2 mi., crossing the bridge to Hutchinson Island.

*accesses open sunrise to sunset.*

*Swimming:* Depending upon the surf, flags at the guard station sometimes limit activity to swimming only or surfing only. These aren't the best beaches for swimming because of sub-merged rocks and a steep bottom slope.

*Sand:* Some crushed shell mingles with the tan sand.

*Amenities:* Lifeguards are on duty at busy times, mostly during winter and summer weekends. Stuart Beach has rest rooms, an outdoor cafe, a playground, outdoor showers, a shaded nature interpretation station, and picnic shelters with grills. Bathtub Park has rest rooms, outdoor showers, and a water fountain.

*Sports:* At Stuart Beach, you can rent Boogie boards, volleyballs, and basketballs. You'll find a volleyball net and basketball courts at the north end of the Stuart Beach parking lot. Snorkelers and divers can explore the 85-acre wormrock coral reef at Bathtub Park, which extends for 1 1/2 miles.

*Parking:* Parking is free. Stuart Beach has the most spaces in paved lots.

## Bathtub Reef Park

Off the main drag, this once-undiscovered beach is now popu-lar with families because the reef near shore, at low tide, makes a calm pond of the Atlantic waters. Small dunes, casuarinas, and sea grapes enhance the view landward, where only a few houses are in sight. The wide beach is terraced from tide erosions. *On McArthur Blvd., about 1 1/2 mi. south of the Rte. A1A intersection.*

## Stuart Beach

The most developed of Stuart's beaches, it nonetheless remains relatively free of unsightly resort overkill. The beach is narrowest here, with big, flat bedrock exposed in spots. Situated next to the Elliott Museum, it provides a variety of amenities, including a playground and beach rentals. This is where the young beachers like to "make the scene." *North of the Stuart causeway on Rte. A1A.*

## Martin County Beach Accesses

These two spots are good choices if you hope to shun the crowds a bit. Both have unpaved parking lots with only outdoor showers, but they're close to Stuart Beach amenities, if you need them. *North of Stuart Beach on Rte. A1A.*

## JENSEN BEACHES

Jensen/Sea Turtle Beach is the main recreational place on this segment of the island. The rest of the beaches range from lightly developed to undeveloped, both with and without parking. Frederick Douglass Memorial Beach, a restful, out-of-the-way

| Beauty | A |
|--------|---|
| Swimming | B |
| Sand | B+ |
| Amenities | B |

spot for picnicking, swimming, and collecting shells, has good facilities. *Most parks are open 8-8.*

*Swimming:* The bottom slope is fairly steep. Rip currents and high surf can pose problems, especially at Jensen Beach.

*Sand:* Narrow sand the color of brown eggshells, strewn with sargasso grass and driftwood. Dunes are lower than to the south.

*Amenities:* Jensen Beach has the most facilities: rest rooms, showers, beach walkovers, food and beach concessions, picnic tables. Lifeguards on duty. Across the road, there are shops and restaurants. Most of the other beaches have rest rooms and boardwalks to the beach.

*Sports:* Surfers like it here. The not-so-daring can rent Boogie boards at Jensen Beach, where there's also volleyball.

*Parking:* Plenty of free parking, paved and unpaved.

### Jensen/Sea Turtle Beach

Outdoors enthusiasts congregate along this 1,500-foot expanse of beautiful beach. Tastefully landscaped, it has closely cropped palms in the parking lot. Sansevieria, sea grasses, and sea grapes proliferate along the dunes. The beach hosts mama turtles during the summer. *At the intersection of Jensen Beach causeway and Rte. A1A.*

### Waveland Public Beach

Near shops and restaurants, this place is convenient, but you may be bothered by having to look at the encroaching civilization while you're trying to enjoy the beach. The sands are wider here than at the main beach. Park structures are modern and attractive. *North of the Jensen Beach causeway on Rte. A1A.*

## Herman's Bay Beach Access

Fairly pristine, this natural beach is narrow and fringed with palmettos and sea grapes. There are picnic tables and a dunes walkover. *About 4 mi. north of Jensen Beach.*

## Walton Rocks Beach

This is for folks who want to get away from it all. To find it, follow a narrow dirt road (no RVs permitted) for less than half a mile through the mangroves and bird nesting areas. Seclusion prevails. The beach has a wild look, with sands sloping sharply to the sea and seaweed all about. Casuarinas provide some shade, but the picnic tables are unsheltered. Grungy rest rooms. Lifeguards on duty when crowds dictate. *North of the St. Lucie Nuclear Plant.*

## Blind Creek Beach

You won't find crowds here. A narrow rock road leads to a carpet of sand, where you park close to the beach. No facilities. *About 9 mi. north of the Jensen Beach causeway.*

## Middle Cove Access

No facilities and a slightly long (five-minute) walk to the beach keep this access lightly used. That plus low dunes and a natural setting lend a reclusive quality to beaching here. *About 12 mi. north of the Jensen Beach causeway.*

## Frederick Douglass Memorial Beach

Prettily landscaped and maintained, this spot offers cement-roofed picnic areas and a lawn edged by pruned sea grapes. The waves are small, and the wide beach is backed by dunes.

This place makes a nice out-of-the-mainstream picnic spot. It's also popular with shell collectors and horseback riders. A lifeguard watches over the 1,000-foot stretch of sand during peak periods. Rest rooms are kept up, and there's a volleyball net. *13 1/2 mi. north of the Jensen Beach causeway.*

## Green Turtle Beach/John Brooks Park

No encroaching high rises here, but no facilities either. It's near the road, thus not as secluded as some of the quieter beaches directly south. *14 1/2 mi. north of the Jensen Beach causeway.*

# HOTELS/INNS/B&Bs

◆ **Indian River Plantation** (very expensive). A grand-scale destination resort, its 200 lush acres encompass secluded beachfront, an 18-hole golf course, 13 tennis courts, a marina, five restaurants, bars, swimming pools, and a variety of lodging options. Beach and bike rentals. The ocean-view studios are nice and have compact kitchenettes. You'll also like the Sandpiper studios, which have their own pool, Jacuzzi, tiki bar, and beach walkover. *555 N.E. Ocean Blvd., Stuart, FL 34996; tel. 407-225-3700, 800-444-3389; fax 407-225-0003. Rte. A1A at McArthur Blvd., on the south end of Hutchinson Island.*

◆ **Hutchinson Inn** (expensive). This motel-style B&B holds 21 rooms, efficiencies, and suites. All have an ocean view, but rooms 11 and 12, and suite 23 have the best. Rooms are moderately priced. Efficiencies include kitchenettes. Suites have a full kitchen. Guests can enjoy the on-property tennis court, swimming pool, and beach. Homey touches: breakfast under the awning; a free weekly barbecue; a cage of song birds; and Emily, a bulldog who wears pearls. *9750 S. Ocean Dr., Jensen Beach, FL 34957; tel. 407-229-2000. On Hutchinson Island, 3 mi. north of the Jensen Beach causeway on Rte. A1A.*

◆ **Harbor Front Inn** (moderate). Ensconced in a 1908-style home of cypress and Florida pine, it recalls the relaxed and breezy vacationing lifestyle of yesteryear. Eight different types of accommodations range from a guest room (inexpensive) to a cottage with kitchen. Most rates include a deluxe home-cooked breakfast. Each unit has a private bath. On the Indian River and close to historic downtown Stuart, it's within walking distance of shopping. *310 Atlanta Ave., Stuart, FL 34994; tel. 407-288-7289; 800-294-1703.*

# HOUSE RENTALS

Home rentals are rare on Hutchinson Island. Condominiums and townhouses are plentiful, however. Most rent for a one-month minimum, for between $2,000 and $3,000 a month in season.

◆ **Hoyt C. Murphy Realtors.** *221 S. Ocean Dr., Fort Pierce, FL 34949; tel. 407-461-1324, 800-289-4698. Open Mon.-Sat.*

# RESTAURANTS

◆ **Scalawags** (expensive). From continental classics to imaginative innovations, the menu offers a wide variety of excellent entrées. The opulent setting overlooks million-dollar yachts bobbing in the resort's marina. Ask for a window seat, then settle in and scrutinize the seafood selections for fresh fare. The Key lime sauce tops fish off nicely. (You get a choice of preparations and sauces.) *555 N.E. Ocean Blvd., Stuart, FL 34996; tel. 407-225-3700; fax 407-225-0003. Open daily for dinner. Across from hotel registration at Indian River Plantation.*

◆ **Conchy Joe's** (moderate). To Bahamians, Conchy Joe means a white Bahamian. Here it means Florida and Bahamian seafood dishes in a setting made to look like a clapboard Bahamian home, complete with a thatched porch roof. Ask for a table on the waterfront to glimpse pelicans and passing river traffic. Grouper marsala with cream sauce is the house specialty. The conch dishes and barbecued boar ribs are tasty, too. *3945 N.E. Indian River Dr., Jensen Beach, FL 34958; tel. 407-334-1130. Open daily for lunch and dinner. On the mainland bank of the Indian River, just north of the Jensen Beach causeway.*

◆ **Jolly Sailor Pub** (moderate). The pick of the local business community for lunch. Sit outdoors or inside in a dark-wood pub setting. The pub grub: burgers, bangers and mash (sausages and mashed potatoes with onion gravy), and steak and kidney pie. It also has a nice selection of salads and a tableau of grilled dinners in various international styles. *1 S.W. Osceola St., Stuart, FL 34994; tel. 407-221-1111. Open daily for lunch and dinner. In downtown Stuart.*

◆ **Prawnbroker** (moderate). Known for its fresh-from-the-sea specialties and prime aged steaks. There's a standard menu, but you'll be better off ordering one of the creative nightly specials featuring the catch of the day. *Harbour Bay Plaza, 3754 S.E. Ocean Blvd., Stuart, FL 34996; tel. 407-288-1222. Open daily for dinner.*

# NIGHTLIFE

◆ **Barn Theatre.** A converted barn serves as playhouse for come-dies, musicals, and dramas. *2400 E. Ocean Blvd., Stuart, FL 34995; tel. 407-287-4884. Box office open Mon.-Fri. Admission.*

◆ **Center For the Arts.** Hosts a changing schedule of dance, music, theater, and visual arts for adults and children. *333 Tressler Dr., Stuart, FL 34994; tel. 407-287-1194. Call for sched-ule. Admission. Take Tressler Dr. off Hwy. 1.*

◆ **Conchy Joe's.** Reggae and calypso bands play four nights a week. *3945 N.E. Indian River Dr., Jensen Beach, FL 34958; tel. 407-334-1130. Open daily. Live music Thu.-Sun. On the mainland bank of the Indian River, just north of the Jensen Beach causeway.*

◆ **Lyric Theater.** Top-name entertainment and regional perform-ers take the stage at this renovated, 600-seat, historic theater. Monday is songwriters' night. *59 S.W. Flagler Ave., Stuart, FL 34994; tel. 407-220-1942. Admission. In downtown Stuart.*

◆ **Scalawags Lounge.** Live, top-40 bands and dancing. *555 N.E. Ocean Blvd., Stuart, FL 34996; tel. 407-225-3700. Open nightly. Live entertain-ment Wed.-Sat. Across from hotel registration at Indian River Plantation.*

# ATTRACTIONS

◆ **Florida Power & Light Energy Encounter.** Hands-on displays and games let visitors walk a treadmill to power a refrigerator, match wits with a computer, and go on an energy treasure hunt. *6501 Rte. A1A, Hutchinson Island, Jensen Beach, FL 34957; tel. 407-468-4111. Open Tue.-Fri., Sun. 10-4. On the north side of the St. Lucie Nuclear Plant, at Gate B.*

# SHOPPING

You'll have the most fun shopping in downtown Stuart, a recharged neighborhood centered around Confusion Corner. A sculptured lady with big jugs (the kind you carry) presides over this baffling roundabout. Shops have a New Age feel, specializing in herbs, pottery, art, books, and stained glass.

◆ **All American Collectibles Animation Art Gallery.** This gallery has a delightful inventory of limited-edition cartoon celluloids, lithographs, and hand-painted cartoon characters. *37 W. Osceola St., Stuart, FL 34994; tel. 407-288-0033. Open Mon.-Sat.*

◆ **Arcade Book Nook.** Specializes in children's stories and Florida books. *Post Office Arcade, 31 S.W. Osceola St., Stuart, FL 34994; tel. 407-220-9465; fax 407-220-1688. Open Mon.-Sat.*

◆ **B&A Flea Market.** Nearly 30 acres of open-air bargains in produce, crafts, souvenirs, and who knows what else. *2885 S. Federal Hwy., Stuart, FL 34997; tel. 407-288-4915. Open Sat.-Sun. On Hwy. 1, north of Indian St.*

◆ **Caramba!** Fashions and home accessories with a tropical and tribal flair. *Post Office Arcade, 15 S.W. Osceola St., Stuart, FL 34994; tel. 407-287-9633; fax 407-287-9633. Open Mon.-Sat.*

◆ **Rare Earth Pottery.** The owner designs and throws the pitchers, fountains, mugs, lamps, and other earthenware sold here. *41 S.W. Flagler Ave., Stuart, FL 34994; tel. 407-287-7744. Open Mon.-Sat.*

# BEST FOOD SHOPS

**SANDWICHES:** ◆ **Plantation Pantry.** *650 N.E. Ocean Blvd., Hutchinson Island, Stuart, FL 34996; tel. 407-225-1100. Open daily.*

**SEAFOOD:** ◆ **Prawnbroker Fish Market.** *3754 S.E. Ocean Blvd., Stuart, FL 34996; tel. 407-288-1222. Open daily.*

**FRESH PRODUCE:** ◆ **O'Dell Citrus.** *10433 S. Ocean Dr., Hutchinson Island, Jensen Beach, FL 34957; tel. 407-229-1387. Open daily.*

**BAKERY:** ◆ **Osceola Bakery.** *38 S.W. Osceola St., Stuart, FL 34994; tel. 407-287-2253. Open Mon.-Sat.; closed Sat. in summer.*

**ICE CREAM:** ◆ **Strawberry's Deli & Ice Cream.** *11037 S. Ocean Dr., Hutchinson Island, Jensen Beach, FL 34957; tel. 407-229-9356. Open daily.*

**BEVERAGES:** ◆ **Treasure Coast Foods.** *1001 Seaway Dr., Hutchinson Island, Fort Pierce, FL 34949; tel. 407-467-1988. Open daily.*

**WINE:** ◆ **Harbour Bay Gourmet.** *3714 S.E. Ocean Blvd., Harbour Bay Plaza, Stuart, FL 34996; tel. 407-286-9463. Open daily.*

# SPORTS
## FISHING
Offshore, wahoo, sailfish, marlin, and dolphinfish await your

bait. In the river, jack crevalle, snook, redfish, sea trout, and tarpon are worth pursuing.

◆ **Free Jumper Charters.** Offshore and river excursions, full- and half-day. *555 N.E. Ocean Blvd., Stuart, FL 34996; tel. 407-283-7787. Open daily. At Indian River Plantation.*

◆ **Hurricane Bait & Tackle.** Fishing equipment sales and rentals. Bait, fishing licenses. *2222 N.E. Indian River Dr., Jensen Beach, FL 34957; tel. 407-334-8771. Open daily. On the mainland, halfway between the Stuart and Jensen Beach causeways.*

◆ **Lady Stuart.** Half-day deep-sea fishing excursions. *Bailey's Boat Marina, 2225 N.E. Indian River Dr., Jensen Beach, FL 34957; tel. 407-286-1860. Open daily. On the mainland, south of the Jensen Beach causeway.*

## BOATING

◆ **Island Princess Cruises.** An 84-foot yacht takes you cruising. *555 N.E. Ocean Blvd., Stuart, FL 34996; tel. 407-225-2100. Open daily. Departs from Indian River Plantation.*

◆ **Rosemeyer's Boat Rental.** Rents powerboats, water skis and other get-wet toys. *3281 N.E. Indian River Dr., Jensen Beach, FL 34957; tel. 407-334-1000. Open daily. On the mainland, southwest of the Jensen Beach causeway at Jensen Beach Blvd.*

◆ **Tropical Visions.** Get out on the water aboard a pontoon boat tour or kayak rental. *600 W. First St., Stuart, FL 34994; tel. 407-223-2097. Open daily. Downtown Stuart.*

## SURFING

Though popular on this wedge of coastline, surfing is not as intense as it is in the Sebastian Inlet area to the north. But there are surf shops to take care of your needs.

◆ **Island Watersports.** Rents and sells surfboards and other beach supplies. *3291 N.E. Indian River Dr., Jensen Beach, FL 34957; tel. 407-334-1999. Open daily. Turn south on the mainland from the Jensen Beach causeway.*

## DIVING

◆ **Deep Six Watersports.** Specializes in scuba instruction, dives, and equipment. Rents and sells Rollerblades and surfboards.

*3289 N.W. Federal Hwy., Jensen Beach, FL 34957; tel. 407-692-2747. Open daily. On Hwy. 1.*

◆ **Dixie Divers.** *1879 S.E. Federal Hwy., Stuart, FL 34994; tel. 407-283-5588. Open daily.*

## BICYCLING
Bike paths run sporadically along Route A1A and down McArthur Boulevard.

◆ **Mac's Bike Shop.** Rents by the day, week, or month. *3742 N.E. Savannah Rd., Jensen Beach, FL 34957; tel. 407-334-4343. Open Mon.-Sat.*

## GOLF
◆ **Indian River Plantation Country Club.** A challenging 18-hole course. *555 N.E. Ocean Blvd., Hutchinson Island, Stuart, FL 34996; tel. 407-225-3700. Admission.*

## TENNIS
◆ **Memorial Park/Sailfish Park.** Lighted tennis courts, handball courts, and other facilities. *E. Ocean Blvd. and Georgia Ave., Stuart, FL 34996. Open daily. Follow Ocean Blvd. west off Hutchinson Island.*

# HISTORY
◆ **Elliott Museum.** Sterling Elliot invented the stamp machine, an automatic knot-tyer, and a four-wheel bicycle that was the predecessor of the Stanley Steamer car. See these and numerous other bits of turn-of-the-century Americana. *825 N.E. Ocean Blvd., Stuart, FL 34996; tel. 407-225-1961. Open daily 11-4. Admission.*

◆ **Gilbert's Bar House of Refuge Museum.** The county's oldest structure, it, along with eight others, harbored 19th-century shipwreck survivors who washed ashore. The only refuge to survive, it displays various marine artifacts and life-saving equipment. There's a seaquarium beneath the house. *301 S.E. McArthur Blvd., Hutchinson Island, Stuart, FL 34996; tel. 407-225-1875. Open Tue.-Sun. 11-4. Admission.*

◆ **Maritime & Yachting Museum.** Exhibits antique and restored vessels, nautical memorabilia, and an assortment of ship models. *2000 N.E. Jensen Beach Blvd., Jensen Beach, FL 34957; tel. 407-334-7733. Open Tue.-Sun. 10-4. Admission. On the mainland. From the Jensen Beach causeway, turn south on Indian River Dr. and west on Jensen Beach Blvd.*

# NATURE

◆ **Environmental Studies Center.** A county facility where you can tour a working beehive, wet lab, fruit tree grove, and plant exhibits. *2900 Indian River Dr., Jensen Beach, FL 34957; tel. 407-334-1262. Open Mon.-Fri. 9-3. Southwest of the Jensen Beach causeway.*

◆ **Heathcote Botanical Gardens.** This three-and-a-half-acre oasis of native and exotic foliage is in a peaceful Oriental setting. *210 Savannah Rd., Fort Pierce, FL 34982; tel. 407-464-4672. Open Tue.-Sat. 9-5; Sun. 1-5. Closed May-Oct. Admission. Off Hwy. 1 south of the Fort Pierce South Bridge.*

◆ **Turtle Beach Nature Trail.** A self-guided tour through native vegetation. *Rte. A1A, Hutchinson Island. Open Tue.-Fri. and Sun. 10-4. 9 mi. north of the Jensen Beach causeway.*

# SAFETY TIPS

Sea lice are the bane of swimmers on this coast. Actually the larvae of thimble jellyfish, they get caught in swimsuits and emit an itch-producing venom that can drive you crazy. Keep an eye out for posted signs at beach entrances that warn of sea lice problems. Shower immediately after you leave the water.

# TOURIST INFORMATION

◆ **Jensen Beach Chamber of Commerce.** *1910 N.E. Jensen Beach Blvd., Jensen Beach, FL 34957; tel. 407-334-3444. Open Mon.-Fri. 9-4.*

◆ **Stuart/Martin County Chamber of Commerce.** *1650 S. Kanner Hwy., Stuart, FL 34994; tel. 407-287-1088, 800-524-9704. Open Mon. 9-5; Tue.-Fri. 8:30-5.*

# CHAPTER 22
# Fort Pierce

The metropolis of Fort Pierce spreads from the mainland onto two different islands separated by Fort Pierce Inlet. They are Hutchinson Island (*see* Chapter 21) to the south, accessible by the South Bridge, and North Hutchinson Island, which is reached via the North Bridge Causeway.

| | |
|---|---|
| Beauty | A- |
| Swimming | A |
| Sand | A- |
| Hotels/Inns/B&Bs | C- |
| House rentals | NA |
| Restaurants | B |
| Nightlife | B- |
| Attractions | B+ |
| Shopping | C- |
| Sports | A- |
| Nature | A |

Beaches at the two areas are a study in contrasts. The southern ones front a tacky resort development. Besides beachgoers, their biggest fans are the fishermen who cast from South Jetty.

North Hutchinson's beaches, however, are pristine beauties that have much to offer water-sports enthusiasts. Nature, swimming, surfing, fishing, and diving are the prime pursuits here. Where civilization has been allowed to intrude, it mainly takes the form of low-impact development. This is not the place to find luxury resorts, countless boutiques, or throbbing nightlife.

The island reveres its importance in history as the birthplace of the Naval frogman program during World War II. Plaques and a museum tell the story of the underwater demolition teams (UDTs) that trained here prior to the D-day invasion in 1944. Other attractions and tourism services can be found on the nearby mainland.

Two main recreational beach complexes anchor the island's southern end: Fort Pierce Inlet State Recreation Area, and

Pepper Park. North of them, there are mainly private beach accesses for condo resorts. The exception is Avalon Park, a small adjunct to the state recreation area. After that, you won't find a good public beach until you get to the Vero Beach area (*see* Chapter 23, Sebastian Inlet).

# OCEAN BEACHES

## FORT PIERCE INLET STATE RECREATION AREA

Hugging the northern shores of Fort Pierce Inlet, this park encompasses 340 acres, with 2,200 feet of beach on the ocean and another 1,500 sandy feet fronting the inlet. Dynamite Point on Inlet Beach marks the training spot for the

| | |
|---|---|
| Beauty | A- |
| Swimming | A- |
| Sand | A- |
| Amenities | B |

Navy's first frogmen. Today, only pelicans and shorebirds invade. Boaters often pull into this beach for sunbathing.

On the other side of the jetty lies the ocean beach, known as Jetty Park or, to locals, North Beach. It is more popular, especially with families, and has bigger waves. Avalon Park, the satellite beach, lies several miles to the north. *Tel. 407-468-3985. Open daily 8-sunset. Entrance to main facility is off Rte. A1A, 1 1/2 mi. from the end of North Bridge Causeway.*
*Swimming:* The water is clear, but swiftly moving in the inlet. Nice, smooth bottom, slightly steep. Little to no wave action. On the ocean, the jetty protects the beach and makes for more

**HOW TO GET THERE**

◆ From Palm Beach International Airport (1 1/2 hours from North Hutchinson Island), go east on Southern Blvd. (Hwy. 98) to I-95 and head north for 55 mi. Take Exit 66 and turn right onto Orange Ave. (Rte. 68). Continue for 4 mi. and turn left on Hwy. 1. Head north for 2 mi. until you see signs for Rte. A1A and North Bridge Causeway. Turn right on Rte. A1A and cross the bridge to North Hutchinson Island.

great swimming conditions. Flag system warns about safety conditions at Jetty Park. Signs at Avalon warn about objects protruding from the bottom, leftovers from frogmen training days. *Sand:* On the inlet front, the sand is very fine and light tan, with seaweed and other natural wash-up. Also, unfortunately, cigarette butts. The beach narrows at the west end and wraps around into deep, lagoon waters. Sand is somewhat coarser oceanside, with more-pronounced dunes. At Avalon, it's much the same, with a more natural flora and dunes on the mend.

*Amenities:* Inlet Beach has a playground and large picnic pavilions with grills. Jetty Park has grills, and the picnic tables are either open or covered with thatched roofs. There are racks for bikes and surfboards. Both beaches have rest rooms and outdoor showers. Lifeguard on duty at Jetty Beach. No facilities at Avalon, but there are boardwalks.

*Sports:* There's a fishing jetty between the two beaches. Many people fish from the shoreline at Inlet Beach. Good surfing off the jetty at the ocean beach. Hiking trail nearby.

*Parking:* Most spaces are at Jetty Park in two large, paved lots. Entrance fee of $3.25 per car of eight or less ($1 per bike rider or pedestrian) covers parking. Avalon has two small, free lots.

## Inlet Beach

Lots of sabal palms and shade trees backdrop the flat beach. The view across the inlet is of South Jetty's highly developed resort domain. *Take the first right after entering the park.*

## Jetty Park

A long, lovely beach trimmed in small dunes, flowering railroad vines, and scrub shrubbery. Boardwalks to the beach from the parking lot and facilities take a few minutes to walk. Some shells and lots of crab holes and bird life. *Continue straight after entering the park.*

## Avalon Park Access

Out in the wilderness of upper North Hutchinson, the state maintains 60 feet of undeveloped beach, which it is working to upgrade with a dunes restoration project. Popular nesting spot for sea turtles. Biting flies can be a nuisance here. *Open daily 8-sunset. About 6 mi. north on Rte. A1A.*

## PEPPER PARK

Route A1A runs right through the middle of this park. On the ocean side is a classic beach park, with sea oats, sea grapes, and scrub vegetation. Across the road, facilities on Wildcat Cove are newer, more landscaped, and geared toward fishermen

| Beauty | A- |
| --- | --- |
| Swimming | A |
| Sand | A- |
| Amenities | A |

and boaters. *Open daily dawn-dusk. 1 mi. north of Fort Pierce Inlet.*
*Swimming:* Good swimming with sandbar offshore. Nice bottom texture and temperatures that usually are warm.
*Sand:* The long, wide beach is carpeted with tan, fairly fine sand plus seaweed and some shell garnish. Hard-packed sand at the water line.
*Amenities:* UDT/Seal Museum (*see* Attractions), rest rooms, picnic shelters with grills, playground, and showers on beach side. More picnic facilities on the cove side. Lifeguard on duty.
*Sports:* Tennis and basketball courts on the beach side; six fishing piers and two boat docks (one for canoes) across the road.
*Parking:* Lots on both sides of the road have a total of 250 free spaces.

# HOTELS/INNS/B&Bs

North Hutchinson Island is light in the accommodations department. You'll find small motels nearby on the other side of the inlet, at Hutchinson Island's north end, which is less than 20 minutes from Fort Pierce Inlet State Recreation Area.

◆ **Mellon Patch Inn** (moderate). Its newness and Southwest U.S. motif sets this apart from most Florida B&Bs. The four rooms are charmingly decorated. The furniture is hand-painted, as are some of the walls: The Tropical Paradise room has a banana-tree-and-birds mural. All rooms look over the canal out back. Gourmet breakfast and use of canoe. No young children. *3601 N. Rte. A1A, North Hutchinson Island, FL 34949; tel. 407-461-5231, 800-656-7824; fax 407-464-9841.*

◆ **Ramada Inn** (moderate). One of the few options near Fort Pierce's northern beaches, it's a low-rise, 149-room hotel with its own beach, pool, whirlpool, restaurant, and lounge. Ocean-front rooms are preferable, but in the expensive range. *2600 N. Rte. A1A, Fort Pierce, FL 34949; tel. 407-465-6000, 800-2-RAMADA. Just north of the Fort Pierce Inlet State Recreation Area.*

# RESTAURANTS

◆ **Mangrove Mattie's** (expensive). South of the Fort Pierce Inlet on Hutchinson Island, its greatest feature is the view of Jetty Park beach and the boat traffic through the pass. Try to get a seat at the bank of windows. Seafood and pasta are the specialties. The dinner menu swims with fish from near and far, done the way you choose. *1640 Seaway Dr., Fort Pierce, FL 34949; tel. 407-466-1044. Open daily for lunch and dinner. Follow Rte. A1A over South Bridge to Hutchinson Island and continue to Seaway Dr.*

◆ **P.V. Martin's Beach Cafe** (expensive). The favorite on North Hutchinson Island, it occupies a vintage beach house with an attitude of refinement and relaxation. Stunning view of the beach; nicely appointed decor. Menu covers all bases, with an emphasis on seafood, plain or fancy. Specialty nights draw crowds, especially the Monday and Friday night seafood buffets. Budgeters should hit the Wednesday and Thursday bargain nights. Sunday champagne brunch. *5150 N. Rte. A1A, North Hutchinson Island, FL 34949; tel. 407-465-7300, 407-569-0700. Open daily for dinner; Mon.-Sat. for lunch; Sun. for brunch. About 5 minutes north of Pepper Park.*

◆ **Fish House Restaurant** (moderate). Great harbor view indoors or out. The nightly seafood specials are more exciting than the regular menu. Boat docking available. *Harbortown Marina, Harbortown Dr., Fort Pierce, FL 34946; tel. 407-466-8732. Open daily for lunch and dinner. West of North Bridge Causeway, turn south at marina signs.*

# NIGHTLIFE

◆ **McAlpin Fine Arts Center.** Home to the Treasure Coast Symphony and host to a variety of lecturers, musicians, and theatrical performances. *Indian River Community College, 3209*

*Virginia Ave., Fort Pierce, FL 34981; tel. 407-462-4750. Call for schedule. Admission. South of South Bridge and west of Hwy. 1.*

◆ **St. Lucie County Civic Center.** A wealth of events happen here, encompassing everything from dog shows to ballet. Home of the Treasure Coast Opera Society. *2300 Virginia Ave., Fort Pierce, FL 34982; tel. 407-462-1530. Call for a schedule of events. Admission. South of South Bridge on Hwy. 1, turn west.*

# ATTRACTIONS

◆ **Fort Pierce Jai-Alai.** Experience the exotic, fast-paced sport that is popular throughout Florida's East Coast. Betting is a major part of the excitement. *1750 South Kings Hwy., Fort Pierce 34945; tel. 407-464-7500, 800-524-2524. Open Wed.-Mon. Dec.-Apr. Call for schedule. Take Orange Ave. west from Hwy. 1 about 6 mi. Turn left on Kings Hwy.*

◆ **Indian River Community College Science Center.** Planetarium shows. Tickets must be purchased in advance. *3209 Virginia Ave., Fort Pierce, FL 34981; tel. 407-462-4750. Open daily Oct.-Jun. Admission. West of Hwy. 1, south of South Bridge.*

◆ **UDT-Seal Museum.** Tells the story of U.S. Navy frogmen or UDTs (Underwater Demolition Teams), including their start at Fort Pierce in 1943 to train for the D-Day invasion, and the beginning of the SEAL (Sea Air Land) program. *3300 N. Rte. A1A, Fort Pierce, FL 34949; tel. 407-462-3597; fax 407-595-1576. Open Tue.-Sat. 10-4; Sun. 12-4. Admission. At Pepper Park.*

# SHOPPING

**S**hopping is not a strong suit for North Hutchinson Island and the Fort Pierce area. Antique-shop browsers will like the drive north of the North Bridge on Highway 1, with its many large antique and consignment shops and flea markets.

◆ **Harbor Branch Oceanographic Gift Shop.** Gifts oriented toward marine education and the environment. *5600 Hwy. 1 N., Fort Pierce, FL 34946; tel. 407-467-7196. Open Mon.-Sat. About 15 minutes. north of North Bridge Causeway.*

# BEST FOOD SHOPS

**SANDWICHES:** ◆ **Sharky's.** *1012 Shorewinds Dr., North Hutchinson Island, FL 34949; tel. 407-466-2757. Open daily. Across from Fort Pierce Inlet State Recreation Area entrance on Rte. A1A.*

**SEAFOOD:** ◆ **Pelican Seafood Market.** *735 N. Fourth St., Fort Pierce, FL 34950; tel. 407-461-2797. Open daily. Off Rte. 1, between North and South bridges.*

**BAKERY:** ◆ **Publix.** *2609 S. Hwy. 1, Fort Pierce, FL 34950; tel. 407-464-8191. Open daily.*

**ICE CREAM:** ◆ **Cumberland Farms Food Store.** *1020 Shorewinds Dr., North Hutchinson Island, FL 34949; tel. 407-465-9089. Open daily. Across from Fort Pierce Inlet State Recreation Area entrance on Rte. A1A.*

**BEVERAGES:** ◆ **Cumberland Farms Food Store.** *1020 Shorewinds Dr., North Hutchinson Island, FL 34949; tel. 407-465-9089. Open daily. Across from Fort Pierce Inlet State Recreation Area entrance on Rte. A1A.*

**WINE:** ◆ **Pelican Liquors.** *709A N. Hwy. 1, Fort Pierce, FL 34950; tel. 407-466-7514. Open daily. South of the North Bridge Causeway on Hwy. 1.*

# SPORTS

## FISHING

◆ **Fancy Rod's.** The full name of the place is Fancy Rods & the Reel World Home of Grand Slam Fishing Center. Get your fishing equipment here. *101 Seaway Dr., Fort Pierce, FL 34950; tel. 407-465-6775. Open daily.*

◆ **Fish Stalker.** Reef fishing for snapper, grouper, cobia, kingfish, dolphin, and others. *1 Ave. A, Fort Pierce, FL 34950; tel. 407-464-4754. Open daily. At Indian River Dr., south of South Bridge.*

◆ **Harbortown Charter Fleet.** *1936 Harbortown Dr., Fort Pierce, FL 34946; tel. 407-466-0947. Open daily. West of North Bridge Causeway, turn south at marina signs.*

## BOATING

◆ **Harbortown Charter Fleet.** *1936 Harbortown Dr., Fort Pierce, FL 34946; tel. 407-466-0947. Open daily. West of the North Bridge Causeway, turn south at marina signs.*

## SURFING

Fort Pierce's Inlet Beach is among the area's top surfing destinations. Northward it gets even better, until it hits a peak at Sebastian Inlet, some 25 miles away (*see* Chapter 23, Sebastian Inlet.).

◆ **Surf School.** Teaches one- or four-day classes. *1085 Morningside Dr., Vero Beach, FL 32963; tel. 407-231-1044. Open daily. At Fort Pierce Inlet Beach.*

## DIVING

The beaches at Fort Pierce Inlet and Pepper Park both rest on ledges close to shore. Only 100 yards from the beach at Pepper Park is the wreck of a Civil War paddle-wheel boat. Be careful when you dive in the inlet, where there's lots of boat traffic. Make sure to display a diver's flag.

◆ **Dixie Divers.** Full-service dive shop and charters. *1717 Hwy. 1, Fort Pierce, FL 34950; tel. 407-461-4488. Open daily. South of South Bridge.*

## BICYCLING

Bicycle paths along the road make Fort Pierce Inlet State Recreation Area a safe and scenic place to pedal. The nearest bike rentals are in Jensen Beach (*see* Chapter 21, Hutchinson Island).

## GOLF

◆ **Indian Hills.** An 18-hole course. *1600 S. Third St., Fort Pierce, FL 34950; tel. 407-461-9620. Open daily. Admission. From the west end of the North Bridge Causeway, follow Hwy. 1 (Fourth St.) south 3 mi. to Georgia Ave. and turn left.*

## TENNIS

◆ **Lawnwood Park Complex.** Six tennis courts open to the public. There's a fee for reserving a court. *1302 Virginia Ave., Fort Pierce, FL 34982; tel. 407-462-1521. Open daily. 13 blocks west of Hwy. 1.*

◆ **Pepper Park.** Two courts. *Rte. A1A, North Hutchinson Island. Open daily.*

# HISTORY

◆ **St. Lucie County Historical Museum.** In charmingly framed vignettes, this county-run museum presents different aspects of local history. A restored house is used to demonstrate the family life of homesteaders. *414 Seaway Dr., Fort Pierce, FL 34949; tel. 407-462-1795. Open Tue.-Sat. 10-4; Sun. 12-4. Admission. On Hutchinson Island, alongside South bridge.*

# NATURE

◆ **Fort Pierce Inlet State Recreation Area.** A 20-minute walk leads through maritime hammock environment. There is also a bird sanctuary with trails penetrating the mysterious world of mangroves. *905 Shorewinds Dr., North Hutchinson Island, FL 34949; tel. 407-468-3985. Open daily 8-sunset. Admission. The entrance to the main park is just east of the drawbridge to North Hutchinson Island. To reach Jack Island, continue north on Rte. A1A about 2 mi.*

◆ **Harbor Branch Oceanographic Institution.** Home port for the Johnson-Sea-Link manned submersibles, it researches and educates in the marine sciences and ocean engineering. Visitors tours take in exhibits, aquariums, and submersible models. *5600 Hwy. 1 N., Fort Pierce, FL 34946; tel. 407-465-2400; fax 407-465-5415. Open Mon.-Sat. Tram and bus tours depart at 10, noon, and 2. Admission. On the mainland, about 15 minutes north of North Bridge Causeway.*

# SAFETY TIPS

Don't stray off the boardwalks as you explore the unique maritime environment at Fort Pierce Inlet State Recreation Area. The boardwalks not only protect dunes and their vegetation, they protect you from sand spurs, prickly pear cactus, and stinging nettles.

# TOURIST INFORMATION

◆ **Fort Pierce/St. Lucie County Chamber of Commerce.** *2200 Virginia Ave., Fort Pierce, FL 34982; tel. 407-461-2700. Open Mon.-Fri. 9-5. West of Hwy. 1, about 1 1/2 mi.*

## CHAPTER 23

# Sebastian Inlet

**N**ot widely known by tourists, the slab of island from Vero Beach to Sebastian Inlet appeals mainly to travelers with specific interests: surfing, art, citrus products, and the Los Angeles Dodgers baseball team. No two of its beaches are alike—from downtown Vero Beach, with its family parks, to Sebastian Inlet State Recreation Area, a dream beach for fishermen and surfers. The Indian River, a name synonymous with citrus groves, separates the island (actually several islands clustered together) from the mainland.

| | |
|---|---|
| Beauty | A- |
| Swimming | B+ |
| Sand | B |
| Hotels/Inns/B&Bs | B |
| House rentals | B+ |
| Restaurants | B- |
| Nightlife | B- |
| Attractions | B |
| Shopping | A- |
| Sports | A |
| Nature | B+ |

Spread along a stretch of Florida's legendary Route A1A, this section shows one of the seaside route's comeliest faces. Driving north from Vero Beach's exclusive, but heavily commercial, village district, you will discover public beaches amongst wilderness and well-groomed beach parks fronting luxury developments in such communities as Indian River Shores and Orchid Island.

Most of the island's tourist services and accommodations are found in Vero Beach, but there are more attractions in the mainland parts of the town and in nearby communities. Allow extra time getting from one place to another. Beach traffic can be heavy, especially in the winter, and finding the best route may be a problem at any time of year. For example, the town of Sebastian is on the mainland, directly across the Indian River from the state recreation area, but it is accessible only by a bridge seven miles to the south.

# OCEAN BEACHES
## VERO BEACH AREA

Right in the thick of things in Vero Beach, Humiston and Jaycee parks are not the most pristine beaches, but they're practical, especially for families. A boardwalk along the waterfront runs a few blocks between the two. Two public accesses without facilities lie a couple of miles to the north.

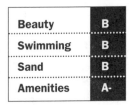

| | |
|---|---|
| Beauty | B |
| Swimming | B |
| Sand | B |
| Amenities | A- |

*Swimming:* Waves are often wild. Somewhat steep bottom.

*Sand:* The beach is normally wide but suffered erosion from Hurricane Erin in late summer 1995. Tan sands are covered with some shell and seaweed debris.

*Amenities:* Both of the parks have rest rooms, outdoor showers, playgrounds, and picnic shelters with grills. Restaurants, shops, and hotels are nearby. Jaycee Park has a food concession and lifeguards on duty.

*Sports:* Good surfing at north beach accesses. No water-sports rentals in the vicinity.

---

## HOW TO GET THERE

◆ From Exit 68 on I-95 (20 minutes from the Vero Beach beachfront), turn east on Rte. 60, which at that point is Osceola Blvd. Continue to follow it for 9 mi., as its name changes to 20th St., Miracle Mile Extension, Indian River Blvd., Royal Palm Blvd., Merrill Barber Bridge, and finally, Beachland Blvd. Beachland Blvd. takes you to the center of Vero Beach village, between Route A1A and Ocean Dr. Sebastian Inlet State Recreation Area lies 13 mi. north, on Rte. A1A.

*Parking:* Street parking at Humiston. The Jaycee Park has two large, paved lots and angle-in street parking. Smaller lots are at the north accesses. All free.

## Humiston Park
Right in downtown Vero Beach, it's handy to everything the village has to offer. With its many amenities, it's a functional beach, but not all that attractive. *South of Beachland Blvd., off Ocean Dr. on Easter Lily Ln.*

## Jaycee Park
Neatly maintained, near downtown's restaurants, shops, and hotels. The beach is bordered by medium-sized dunes, trimmed with sea oats and sea grapes. *Open daily 6-10. North of Beachland Blvd., at Rte. A1A and Mango Rd.*

## North Accesses
Two public accesses, named Turtle Trail and Sea Grape Trail, lie within the six miles of beach north of Jaycee Park. Popular with surfers, they have no facilities, fewer people, and a less-developed shoreline. Nicely maintained with scaevola and sea grapes tumbling down tall dunes. *Look for signs on the right as you drive north.*

## INDIAN RIVER SHORES
Wabasso Park is the main beach facility on this part of the island, north of Vero Beach, where the landscape turns manicured around cloistered, upscale communities. The two parks directly north of Wabasso are much more appealing to the

| Beauty | A |
|---|---|
| Swimming | B+ |
| Sand | B |
| Amenities | A- |

eye, with carefully tended landscaping. There, the beaches seem to stretch to infinity, just the way great beaches should.

*Swimming:* Low to high breakers please both swimmers and surfers.

*Sand:* Coarse, natural sand that flares into a wide beach.

*Amenities:* All but Ambersand have rest rooms, picnic shelters and grills, outdoor showers, and lifeguards on duty. There are food concessions at Wabasso.

*Sports:* Popular with surfers. No equipment rentals or facilities.

*Parking:* There is plenty of free, paved parking available at all beaches.

## Wabasso Beach Park

Close to a new Disney Resort development, its view now includes a number of large houses atop the tall dunes. *At the east end of the Wabasso Bridge, at Rte. A1A.*

## Golden Sands County Park

A playground amid clean, well groomed, flowery grounds makes this a family favorite. *Less than 2 mi. north of Wabasso Park, on Rte. A1A.*

## Treasure Shores Park

Another picture-pretty prototype of the perfect beach park, its playground hides under a canopy of live oak. Not as flowery as Golden Sands, it's given more to shady native vegetation. *About 3 mi. north of Wabasso Park, on Rte. A1A.*

## Ambersand Beach Access

It has the same wide, long beach, but no facilities and less likelihood of crowds. Surfers unite. *5 mi. north of Wabasso Park, on Rte. A1A.*

## SEBASTIAN INLET STATE RECREATION AREA

Sliced in two by a man-made inlet, the park encompasses a total of 587 acres devoted to fishing, boating, nature appreciation, beaching, and a treasure museum (*see* History). Its three miles of beach, split by the inlet, are fine for swimming, snor-

| Beauty | A |
|---|---|
| Swimming | B+ |
| Sand | B+ |
| Amenities | A- |

keling, scuba diving, and surfing. These beaches get heavily populated in winter and on summer weekends.

*Swimming:* Best swimming is on the north beach among smaller waves.

*Sand:* Soft, fine white sand at the south-side Day Use Area. Coarser

on the north side, and stubbled with bits of shell and driftwood.
*Amenities:* Rest rooms, outdoor showers at both beaches. Food and gift concessions near the Day Use Area at the south entrance and at the north-side beach. North Use Area has shaded picnic tables and grills. No lifeguard at either beach.
*Sports:* Excellent fishing from the pier on the south side, the jetties on the north side, and the catwalks under the bridge that spans the inlet. Concessions sell fishing supplies and rent snorkeling equipment and dive flags. Great surfing, but it's restricted to the Day Use Area Beach. Boat ramps.
*Parking:* The Day Use Area has a small unpaved lot that's free of charge. If you choose to enter the park proper, where the concessions are, there's a fee of $3.25 per car of eight persons or less ($1 for bike riders and pedestrians).

## Day Use Area Beach

Swimming conditions vary here. Waves may lap or roar, and surfers turn out in great numbers when they do the latter. Beautiful vista and a wide, natural beach with medium-high dunes fringed in sea grasses. *South side of Sebastian Inlet, on Rte. A1A.*

## North Use Area Beach

The more developed of the two beaches, it's also more family-friendly, with picnic facilities, better swimming conditions, and concessions near at hand. The wide beach is edged in low dunes, grassy and well-vegetated. *Just north of the bridge over the inlet, on Rte. A1A.*

# HOTELS/INNS/B&Bs

◆ **Aquarius Resort** (moderate). An older white-brick hotel with character, a beach, a pool, and kitchen facilities in each room. For extra comfort and ambience, get an ocean-front efficiency (expensive). Close to downtown shops and restaurants. *3544 Ocean Dr., Vero Beach, FL 32963; tel. 407-231-1133.*
◆ **Capt. Hiram's Islander Resort** (moderate). This charming, colonial-Caribbean building in Vero Beach's shopping district holds 16 guest rooms, all with refrigerators. Each colorfully decorated room opens onto either the courtyard or the pool and

barbecue area. Rental bikes, library, close to beach. *3101 Ocean Dr., Vero Beach, FL 32963; tel. 407-231-4431, 800-952-5886.*

◆ **Driftwood Resort** (inexpensive). One of Vero Beach's most popular hostelries, it looks as if it's dressed for the frontier. Legend has it that it was built in the early 1900s out of washed-up timber—without a plan. Through the years, it has accumulated a jumble of memorabilia and antiques. Standard rooms, efficiencies, and two-bedroom apartments (expensive) on a stretch of prime beachfront. Ocean-front units are best, but also most expensive. Pools, restaurant. *3150 Ocean Dr., Vero Beach, FL 32963; tel. 407-231-0550.*

◆ **Sebastian Inlet State Recreation Area** (inexpensive). 51 campsites with electricity and water, near boating and fishing facilities. *9700 S. Rte. A1A, Melbourne Beach, FL 32951; tel. 407-589-9659. Registration open daily 8-10. From Vero Beach village, drive north 13 mi. on Rte. A1A.*

# HOUSE RENTALS

**M**any homes and condos require a minimum stay of one to three months. Homes on the beach begin at about $1,200 a month, but lower prices are available for longer stays. Vacation homes are fairly plentiful.

◆ **Beach & Beyond Rentals.** *2945 Cardinal Dr., Vero Beach, FL 32963; tel. 407-234-3379, 800-330-3379. Open Mon.-Fri.; monitored answering machine Sat.-Sun.*

# RESTAURANTS

◆ **Black Pearl** (expensive). Tops the fine-dining list in this area. Known for its mesquite-grilled fish and homemade desserts and pastries. Elegant, but not snooty. *1409 Rte. A1A, Vero Beach, FL 32963; tel. 407-234-4426. Open daily for dinner.*

◆ **Village South** (moderate). In an intimate Swiss atmosphere reminiscent of a wine cellar, dine grandly on specialty pasta dishes, steak au poivre, stuffed shrimp, Long Island duckling, and other classics. *2900 Ocean Dr., Vero Beach, FL 32963; tel. 407-231-6727. Open daily for lunch and dinner. Closed Sun. in summer.*

◆ **Crusty's** (inexpensive). Casual, with a gorgeous view of the ocean, it excels at raw bar items, sandwiches, and pizza. Also serves dinners (moderate) from spaghetti and meatballs to coquille St. Jacques. *1050 Easter Lily Ln., Vero Beach, FL 32963; tel. 470-231-4728, 407-234-3923. Open daily for lunch and dinner. Off Ocean Dr., at Humiston Park.*

# NIGHTLIFE

In privileged Vero Beach village and environs, there are no nightclubs or discos with rock music. Nightlife is about culture, not carousing.

◆ **Mashed Potato Players.** This professional company performs original comedies throughout the area. *Box 2612, Vero Beach, FL 32961; tel. 407-589-3555. Call for schedule and venues. Admission.*

◆ **Riverside Theatre & Wahlstrom Children's Theatre.** Adult and juvenile comedies and other plays in winter. *3250 Riverside Park Dr., Vero Beach, FL 32963; tel. 407-231-6990. Box office open Mon.-Fri. Admission. In Riverside Park, north of Beachland Blvd.*

# ATTRACTIONS

◆ **Indian River Citrus Museum.** Photographs, antiques, and memorabilia tell how Indian River citrus gained its reputation starting in the early 1800s. Includes guided citrus tour and video. *2140 14th Ave., Vero Beach, FL 32960; tel. 407-770-2263. Open Tue.-Sat. 10-4; Sun. 1-4. Admission. Follow Rte. 60 (Beachland Blvd.) off the island to 14th Ave.*

◆ **Los Angeles Dodgers Spring Training Camp.** The days of Sandy Koufax and Don Drysdale have long been gone, but veteran manager Tommy LaSorda keeps coming back for more. For decades, this has been the preseason home of professional baseball's Dodgers, bringing much excitement to the area every February and March. After that, local teams take over. *Dodgertown, Box 2887, Vero Beach, FL 32961; tel. 407-569-4900, 407-569-6858. Admission. Follow Rte. 60 about 3 1/2 mi. off island. Turn right on Clemans Ave., and again on Dodger Rd.*

# SHOPPING

**V**ero Beach, recently rated one of America's best small art towns, has more than just its renowned galleries to attract shoppers. Its village shopping district holds all sorts of gift and clothing shops of interest.

◆ **Artists Guild Gallery.** Fine art by local artists and others in various media. *2855 Ocean Dr., Vero Beach, FL 32963; tel. 407-231-7551. Open daily in winter; Tue.-Sat. Memorial Day-Labor Day. In Portales de Vero shopping arcade.*

◆ **Bottalico Gallery.** Custom hand-painted and trompe l'oeil furniture and accessories. *3121 Ocean Dr., Vero Beach, FL 32963; tel. 407-231-0414. Open daily.*

◆ **Four Seasons Gift Shoppe.** Christmas-themed, it also carries local jams, jellies, and other gifts. *3117 Ocean Dr., Vero Beach, FL 32963; tel. 407-234-1984; fax 407-234-4140. Open daily.*

◆ **Roundabout.** Full of novelty toys and gifts, greeting cards, frames, and all kinds of fun stuff. *2855 Ocean Dr., Vero Beach, FL 32963; tel. 407-221-3323. Open daily. In Portales de Vero shopping arcade.*

# BEST FOOD SHOPS

**SANDWICHES:** ◆ **Crusty's.** *1050 Easter Lily Ln., Vero Beach, FL 32963; tel. 407-231-4728; fax 407-234-3923. Open daily. Off Ocean Dr. at Humiston Park.*

**SEAFOOD:** ◆ **Orchid's Delicatessen & Seafood Shoppe.** *1025 Easter Lily Ln., Vero Beach, FL 32963; tel. 407-234-5650. Open daily. Next to Humiston Park.*

**FRESH PRODUCE:** ◆ **Hale Indian River Groves.** *615 Beachland Blvd., Vero Beach, FL 32963; tel. 407-231-1752. Open Mon.-Sat. West of Rte. A1A, before the bridge.*

**BAKERY:** ◆ **Apples Bakery.** *1025 Easter Lily Ln., Vero Beach, FL 32963; tel. 407-234-5600. Open Tue.-Sat.*

**ICE CREAM:** ◆ **Cravings.** *3149 Ocean Dr., Vero Beach, FL 32963; tel. 407-231-0208. Open daily.*

**BEVERAGES:** ◆ **Village Beach Market.** *4905 Rte. A1A, Vero Beach, FL 32963; tel. 407-231-2338. Open daily.*

# SPORTS

## FISHING

The man-made cut through Sebastian Inlet State Recreation Area creates optimal fishing conditions for shrimp, clams, and various types of saltwater fish. Cast from the jetties or catwalk on the north side underneath the bridge, or from the pier on the south side of the park.

◆ **Miss Sebastian Fleet.** Fishing charters. *7575 131st St., Sebastian, FL 32958; tel. 407-589-3275. Open daily. At Sembler Marina, on Indian River Dr. in Sebastian.*

## BOATING

Most boat charters and rental opportunities are found in the town of Sebastian on the mainland. There are boat ramps at Sebastian Inlet State Recreation Area.

◆ **Breakaway Charters.** Sunning and waterskiing charters. *615 11th St., Vero Beach, FL 32962; tel. 407-569-6484. Open daily.*

## SURFING

Sebastian Inlet hosts several national surfing tournaments annually. Surfing is allowed on the south side of the inlet.

◆ **Surf School.** Surfing courses with board rentals and sales. *1085 Morningside Dr., Vero Beach, FL 32963; tel. 407-231-1044. Open daily.*

## DIVING

The water in this area are is generally too murky for diving. Most charters take you to southern waters.

◆ **Breakaway Charters.** Divers with their own equipment can visit the wrecks and reefs of Fort Pierce Inlet and beyond. *615 11th St., Vero Beach, FL 32962; tel. 407-569-6484. Open daily.*

◆ **Deep Six Dive & Water Sports.** Arranges boat charters and rents, sells, and services diving equipment. *416 Miracle Mile Extension, Vero Beach, FL 32960; tel. 407-562-2883, 800-732-9685. Open daily. Follow Rte. 60 off the island, until it becomes Miracle Mile.*

## BICYCLING

A bike path parallels Route A1A north of Vero Beach to Sebastian Inlet for about eight miles.

## GOLF

◆ **Dodger Pines.** The closest 18-hole course that's open to the public. *4600 26th St., Vero Beach, FL 32960; tel. 407-569-4403. Open daily. Admission. North of Rte. 60, west of the Beachland bridge.*

## TENNIS

◆ **Riverside Tennis Courts.** Ten hard-surface courts, six of them lighted. *Riverside Park, Vero Beach, FL 32963; tel. 407-231-4787. Open daily. Admission. South of Beachland Blvd; turn before the bridge.*

# HISTORY

◆ **McLarty Treasure Museum.** In 1715, a hurricane dashed to bits a treasure-laden Spanish fleet returning from Mexican waters. This museum, erected on the site of the survivors' camp, relates the story of the wreck and displays some of its recovered treasure. *Sebastian Inlet SRA, 9700 S. Rte. A1A, Melbourne Beach, FL 32951; tel. 407-589-2147. Open daily 10-4:25. Admission.*

# NATURE

◆ **Sebastian Inlet State Recreation Area.** Nature walks into man-groves, maritime forest, coastal hammocks, dunes, and beach. Summer sea turtle walks. *9700 S. Rte. A1A, Melbourne Beach, FL 32951; tel. 407-984-4852. Open daily 8-sunset. Admission.*

# SAFETY TIPS

The best surfing beaches are not normally ideal for swimmers because of turbulence, strong undercurrents, and the danger of getting hit by a surfboard.

# TOURIST INFORMATION

◆ **Vero Beach-Indian River County Chamber of Commerce.** *1216 21st St., Box 2947, Vero Beach, FL 32961; tel. 407-567-3491, 800-338-2678; fax 407-778-3181. Open Mon.-Fri. 9-5. On the mainland, follow Rte. 60 to Miracle Mile Extension and 21st St.*

## CHAPTER 24

# Playalinda

**S**pace-age wonders and the awe-inspiring beauty of an unspoiled beach are joined on Canaveral National Seashore, a sliver of land 25 miles long, sandwiched between the Atlantic Ocean and wide, brackish Mosquito Lagoon. Playalinda Beach, the southernmost of three beaches on the island, is also the most popular because it's closest to the nature preserve's far-out neighbor, the Kennedy Space Center.

Although rocket launches periodically shut down the beach, the rela-tionship between beach and base gen-

| | |
|---|---|
| **Beauty** | A+ |
| **Swimming** | B+ |
| **Sand** | B+ |
| **Hotels/Inns/B&Bs** | B- |
| **House rentals** | B |
| **Restaurants** | B+ |
| **Nightlife** | B- |
| **Attractions** | A |
| **Shopping** | B |
| **Sports** | B- |
| **Nature** | A+ |

erally works well. The space center is quiet most days, and beach-goers can take the tour there when they tire of sun and surf.

If you don't count the space center, Playalinda is blissfully far from everything except nature. The national seashore abuts 140,000-acre Merritt Island National Wildlife Refuge, creating a vast haven for countless wildlife species, many of which are on the endangered list.

Because of its remoteness, there is no true beach town asso-ciated with Playalinda. The nearest civilization is in Titusville, a 20-minute drive from Playalinda's southern boundary, and worlds removed from being a resort town. It's a quiet oasis between the clamor of Orlando and Cocoa Beach. Folks are most likely to come here on a day trip to the space center, or for an overnight before a NASA launching.

Although there are plenty of other attractions in the area, space is the town's theme. Wherever you look, pieces of old space ships are lying around like lawn sculptures. But there's also an historic downtown on the upswing, good restaurants, and great bird-watching nearby.

As for the beach, its calm waters endear it to families with small children. Serious boardsters head south to the surfing capital, Cocoa Beach.

# OCEAN BEACHES
## PLAYALINDA

Tall, well-established dunes slope into a slanting beach and ocean bottom. The view is absolutely gorgeous: sea grape trees, palmettos, dunes tufted with sea oats. There are many types of birds to watch and, in the distance, the best view you can get of launch pads without going on a Spaceport tour.

| | |
|---|---|
| Beauty | A+ |
| Swimming | B+ |
| Sand | B+ |
| Amenities | C- |

The north end of the beach was "clothing optional" until county officials recently legislated against nudity. Posts mark loggerhead nests in summer. The beach may close when the parking lots are full—or if someone is launching a space shuttle next door.

*Swimming:* Gentle waves, sometimes big enough to satisfy surfers. Clean, clear, generally warm water. Slightly steep bot-

**HOW TO GET THERE**

◆ From Orlando International Airport (50 minutes from Playalinda Beach), head north on Semoran Blvd. for 6 mi. Turn right on Colonial St. (Rte. 50) and drive 32 mi. to Hwy. 1 in Titusville. To get to Playalinda, turn left and drive 4 mi. to Garden St. (Rte. 406). Turn right and drive 3 mi. Turn right again on Rte. 402 and continue across Merritt Island for another 9 1/2 mi. to the beach.

tom slope.

*Sand:* Light tan, shell-speckled sand.

*Amenities:* Pit toilets and beach walkovers at all parking lots except No. 10. No lifeguard.

*Sports:* Boat ramp near lot No. 8 at Eddy Creek. Fishing is good from the beach or in the lagoon. Hikers find lots of nearby trails. You can hike or bike five miles north to Klondike Beach, which is not accessible by car.

*Parking:* Park only in the 13 lots along the four-mile beach. No. 2 is designated for oversized vehicles.

# HOTELS/INNS/B&Bs

L odging falls into the family-run and franchise-owned categories, plus a few campgrounds. Nothing spectacular, but easy on the wallet. Prices generally stay the same year-round, except for increases the night before a NASA launching or during big racing events in Daytona Beach. Most hotels are near the Spaceport or Interstate 95.

◆ **Best Western Space Shuttle Inn** (inexpensive). Convenient to Orlando, Playalinda, and the Spaceport, it has a heated pool, sauna, exercise room, restaurant, and comfortable accommodations. *3455 Cheney Hwy., Titusville, FL 32780; tel. 407-269-9100, 800-523-7654. On Rte. 50, 3 mi. west of Hwy. 1, just east of I-95.*

◆ **Howard Johnson Kennedy Space Center** (inexpensive). Closest of the chain hotels to the beach. Your basic HoJo, situated where Highway 1 meets Riverside Drive, a lovely residential way along the Indian River. A great place to catch the shuttle launches, but the rates are higher then. Pool, restaurant, lounge, workout gym, fishing pier, boat docks. Poolside rooms are nicest. *1829 Riverside Dr., Titusville, FL 32780; tel. 407-267-7900, 800-654-2000; fax 407-267-7080.*

# HOUSE RENTALS

◆ **Great Outdoors.** You can rent manufactured homes in a developed RV community with golfing, tennis, pool, health club, shuffleboard, and other amenities. Daily to monthly rates. Weekly in season:

about $450. *4505 Cheney Hwy. (mailing address: 135 Plantation Dr.), Titusville, FL 32780; tel. 407-269-5004, 800-621-2267. Open daily. Off Cheney Hwy. (Rte. 50), east of Hwy. 1.*
◆ **Treder Realty.** Has an inventory of about 35 homes that rent by the week or month at $800 to $1,600 a month. *2110 S. Washington Ave., Titusville, FL 32780; tel. 407-267-6616. Open Mon.-Fri.*

# RESTAURANTS

Restaurant prices are reasonable in the Titusville area. Citrus and seafood are the key dietary components. Many restaurants tout their rock shrimp, a species available, but not widely used, throughout Florida. The name comes from the shrimp's tough shell. Some compare the taste of its meat (drier, chewier, and sweeter than its cousins) to lobster.
◆ **Alexandria's** (expensive). A Victorian home holds the area's proudest get-dressed-up-and-go-out restaurant. Continental cuisine prevails, with creative twists to the tried and true. Reservations suggested. *2543 Hwy. 1, Mims, FL 32754; tel. 407-264-1134. Open Tue.-Sat. for dinner in winter; Fri.-Sat. Memorial Day-Labor Day.*
◆ **Paul's Smokehouse** (moderate). The best prices anywhere for filets, prime rib, and barbecue. Some meats are paired with seafood, surf-and-turf style. Pies and cakes in many varieties are made from scratch. The atmosphere is dressier than the picnic-table style you find at most barbecue houses. Great view of the river and Spaceport. *3665 S. Washington Ave., Titusville, FL 32780; tel. 407-267-3663. Open Tue.-Sun. for lunch and dinner.*
◆ **Steamers Riverside Eatery** (moderate). The hands-down best place for seafood and a view in the area. Ask for a porch seat or air-conditioned table along the bank of windows looking onto the Indian River and Merritt Island. Tasty, powdered-sugar-dusted corn fritters come as you're seated. To get your fill of local seafood, order one of the sampler platters. Children eat free with an adult. Reservations advised. *801 Marina Rd., Titusville, FL 32796; tel. 407-269-1012; fax 407-264-2422. Open daily for lunch and dinner. North of the bridge to Playalinda off Hwy. 1. Turn*

*east across from Sand Point Plaza (watch for sign) and take a quick left.*

◆ **Kloiber's Cobbler Eatery** (inexpensive). The red brick exterior dates from 1890 when this downtown building held a department store. Ask for a loft table that overlooks the stylish restoration and open kitchen. Fresh baked goodies, great salads, quiche, sandwiches, and espresso. Homemade soup special daily. Save room for the cobbler or homemade bread pudding. *337 S. Washington Ave., Titusville, FL 32796; tel. 407-383-0689; fax 407-383-0656. Open daily for breakfast, lunch, and dinner. Downtown, on Hwy. 1 N.*

# NIGHTLIFE

ead to Cocoa Beach for the wild parties. Titusville is quieter about its after-hours fun. Many bars are oriented to the country-music or Harley-Davidson crowd.

◆ **Steamers Riverside Eatery.** Live acoustic guitar music on weekends. *801 Marina Rd., Titusville, FL 32796; tel. 407-269-1012; fax 407-264-2422. Open daily. Turn east off of Hwy. 1 across from Sand Point Plaza (watch for sign) and take a quick left.*

◆ **Titusville Playhouse.** A professional troupe and a children's theater are lodged in this historic silent-movie house, built in 1905. Call for schedule of performances. *Emma Parrish Theatre, 301 Julia St., Titusville, FL 32780; tel. 407-268-1125. Admission. Downtown, off Hwy. 1.*

◆ **TJ's Lounge.** Live country bands and line dancing keep this place stepping. *4702 S. Washington Ave., Titusville, FL 32780; tel. 407-269-9883. Open Wed.-Sat. Admission.*

# ATTRACTIONS

◆ **Astronaut Hall of Fame.** The highlight of this tribute to America's astronauts is the new Shuttle to Tomorrow. It simulates the feel and excitement of lift-off, space walking, re-entry, and landing through audio, visual, and sensory presentations. *6225 Vectorspace Blvd., Titusville, FL 32780; tel. 407-269-6100. Open daily 9-6. Admission. On Rte. 405, 1 mi. east of Hwy. 1, and*

*6 mi. west of Kennedy Space Center.*

◆ **Kennedy Space Center Spaceport USA.** Plan on spending a couple of hours, more if you want to see an IMAX movie or take a guided bus tour (admission for both). Exhibits are devoted to manned spaceflight, the Merritt Island Wildlife Refuge, and the effect of space travel on our lives. The highlights are the IMAX movie and a mock-up of the space shuttle *Explorer*. A suited astronaut circulates for picture-taking, and a space-age playground keeps the littlest ones entertained. *DNPS, Kennedy Space Center, FL 32899; tel. 407-452-2121. Open daily 9-dusk. Take Rte. 405 east off Hwy. 1 for 7 mi. Follow signs to turn at Rte. 3.*

◆ **Titusville Parachute Center.** A new perspective on the Space Coast. You can learn to jump in 20 minutes and take your first plunge. Must be 18 or older. No reservations. *Dunn Airfield, 476 N. Williams Ave., Titusville, FL 32796; tel. 407-267-0016. Open Wed.-Fri. noon-sunset; Sat.-Sun. 9-sunset. Take Williams Ave. north off Garden St. (Rte. 406).*

◆ **Warbird Air Museum.** Large collection of vintage military flying gear, uniforms, artwork, and aviation memorabilia. *6600 Tico Rd., Titusville, FL 32780; tel. 407-268-1941. Open daily 10-6. Admission. At the Space Center Executive Airport off Rte. 405, just west of Hwy. 1.*

# SHOPPING

Old downtown Titusville is being born again as a shopping district where the accent is on antiques and homey things. Washington Avenue and Main Street form the core.

◆ **Gift Gantry.** Everything you ever wanted to buy about space: books, collectibles, prints, toys, T-shirts, even space food. *TWRS, Kennedy Space Center, FL 32899; tel. 407-452-2121. Open daily. At Kennedy Space Center Spaceport USA, off Rte. 405 on Rte. 3.*

◆ **Linger Awhile Antiques.** Specializes in primitive, Victorian, and country antiques, quilts, bears, pottery, glassware, and arts and crafts. *335 S. Washington Ave., Titusville, FL 32796; tel. 407-268-4680. Open Wed.-Sun. Downtown, on Hwy. 1 N.*

◆ **River Road Mercantile.** Antiques, mostly in a country vein. *342*

*S. Washington Ave., Titusville, FL 32796; tel. 407-264-2064. Open Mon.-Sat. Downtown, on Hwy. 1 N.*

# BEST FOOD SHOPS

**SANDWICHES:** ◆ **Mr. Submarine & Salads.** *2400 S. Hopkins Ave., Titusville, FL 32796; tel. 407-383-1616. Open daily. On Hwy. 1 S., behind Miracle City Mall.*

**SEAFOOD:** ◆ **Winn-Dixie.** *700 Cheney Hwy., Titusville, FL 32780; tel. 407-269-9972. Open daily. On Rte. 50.*

**FRESH PRODUCE:** ◆ **May Groves.** Sells citrus on-site and by shipment. *1885 Hwy. 1 N., Titusville, FL 32796; tel. 407-267-7159, 800-237-7159. Open daily. North of the bridge to Playalinda.*

**BAKERY:** ◆ **Kloiber's Cobbler Eatery.** *337 S. Washington Ave., Titusville, FL 32796; tel. 407-383-0689; fax 407-383-0656. Open daily. Downtown, on Hwy. 1 N.*

**ICE CREAM:** ◆ **Carvel Ice Cream.** *2500 S. Washington Ave., Titusville, FL 32780; tel. 407-269-9771. Open daily.*

**BEVERAGES:** ◆ **7-Eleven.** *1500 Garden St., Titusville, FL 32796; tel. 407-269-3331. Open daily. Turn right after the bridge to Playalinda.*

**WINE:** ◆ **ABC Liquors.** *1293 S. Washington Ave., Titusville, FL 32780; tel. 407-269-1591. Open daily.*

# SPORTS
## FISHING

The national parks offer fishing in freshwater and saltwater for anything from bass to Spanish mackerel. For information on sport fishing in the Merritt Island National Wildlife Refuge, call 407-861-0667.

◆ **Fly Fisherman.** Come here for fly fishing tackle and supplies. *1114 S. Washington Ave., Titusville, FL 32780; tel. 407-267-0348. Open Tue.-Sat.*

◆ **Titusville Veteran's Pier.** Free pier fishing, rod and reel rentals, bait and tackle. *Veteran's Memorial Park, Titusville, FL 32782; tel. 407-383-2464. Open daily.*

## BOATING

You'll find the closest charter boat activity at Port Canaveral, about an hour from Playalinda.

◆ **Titusville Municipal Marina.** Rent a 24-foot pontoon boat. *451 Marina Rd., Titusville, FL; tel. 407-269-7255. Open daily. North of the bridge to Playalinda. Turn east across from Sand Point Plaza.*

## SURFING

Fanatical surfers will naturally want to make the pilgrimage to Ron Jon Surf, the ultimate surf shop. It's open 24 hours and qualifies as a tourist attraction. But it's about an hour's drive away, on Cocoa Beach, one of Florida's most challenging surfing beaches. Playalinda holds its own, but shops are few.

◆ **Stikee Surf Shop.** Surfboards and other supplies. *9 Main St., Titusville, FL 32796; tel. 407-383-1633. Open daily.*

## DIVING

◆ **American Divers International.** The nearest dive shop to Playalinda, it is about 45 minutes away. *691 N. Courtenay Pkwy., Merritt Island, FL 32953; tel. 407-453-0600. Open Mon.-Sat.*

## BICYCLING

Beach and nature trails in Merritt Island National Wildlife Refuge and Canaveral National Seashore afford cyclists opportunity to commune with nature off-road. There are no bike rentals in the vicinity.

## GOLF

◆ **Great Outdoors.** 18 holes of golf open to the public. Call to reserve tee times three days in advance. *135 Plantation Dr., Titusville, FL 32780; tel. 407-269-5524. Open daily. Admission. 4 mi. west of Hwy. 1 on Rte. 50 (Cheney Hwy.), just west of I-95.*

◆ **Royal Oak.** Semi-private, 18 holes. *2150 Country Club Dr., Titusville, FL 32780; tel. 407-269-4500. Open daily. Admission. North of Searstown Mall, turn west on Hwy. 1.*

## TENNIS

◆ **Singleton Courts.** *540 N. Singleton Ave., Titusville, FL 32796; tel. 407-264-5036. Open daily. Admission.*

# HISTORY

**D**owntown Titusville, along Highway 1 between Main and Julia streets, is being perked up with renovation of turn-of-the-century buildings and flowery courtyards.

◆ **North Brevard Historical Museum.** Photographs, furniture, clothing, and other memorabilia in this museum depict early lifestyles in the Titusville area. *301 S. Washington Ave., Titusville, FL 32796; tel. 407-269-3658. Open Tue.-Sat. 10-2 Downtown, on Hwy. 1 N.*

# NATURE

◆ **Merritt Island National Wildlife Refuge.** Bald eagles soar through the sky where space shuttles launch. Merritt Island's 140,000 acres, along with the abutting Canaveral National Seashore, is a habitat for 1,000 plants species, 310 bird species, and 21 threatened or endangered animals. *Box 6504, Titusville, FL 32782; tel. 407-861-0667. Refuge open daily during daylight hours. Visitors center open Mon.-Fri. 8-4:30; Sat. 9-5. 5 mi. from Titusville via Rte. 406 east and Rte. 402.*

# SAFETY TIPS

**S**igns in the area warn about car theft and carjackers. Heed them. Lock your car even while driving, and keep the windows up.

# TOURIST INFORMATION

For launch information, call NASA at 407-867-4636 or Spaceport USA at 800-572-4636.

◆ **Canaveral National Seashore Headquarters.** *308 Julia St., Titusville, FL 32796; tel. 407-267-1110. Open Mon.-Fri. 8-4:30. Downtown, off Hwy. 1.*

◆ **Florida's Space Coast Office of Tourism.** *2725 St. John's St., Melbourne, FL 32940; tel. 407-633-2110, 800-872-1969. Open Mon.-Fri. 9-5.*

◆ **Titusville Chamber of Commerce.** *2000 S. Washington Ave., Titusville, FL 32780; tel. 407-267-3036. Open Mon.-Fri. 9-5.*

## CHAPTER 25

# Amelia Island

**A**melia Island, a beach with a past, has been seducing travelers for a century and a half. Florida's first resort island, it played host in the 1850s to Ulysses S. Grant and other northern notables, who were entertained in the gracious Victorian homes of its residents.

| | |
|---|---|
| Beauty | A |
| Swimming | B+ |
| Sand | A- |
| Hotels/Inns/B&Bs | A+ |
| House rentals | A |
| Restaurants | A+ |
| Nightlife | B |
| Attractions | B+ |
| Shopping | A |
| Sports | A- |
| Nature | A |

The frilly architecture remains in downtown Fernandina Beach's Silk Stocking District. Historic buildings house quaint shops, antique marts, restaurants specializing in local shrimp, and Florida's oldest tavern, The Palace Saloon. Many vintage homes still open their doors to guests as charming bed-and-breakfasts.

At the west end of Centre Street, docks accommodate one of the island's most prominent institutions: its celebrated shrimping fleet. You'll be able to sample the proceeds at just about any restaurant in town.

To the north, Old Town recalls a rowdier Fernandina past, when President James Monroe branded the town a "festering fleshpot." Between 1807 and 1821 (the year Florida joined the United States), the island was controlled by pirates and served by some 50 saloons and bordellos.

Before then, the island was shuffled back and forth between various ruling factions. France was the first, after Jean Ribault landed here in 1562. The United States became the seventh. The Confederacy, for a short time, ruled as the eighth.

A substantial reminder of the Civil War era—Fort Clinch—stands at the island's northernmost end. It eventually was occupied, along with the rest of the island, by Union troops in 1862. Indirectly, the occupation led to Fernandina's development, as awed soldiers returned home with fantastic tales about Florida's northernmost island. Today, Fort Clinch State Park is the site of one of the island's nicest beaches.

Amelia's 13 miles of bleach-blond beach are characterized by a broad expanse of shell-strewn, quartz sand and a backdrop of rolling dunes. The dunes are as steep and tall as cliffs at the island's south end, where luxury resorts share the beachfront with public beaches and the historic African-American settlement of American Beach.

Pets on leashes are allowed on the island's public beaches. At some of them, cars can drive onto the sands and park, but that requires a permit. For more information, contact the county courthouse or drop into Hall's Beach Store (*see* Tourist Information or Best Food Shops).

# OCEAN BEACHES

## FORT CLINCH STATE PARK

On the grounds of the old fort, this exquisite, 4,000-foot-long beach at the island's north end is usually uncrowded and quiet. It is gently sculpted like a cove. Rolling dunes, topped with shrubs, edge

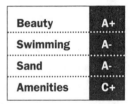

| Beauty | A+ |
|---|---|
| Swimming | A- |
| Sand | A- |
| Amenities | C+ |

the wide beach, which is a good five-minute walk from the parking lot via a boardwalk. The view is unscathed by high rises, a flashback to pre-development Florida. *Open daily 8-sunset. Park*

## HOW TO GET THERE

◆ From Jacksonville International Airport (40 minutes from Amelia Island), take Airport Rd. to I-95. Drive north 15 mi. on I-95 to Exit 129 (Rte. A1A). Turn right on Rte. A1A and drive 12 mi. to Amelia Island.

*entrance is on Atlantic Ave., just east of Fletcher Ave. Beach is 3 mi. from entrance (follow signs).*

*Swimming:* Cool, fairly clear water. Playful waves. Smooth bottom.

*Sand:* This white-sand beach has two levels. Bits of sticks and ground shell are scattered on the wide, flat upper shelf, which drops sharply at the high tide line. Lots of shells lie along the hard-packed sand on the lower level.

*Amenities:* Rest rooms and outdoor showers. Tours of Fort Clinch and guided nature walks are also available. No lifeguard.

*Sports:* At the north end of the beach, a jetty and a pier jutting into Cumberland Sound are popular with fishermen.

*Parking:* It costs $3.25 per car of eight or less to enter the park ($1 per pedestrian or bicyclist). The number of spaces is ample.

## FERNANDINA BEACHES

The high dunes of the island's south end level off here and have been augmented in some places to repair erosion. Along South Fletcher Avenue (Route A1A) are a series of small parking lots with beach boardwalks maintained by the city. They have no facilities.

| | |
|---|---|
| Beauty | B+ |
| Swimming | B+ |
| Sand | B+ |
| Amenities | A |

Main Beach is the center of beach activity on the island. When the wind is from the wrong direction, however, the unpleasant aroma from a nearby paper mill assaults the senses.

*Swimming:* Good swimming, with low to high surf action. Easy-sloping bottom.

*Sand:* A wide, long spread of taupe sand, thick and fluffy except where hard-packed at water's edge.

*Amenities:* Main Beach has rest rooms, outdoor showers, picnic shelters, a food concession, a playground, miniature golf, a water slide, and a game room (fees charged for the last three). There are restaurants and shops nearby. A lifeguard is on duty.

*Sports:* Volleyball at Main Beach. Surfing is forbidden on Main Beach, where there are usually a lot of swimmers, but there is a surf shop close by.

*Parking:* You will find plenty of free, paved parking at Main Beach. Smaller lots are located at other public accesses.

## Main Beach

Also known as Oceanfront Park and Dr. Ralph Wolff Beach Park, it's popular with families because of the amenities and nearby attractions. Nice grassy grounds and low dunes with tufts of sea oats. *On N. Fletcher Ave. (Rte. A1A) and Trout St.*

## South Beaches

This swath of beach appears endless and in fact, is perfect for long walks and jogs. Scrub vegetation and flowering railroad vines crisscross the 40-foot-high dunes.

| | |
|---|---|
| Beauty | A |
| Swimming | B+ |
| Sand | A- |
| Amenities | B |

*Swimming:* Docile breakers can build to surfing size. Good, smooth bottom with a gentle slope. The water can be cold in winter.

*Sand:* The fine, white sand is covered with crushed shells, deposited by dredges brought in to renourish the beach. Dunes level off into an extremely wide, flat beach that is hard-packed at water's edge. Good place to collect shells and shark teeth.

*Amenities:* No facilities at the county beach access or Scott Road. Burney has picnic shelters, outdoors showers, and rest rooms with indoor showers that look decrepit from the outside but are clean inside. Peter's Point has similar amenities but in better condition. If you forget your picnic, the beach restaurant and bar at The Ritz-Carlton are only a quarter-mile away. No lifeguard at any of the beaches.

*Sports:* Good surfing. Trucks rent Jet Skis on the beach.

*Parking:* Small, unpaved lot at county beach access. Large, paved lots at Burney and Peter's Point; a smaller one at Scott Road. All parking is free.

## Peter's Point Beach Front Park

This is the nicest of the south-end public beaches, with blue, tin-roofed picnic shelters and rest rooms. There is some commercial development nearby, but it's tasteful. *On S. Fletcher Ave. at the south end, before the road turns west.*

## Scott Road Beach Access

Lack of facilities (there's only a portable toilet) keeps crowds away. Scrub oaks and rolling dunes, with lots of buildings in sight. *Turn east off Rte. A1A. 5 1/2 mi. north of the south bridge.*

## Burney Beachfront Park

Near American Beach, which in the past has experienced crime problems, this beach is still lightly visited, even though the problems are being addressed. Lots of dunes and scrub oak. *Turn east off Rte. A1A, 4 1/2 mi. north of the south bridge.*

## Nassau County Beach Access

It takes about five minutes to walk the steps and trail from the parking lot to the beach. The view is pleasant: a few homes, and the low-rise resort buildings of Amelia Island Plantation in the distance to the north. Few people congregate here, so it's good for seclusion-lovers. *Off Rte. A1A, 3 mi. north of the south bridge.*

# HOTELS/INNS/B&Bs

**K**nown for its lovely Victorian B&Bs, Amelia Island is also home to renowned destination resorts that specialize in pampering guests with every imaginable service.

◆ **The Ritz-Carlton** (very expensive). With typical Ritz grandeur, the hotel rules a stretch of lovely beach at Amelia Island's south end. Its 449 rooms spell elegant comfort with marble bathrooms, three phones, twice-daily maid service, robes, ocean view, and classic furnishings. Three restaurants, bars, an 18-hole golf course, tennis, a fitness club, spa, children's program, playground, beach rentals, swimming pools, whirlpool, and shops provide the makings of a perfect beach vacation. *4750 Amelia Island Pkwy., Amelia Island, FL 32034; tel. 904-277-1100; fax 904-277-1145. From the north bridge, turn right off Rte. A1A onto Amelia Island Pkwy.*

◆ **Amelia Island Plantation** (expensive). This top resort takes care of all your beach vacationing needs. It caters to families, with an excellent children's program, gorgeous beachfront, beach and bike rentals, suite options, and multi-bedroom villas (very expensive). Other features: golf course, tennis, bike and running trails, restaurants, bars, shops, swimming pools, charter boats, and land tours. *Box 3000, Amelia Island, FL 32035; tel. 904-261-*

*6161, 800-874-6878. On Rte. A1A, at the island's south end.*

◆ **Bailey House** (moderate). One of Amelia's first Victorian B&Bs, the Bailey was built in Queen Anne style in 1895. Period furniture recalls the era in the lavish public rooms and five guest rooms, each of which has a private bath and TV. The Victorian Room is a favorite because it's inside one of the house's turrets. The Rose Room (expensive) is the most expensive, with a fireplace and an antique-footed tub. *Box 805, 28 S. Seventh St., Fernandina Beach, FL 32035; tel. 904-261-5390. Downtown, off Centre St.*

◆ **Florida House Inn** (moderate). Built in 1857 as one of Florida's first hostelries, it's been restored to pre-Civil-War simplicity with 11 rooms minus all the Victorian embellishment common to Fernandina. All rooms have antique furnishings, private baths, air-conditioning, TVs, and phones. Room No. 10 (expensive) is upstairs with a fireplace, Jacuzzi, and a shower. Full Southern-style breakfast is complimentary. Lunch and dinner also available. *Box 688, 22 S. Third St., Fernandina Beach, FL 32035; tel. 904-261-3300, 800-258-3301. Downtown, off Centre St.*

◆ **Fort Clinch State Park** (inexpensive). 62 campsites available either near the river or a short walk away from the beach. Laundry and sanitary pump station. *2601 Atlantic Ave., Fernandina Beach, FL 33034; tel. 904-277-7274. Entrance on Atlantic Ave., just east of Fletcher Ave. (Rte. A1A).*

# HOUSE RENTALS

Amelia Island's selection of rental homes is vast, ranging from humble beach-view cottages to grand seaside palaces. There's even one in the shape of a lighthouse. Most are rentable by the day, week, or month. Monthly rates range from $750 to $6,500.

◆ **Amelia Island Lodging Systems.** *584 S. Fletcher Ave., Fernandina Beach, FL 32034; tel. 904-261-4148, 800-872-8531. Open daily.*

◆ **Amelia Island Rental & Management Services.** *5137 First Coast Hwy. S., Amelia Island, FL 32034; tel. 904-261-9129, 800-874-8679. Open daily. On Rte. A1A.*

# RESTAURANTS

The sweet, white shrimp harvested from local waters show up on most menus. Another local ingredient you'll find on some tables is Datil pepper, which is made into sauce, pickled chiles, and jelly. Southern-style cooking asserts its influence. Don't count on finding anything "light" on most menus.

◆ **The Grill** (very expensive). Fresh seafood and wild game form the foundation of cutting-edge cuisine. The view of Atlantic breakers adds romance to the intimate setting and live piano music. A window seat is a must for the perfect experience. Jackets required. *4750 Amelia Island Pkwy., Amelia Island, FL 32034; tel. 904-277-1100; fax 904-277-1145. Open Mon.-Sat. for dinner. At The Ritz-Carlton.*

◆ **1878 Steak House** (moderate). Order a filet mignon, strip steak, or rib eye by the ounce, from a selection presented at your table. Top with forrestierre (brown peppercorn and mushroom) sauce. There's also shrimp and seafood selections, plus surf-and-turf combinations. The atmosphere is pure Fernandina, with Victorian trappings. Of course, there's a story behind the name of the restaurant. Read the back of the menu. *12 N. Second St., Fernandina Beach, FL 32034; tel. 904-261-4049. Open daily for dinner.*

◆ **Brett's Waterway Cafe** (moderate). Lots of windows brighten the dark wood interior and look onto the bobbing boats in the harbor. The menu is designed to enhance, not camouflage, the fresh flavor of the local shrimp, as well as other fish, poultry, and meat. For an offbeat lunch, the grilled chicken and brie salad is a good choice. At dinner, try the broiled shrimp with sun-dried tomato butter. *Box 1496, 1 S. Front St., Amelia Island, FL 32035; tel. 904-261-2660. Open daily for dinner; Mon.-Sat. for lunch. On Fernandina Harbour Marina, at the west end of Centre St.*

◆ **Sandbar** (moderate). An island classic, it hides from modern times behind Spanish moss at the river's edge. Its cypress interior, red clapboard siding, and Southern-style fish entrees have remained unchanged over the years. A favorite of locals and visitors. Fried shrimp, oysters, and other seafood and fish items are served in queen and king portions, complete with hush puppies. *Forrest Rd., Amelia Island, FL 32034; tel. 904-261-4185. Open*

*Tue.-Sun. for dinner. In Amelia City, turn west at the Lil' Champ store on an unmarked road called Gerbing Rd. A large red sign advertising the restaurant points the way. Follow the narrow lane through the neighborhood and woods.*

◆ **Florida House Inn** (inexpensive). Family-style feasts served in a pre-Civil-War setting. Meals showcase Southern food and hospitality. *Box 688, 22 S. Third St., Fernandina Beach, FL 32035; tel. 904-261-3300. Open Mon.-Sat. for lunch; Tue.-Sat. for dinner; Sun. for brunch. Downtown, off Centre St.*

# NIGHTLIFE

◆ **Brass Rail Saloon.** Part of the 1878 Steak House, it features local bands playing country music and other contemporary styles. *12 N. Second St., Fernandina Beach, FL 32034; tel. 904-261-4049. Open Mon.-Sat. Off Centre St.*

◆ **Palace Saloon.** Florida's oldest bar boasts historic (circa 1900) digs, a pressed-tin ceiling, and memories of such patrons as the Carnegies and DuPonts. There's also a mahogany back bar, literary murals, live music, and a ghost named Charlie. *117 Centre St., Fernandina Beach, FL 33034; tel. 904-261-6320. Open daily.*

◆ *Stardancer.* This small cruise ship sails for dinner and dancing. Also casino cruises. *11 S. Second St., Fernandina Beach, FL 32034; tel. 904-277-8980, 800-842-0115; fax 904-277-8249. Open Tue.-Sun. Admission.*

# ATTRACTIONS

◆ **Eight Flags Water Slide.** A giant water slide with game room next door. *35 N. Fletcher Ave., Fernandina Beach, FL 32034; tel. 904-261-8212. Open daily 10-7 Memorial Day-Labor Day. Admission. Across the street from Main Beach.*

◆ **Island Falls Adventure Golf.** A waterfall and streams add challenge to this miniature-golf course. *1550 Sadler Rd., Fernandina Beach, FL 32034; tel. 904-261-7881. Open daily 10 a.m.-11 p.m. Hours vary in winter according to weather conditions. Admission. Across from K-mart.*

◆ **Old Towne Carriage Company.** Narrated, horse-drawn carriage tours of downtown Fernandina Beach and Old Town.

*Fernandina Beach, FL 32034; tel. 904-277-1555. Call for hours of operation. Admission. At the waterfront, on Centre St.*

# SHOPPING

**D**owntown Fernandina Beach, with its vintage store fronts and charming boutiques, is lots of fun. On the south end of the island, Palmetto Walk provides a more modern shopping experience beneath a canopy of live oaks. Antiques, home accessories, crafts, art, and books are the specialties. To purchase everyday necessities, head to Sadler Road and 14th Street.

◆ **Eight Flags Antique Market.** A daily antique fair. More than 50 antique dealers sell everything imaginable. *602 Centre St., Fernandina Beach, FL 32034; tel. 904-277-8550. Open daily.*

◆ **Gallery.** A co-op art gallery representing artists of the Island Art Association. *Box 1251, 205 Centre St., Fernandina Beach, FL 32035; tel. 904-261-7020. Open daily.*

◆ **The Unusual Shop.** Handcrafted works by the store's owners and other artisans include hand-painted ceramic tiles, pottery, jewelry, puppets, Haitian art, and tropical clothing. *308 Centre St., Fernandina Beach, FL 32034; tel. 904-277-9664. Open daily.*

# BEST FOOD SHOPS

**SANDWICHES:** ◆ **As You Like It.** *316A Centre St., Fernandina Beach, FL 32034; tel. 904-277-2005. Open Mon.-Sat. Downstairs.*

**SEAFOOD:** ◆ **Atlantic Seafood.** *10 Ash St., Fernandina Beach, FL 32034; tel. 904-261-4302. Open daily. One block off Centre St., at Fernandina Harbour Marina.*

**FRESH PRODUCE:** ◆ **Winn-Dixie.** *1745 Eighth St., Fernandina Beach, FL 32034; tel. 904-277-2539. Open daily. South of Atlantic Ave.*

**BAKERY:** ◆ **Amelia Island Gourmet Coffee Co.** *3 N. Fourth St., Fernandina Beach, FL 32034; tel. 904-321-2111. Open daily. Off Centre St.*

**ICE CREAM:** ◆ **Water Turkey Gifts & Ice Cream.** *207 Centre St., Fernandina Beach, FL 32034; tel. 904-261-6474. Open daily.*

**BEVERAGES:** ◆ **Hall's Beach Store.** Also sells beach driving/parking permits. *2021 Fletcher Ave., Fernandina Beach,*

*FL 32034; tel. 904-261-7007. Open daily.*
**WINE:** ◆ **Amelia Liquors South.** *Palmetto Walk, 4924 First Coast Hwy., Amelia Island, FL 32034; tel. 904-261-7701. Open daily. 2 11/2 mi. north of Amelia Island Plantation on Rte. A1A.*

# SPORTS

## FISHING

Fish Cumberland Sound from the pier at Fort Clinch State Park. Amelia Island State Recreation Area provides some parking for fishermen who cast into waters south of the island. Get your fishing license at Wal-Mart or K-mart.

◆ **Amelia Island Charter Boat Association.** Call about specialty fishing charters for deep water and backwater. Trips just to hook large-mouth bass. Party boats. *3 S. Front St., Fernandina Beach, FL 32034; tel. 904-261-2870. Open daily.*

◆ **Atlantic Seafood.** Live and dead bait, tackle, and other supplies. *10 Ash St., Fernandina Beach, FL 32034; tel. 904-261-4302. Open daily. One block off Centre St., at the Fernandina Harbour Marina.*

## BOATING

◆ **Amelia Island Charter Boat Association.** Sightseeing, sailing, cocktail, and other excursions. *3 S. Front St., Fernandina Beach, FL 32034; tel. 904-261-2870. Open daily.*

## SURFING

Surfing conditions are often favorable. Surfing is not allowed on Main Beach. On other beaches, surfboards must be leashed.

◆ **Driftwood Sun & Surf.** Surfboards, surfwear, and other beach necessities. *31 S. Fletcher Ave., Fernandina Beach, FL 32034; tel. 904-321-2188. Open daily.*

◆ **Pipeline Surf Shop.** Surfboards, body boards, skim boards, Boogie boards, and rentals. *2856 Sadler Rd., Fernandina Beach, FL 32034; tel. 904-277-3717. Open daily.*

## DIVING

◆ **Aqua Explorers Dive Center.** Teaches certification courses, arranges charters, and sells and rents equipment. *2856 Sadler*

Rd., *Fernandina Beach, FL 32034; tel. 904-261-5989. Open Mon.-Sat.*

## BICYCLING
Many resorts rent bikes for beach riding and pedaling along the jogging path on Amelia Island Parkway.

## GOLF
◆ **Fernandina Municipal Golf Course.** An 18-hole course. *2800 Bill Melton Rd., Fernandina Beach, FL; tel. 904-277-7370. Open daily. Admission. Off S. Fletcher Ave. (Rte. A1A).*

## TENNIS
Amelia Island Plantation has hosted several professional tournaments. Many resorts provide fine facilities for guests. Two courts at the municipal park in Fernandina Beach (Atlantic Avenue and 11th Street) are open to the public.

## HORSEBACK RIDING
◆ **Seahorse Stables.** Trot along five miles of beach at the island's south end. *7500 Rte. A1A, Amelia Island, FL 32034; tel. 904-261-4878. Open daily. Turn off Rte. A1A at Amelia Island State Recreation Area, just north of the south bridge.*

# HISTORY
Downtown holds almost 50 pre-1900 structures in a 50-block area around Centre Street and the Silk Stocking residential area. Pick up a copy of *Amelia Now* in most stores for a walking or driving tour of the historic district.

◆ **Amelia Island Museum of History.** The old county jailhouse serves as a museum that tells the story of Amelia's past via living history tours. *233 S. Third St., Fernandina Beach, FL 32034; tel. 904-261-7378. Open Mon.-Sat. 10-5; tours at 11 and 2. Two walk-in tours daily. Admission. Downtown, off Centre St.*

◆ **Fort Clinch.** Reenactments demonstrate fort life under both Union and Confederate forces, which controlled it at different times. *Fort Clinch State Park, 2601 Atlantic Ave., Fernandina Beach,*

*FL 32034; tel. 904-277-7274. Open daily. Admission. Entrance to the state park is on Atlantic Ave., just east of Fletcher Ave. (Rte. A1A).*

# NATURE

Two entirely different waterfronts embrace Amelia Island: on one side, the wild Atlantic; on the other, the slow, marshy Amelia River. Both have a wealth of wildlife on their shores, and there are several distinct levels of maritime vegetation inland. Guided nature tours are held at Fort Clinch State Park.

# SAFETY TIPS

Rip tides are especially dangerous in the vicinity of American Beach, which is near Burney Beach Front Park. This same area has been the site of violent crime. Its bad reputation is on the mend, but the best advice is to avoid it after dark.

# TOURIST INFORMATION

◆ **Amelia Island Tourist Development Council.** *Box 472, Fernandina Beach, FL 32035; tel. 904-261-3248, 800-226-3542. Open Mon.-Fri. 9-5. Welcome center is in the old train depot at Centre St. and Front St.*

◆ **Nassau County Courthouse.** Sells beach driving/parking permits. *416 Centre St., Fernandina Beach, FL 32034; tel. 904-321-5700. Open Mon.-Fri. 8:30-5.*

◆ **TelEvent.** Call for 24-hour information on attractions, restaurants, accommodations, and events. *Tel. 904-277-1599.*